1000 English History Facts and 50 True Tales

A Journey Through England's Defining Moments and Figures

Welcome Aboard, Check Out This Limited-Time Free Bonus!

Ahoy, reader! Welcome to the Ahoy Publications family, and thanks for snagging a copy of this book! Since you've chosen to join us on this journey, we'd like to offer you something special.

Check out the link below for a FREE e-book filled with delightful facts about American History.

But that's not all - you'll also have access to our exclusive email list with even more free e-books and insider knowledge. Well, what are ye waiting for? Click the link below to join and set sail toward exciting adventures in American History.

Access your bonus here: https://ahoypublications.com/

Or, Scan the QR code!

Table of Contents

Part 1: English History
1000 Interesting Facts About England

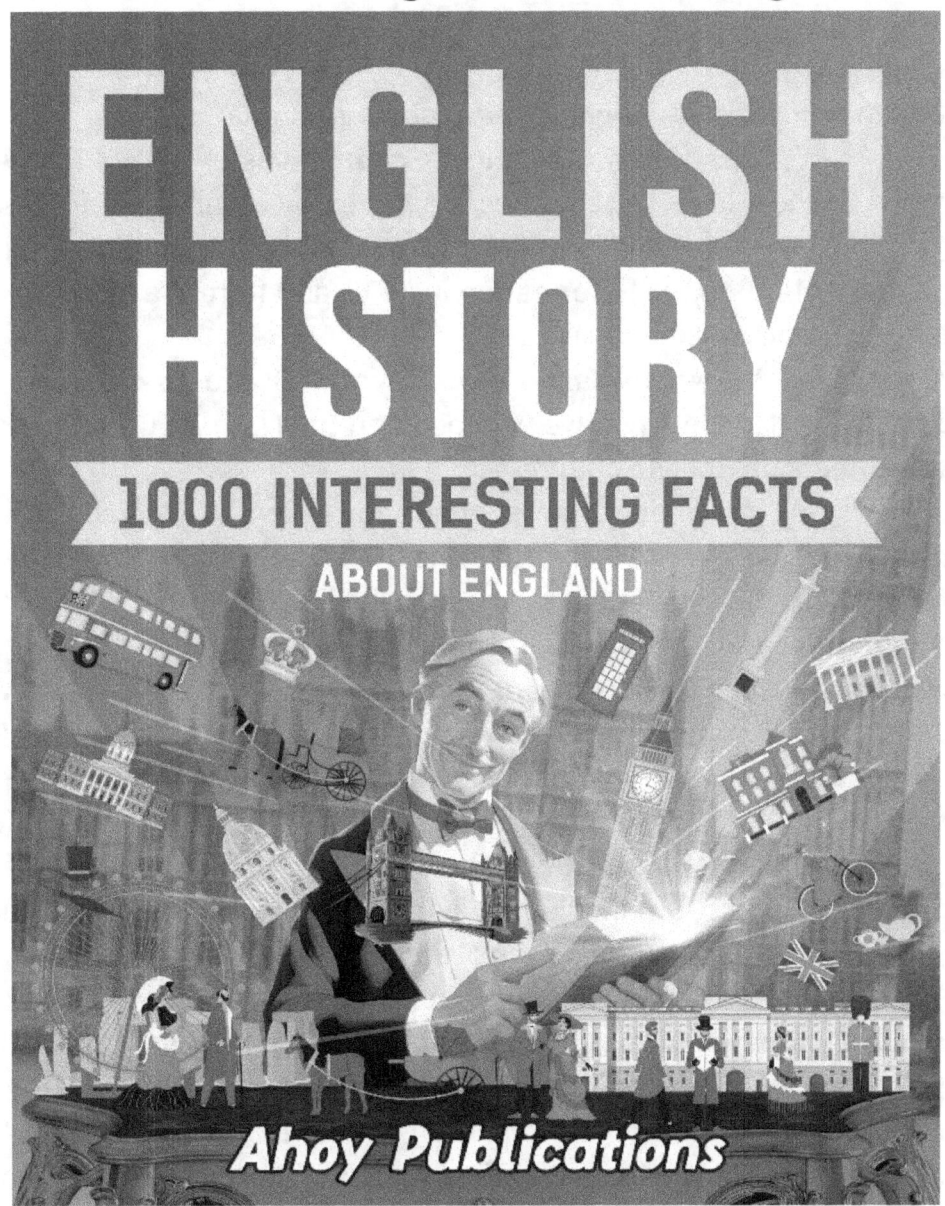

Introduction

*For centuries, the **history of England** has been tumultuous, filled with invasions, conquests, and revolutions.* **From the Anglo-Saxon invasion of 449 to present-day Brexit**, England's political landscape has been shaped by a variety of forces. This book will explore the major events and eras that have shaped **England's history**, from **the Norman Conquest** in 1066 **to the Reformation in 1517** and from **the Industrial Revolution** of the 18ᵗʰ century to **the Brexit vote** in 2016.

*You'll first learn about the **Anglo-Saxon invasion*** of 449 and its impact on England's political and social landscape. Then we will focus on the Norman Conquest of 1066 and its long-lasting effects on English culture.

*From there, you'll find fascinating facts about the reign **of William the Conqueror**,* including an in-depth look at how his rule changed England. We'll move on to some interesting facts about **the Plantagenet dynasty**, which ruled England beginning in 1154 and ended with **the Hundred Years' War** in 1453.

*And there were so many wars in **English history!*** We'll also explore **the Wars of the Roses**, a series of **civil wars** fought between two rival branches of **the Plantagenet dynasty**, and **the Reformation**, a period of religious upheaval that began in 1517.

*In the second section, we'll delve into **the Elizabethan era**, **the English Civil War**, **the Restoration, and the Glorious Revolution**.* You'll learn some interesting facts about the **Age of Enlightenment**, a period of intellectual and scientific progress that began in 1715.

*From there, **the Industrial Revolution*** and the abolition of the slave trade will be *discussed—you'll be surprised by the facts on those!* Afterward, we will look at **the Reform Acts, the Victorian era, the Crimean War, the Great Exhibition, the Irish Potato Famine, and the Boer Wars.**

Speaking of wars, you'll learn some interesting tidbits about the two world wars, **the welfare state, the Suez Crisis, decolonization, and the Thatcher years.** Finally, our last two chapters will cover **the Good Friday Agreement** and **Brexit**, respectively.

*By reading this book, you will gain an appreciation for how **England's history** has been shaped by a variety of forces over the past few centuries.* **From invasions to revolutions,** England's political landscape has been marked by tumultuous events and moments of progress. **You will surely find this book informative and intriguing.** We hope you'll continue your journey after finishing the book to learn more about **England's history!**

Section 1: Exploring Pre-Modern England
Roman Britain
(43–c. 410 CE)

Explore the fascinating history of Roman Britain. This unique collection of facts will shed light on the pivotal moments that shaped this captivating period.

Though Roman forces under Julius Caesar landed in Britain, they did not stay long. The Roman occupation began in 43 CE when Roman Emperor Claudius initiated the invasion that would establish Roman authority in Britain. You'll read about the rise of a new civilization in Britain and the Romans' eventual withdrawal when Rome declined in power.

1. **Around 55 BCE, Julius Caesar** they were unsuccessful in establishing lasting Roman control.

2. **In 43 CE, Emperor Claudius ordered the Roman invasion of Britain**, which was led by **Aulus Plautius**. This marked **the official beginning of Roman rule**.

3. **Roman forces established the city of Londinium** (now London) **around 47 CE**, which became an important center of commerce and administration.

4. **Hadrian's Wall**, a fortification **built in 122 CE**, marked the northernmost boundary of **Roman Britain**, providing defense against northern tribes.

5. **The construction of the Antonine Wall began in 142**. It was located farther north in **modern-day Scotland**, but it was abandoned just a few decades later.

6. **Boudicca, queen of the Iceni tribe, led a major rebellion against Roman rule in 60 or 61**, resulting in the significant destruction of Roman settlements.

7. **Roman Britain experienced a period of relative peace and prosperity during the 2nd century CE, known as the Pax Romana.**

8. **By the 3rd century CE, Roman Britain had developed a thriving economy**, with trade networks and the production of various goods, including pottery and metalwork.

9. **Christianity began to spread in Roman Britain during the 3rd century**. By the 4th century, it had become the dominant religion.

10. **In 410, the Roman Empire withdrew its troops from Britain**, leaving the region vulnerable to raids by invading **Germanic tribes**.

11. **The departure of the Romans marked the beginning of the period known as sub-Roman Britain,** which was characterized by a decline in central authority.

12. **The legendary King Arthur**, often associated with **the period of sub-Roman Britain**, is believed by some to have led a **resistance against invading forces**.

13. **The Anglo-Saxon migration from continental Europe increased in the 5th and 6th centuries,** gradually replacing Roman-British culture.

14. **The Lindisfarne Gospels**, a remarkable illuminated manuscript, **was created around 700 CE,** showcasing **the blending of Celtic and Anglo-Saxon artistic traditions.**

15. **The legacy of Roman Britain can be seen today in the surviving archaeological sites,** Roman roads, and the influence of Latin on the English language.

Anglo-Saxon Invasion
(449–1066)

From 449 to 1066 CE, Britain was invaded by the Anglo-Saxons. The Anglo-Saxons were Germanic tribes. They were mostly farmers and craftsmen, but they were also warriors who fought against the native Britons, eventually dividing the land into several kingdoms, such as Wessex, Essex, Sussex, and Mercia. They were often at odds with each other. "Britons" is the name for the people who lived in England before the Anglo-Saxon invasions.

This era saw great artistic achievements, including literature like Beowulf and the Anglo-Saxon Chronicle, and advancements in metalworking skills and architecture. In 1066, these advances were halted when the Anglo-Saxons were defeated by the Normans, leading to significant changes politically, economically, and socially.

16. **The Anglo-Saxons began migrating to England around 449.** The Anglo-Saxons shortly became the dominant force in England. **They ruled until 1066**.

17. **Three Germanic tribes made their way to England: the Angles, Saxons, and Jutes.**

18. **They were collectively called the Anglo-Saxons.** They were the first people to be called **"English."**

19. **They came from northern Europe to England** in search of new land from their original homes in what is today **northern Germany and Denmark**. These places were too crowded. Too many tribes lived in the areas around their homelands.

20. **Though the Jutes, a Germanic tribe from Denmark, joined the Angles and Saxons migrating to England**, it is believed they were assimilated into Anglo-Saxon culture about a century after their arrival.

21. **The Anglo-Saxon invasion changed England forever**. They brought their language (which became Old English), customs, beliefs, and laws.

22. Important figures who lived during this era include **Alfred the Great**, who defended **England against Viking invasions**; **Bede, a monk** and **scholar**; **Offa of Mercia**, regarded as one of the most powerful kings in England during his time; **and Ethelbert of Kent**, who became **the first Anglo-Saxon king to convert to Christianity**.

23. One famous battle during this time was the **Battle of Edington (878)**, in which King **Alfred the Great of Wessex** defeated a large Viking army.

24. **Danish and Norwegian Vikings began raiding along British** coastlines from the 8th century onward.

25. **The Anglo-Saxon tribes were divided into seven small kingdoms known as the Heptarchy**. These kingdoms were independent of each other. They often fought one another.

26. Eventually, **the Kingdom of Wessex became the most powerful**. It unified all seven into one large kingdom known as **England or the "Land of the Angles."**

27. **Strong kings had control over laws, taxes, military matters, and government decisions.** They were responsible for the people's welfare. However, kings often sought advice from their ealdormen, a type of governor.

28. **Wergild ("man price") determined how much compensation a person** should receive if they were wronged or injured or if a family member was killed.

29. **Important literary works from this era include** *Beowulf* (a heroic epic poem) and **Bede's** *Ecclesiastical History of the English People* (an important sourcebook about early Christianity in Britain). **The** *Anglo-Saxon Chronicle*, a record of events that took place during the reign of **Alfred the Great** (r. 871-899), is one of the most important Anglo-Saxon references.

30. The later **Anglo-Saxon period saw an increase in literacy and education**. Schools were established to teach **Latin and Greek literature**, **mathematics**, and **philosophy** to the upper class.

31. **The Anglo-Saxons originally believed in the many Germanic gods**, like **Woden/Odin** (the father of the gods), **Thunor/Thor** (the god of thunder), **Freya** (the goddess of love), and **Tiw/Tyr** (the god of war). All of these gods were venerated by the Anglo-Saxons' later enemies, the Vikings.

32. **Their beliefs changed once Christianity started to spread**. The religion was first introduced by **St Augustine of Canterbury in 597 when Pope Gregory** I sent him on a mission to convert the Anglo-Saxons.

33. **The Anglo-Saxons were very skilled craftsmen**. They worked with wood, stone, metal, leather, and textiles to create beautiful works of art and practical items, such as **weapons and tools.**

34. **Anglo-Saxon architecture was characterized by timber buildings** with thatched roofs. Later periods saw the introduction of more lasting materials like **brick and stone**.

35. **Homes during this era varied depending on social class**. Kings and nobles lived in fancy halls, but most people lived in very simple huts and cottages.

36. **The Anglo-Saxon period saw the construction of burghs**, fortified towns. Any British town with "burgh" at the end was founded during this time.

37. **Their most important form of entertainment was storytelling**, which would often include elements of mythology and heroic deeds.

38. **Pre-Christian Anglo-Saxons believed in a variety of magical creatures**, including elves, dragons, fairies, and giants, which were often mentioned in stories from this era.

39. **Music was popular among all classes**. Instruments included drums, flutes/pipes, harps, and lyres. Music styles ranged **from folk songs to epic poems** set to primitive melodies.

40. **Games were also played. Dice games like knucklebones**, which was similar to modern-day jacks, were popular.

41. **Drinking alcohol was common**. Mead, a beverage made with honey, and ale, a **beer made from barley,** were very popular. **Alcoholic drinks were often drunk instead of water**. Water often carried bacteria, which made people sick.

42. **Traditional clothing at this time consisted mostly of woolen garments for men and women.** They wore **tunics** (long shirts), **cloaks or coats**, or **trousers or hose**. Women wore linen shifts, usually a long shirt tied at the waist. **Wealthy women wore dresses**. Almost everyone wore leather shoes or boots.

43. **The average lifespan in Anglo-Saxon England was less than forty years** for most people. Royalty, especially kings, tended to live a bit longer.

44. **By the end of the Anglo-Saxon period, England was a very wealthy nation**. Foreign rulers sought to control it, such as the Normans and the Vikings.

45. **The Anglo-Saxon period ended in 1066 when William of Normandy, later known as William the Conqueror, invaded England.**

Vikings in England
(793–1066)

The Vikings were people from Norway, Denmark, and Sweden who began to sail from their Scandinavian homes to explore and raid the world around them in the 8th century CE. Most Swedish Vikings traveled east to Russia and Ukraine, but **the Danes and Norwegians traveled west**. Initially, **they raided England** for riches but later came to settle.

Over the years, **the Vikings and the English fought many battles**. At one point, **the Scandinavians controlled much of England. Their chief city was Jorvik**, today's York, in northeastern England. The area around the city and across the country to the Irish Sea was called the **Danelaw** by the Anglo-Saxons. Learn more about this adventurous and dangerous time with these thirty facts!

46. **Vikings raided, traded, and then settled in many parts of Britain and Ireland.**

47. **In the 800s, many Vikings and their families began to settle in England**, especially in the north and the southeastern part of the country known as **East Anglia**.

48. **Most of the Vikings who settled in the northeastern part of England were Danes. Norwegian Vikings, called the Norse**, settled in the northwest part of England and the southwest part of Scotland, along with the northern Orkney and Hebrides islands. **Vikings also established bases and cities in Ireland.**

49. **Though the Vikings controlled islands off the coast of Scotland** and some towns in the English/Scottish border regions, **they never controlled Scotland like they did parts of England.**

50. **When battles between the Vikings and Anglo-Saxons began**, the Vikings had an advantage. Many Vikings had been in battle before. Many of the early **Anglo-Saxon armies they met were largely made up of the *fyrd*** (pronounced similar to "feared"), who were **farmers and peasants** ordered to serve in the army. **Most of them had no training or experience.**

51. **No place was safe from Viking raiders, as their ships were capable of traveling even shallow rivers.**

52. **Monasteries were the prime targets of Viking raids in the initial Viking period.** These buildings were often very rich in gold coins and religious items.

53. **The most famous raid of a monastery was the first raid on the island of Lindisfarne** on the northern coast of England in 793.

54. **As the interaction between the Anglo-Saxons and Vikings grew**, so did **the spread of Christian beliefs among the Vikings.**

55. **Contrary to what many people believe, the Vikings and English often lived in the same areas.** They traded with one another and occasionally intermarried.

56. **The Vikings didn't bring death and destruction to England.** Because many Vikings established trading networks, England began to trade with many more cultures.

57. **Many archaeological finds in England from this period** came from as far away as the Middle East, Russia, and Ukraine, places where the Vikings had settled or had trading stations.

58. **Viking art in the form of woodwork and jewelry was very similar to pre-Christian Anglo-Saxon artwork**. This is not surprising since some **Vikings came from the same areas as the Angles, Saxons, and Jutes** before they traveled to Britain.

59. **The modern city of York was known to the Vikings as Jorvik.** It was the most important Viking city and fortress in England.

60. **Control of York ("Jorvik") went back and forth between the Vikings and Anglo-Saxons from about 850 to 954**, when the Anglo-Saxons took control of the city. Even under Viking King Canute, York was governed by the Anglo-Saxons.

61. **Today, it's easy to identify towns in England that were founded by the Vikings.** For example, towns and cities that end in "by" were founded by the Danes.

62. **Though the land in England controlled by the Vikings grew, shrank, and moved over time,** the northeastern and north-central **part of England became known as the Danelaw**, the area where the law of the Danes was in effect.

63. **The area of England north of Liverpool and into the famous Lake Country was controlled by Norwegian Vikings** during the Viking period rather than the Danes.

64. **The Great Heathen Army, also known as the Great Viking Army, invaded England in 865.** Before this, most Viking invasions of England were smaller raids.

65. **Legend has it that the legendary Viking Ragnar Lothbrok's three sons led the Great Heathen Army.** Historians aren't sure if Ragnar was a legend or a real person.

66. **One of the men who claimed to be Ragnar's son was Ivar the Boneless.** Some historians and archaeologists believe **that Ivar was killed in a battle near Repton**, where a mass grave with Viking bodies was found in the early 1970s.

67. **One of the ways we study Viking history is by finding and studying the many hoards of coins, jewelry, weapons, and precious metals the Vikings buried underground.** Hoards are still being found in England and other places to this day.

68. **By the mid-9th century, the Vikings controlled much of England.** The only Anglo-Saxon kingdom left was Wessex.

69. **For fifteen years, the king of Wessex, later known as Alfred the Great, united the Saxon kingdoms, fought the Vikings,** and pushed them away from the borders of his kingdom.

70. **In 1002, the king of Wessex, Æthelred (eh-thel-red) the Unready, ordered a massacre of Danes in England.** Historians aren't sure how many Danes were killed in the **St. Brice's Day massacre.** Thousands could have been killed.

71. Although many people believe that **Æthelred's nickname means that he was unready, the title has its roots in the Saxon word** *redeless,* which means **"without counsel"** or "without advice."

72. **In 1016, Viking King Canute became king of England, Denmark, and Norway.** However, he named **the English Harold I** as his successor as king of England.

73. A famous **tale about King Canute** tells the story of how he **ordered the tides to stop coming in.** Many people today think this might be because he was crazy, but he did this to show his men that there were things he could not do.

74. **Before William of Normandy launched his invasion of England** in the fall of 1066, the last great Viking invasion of England took place in northeastern England. **Famous Viking warrior** (which means **"hard ruler"** in Old Norse) believed he had a claim to the English throne.

75. **Hardrada** was defeated and killed by **English King Harold Godwinson** at the **Battle of Stamford Bridge** on September 25th, 1066, just three weeks before **the Battle of Hastings.**

Norman Conquest
(1066–1075)

In this chapter, we'll explore **the Norman Conquest of England**. Let's look at the culture, language, laws, government, and architecture introduced **by William the Conqueror** and his sons. **The Norman Conquest** impacted **the economic and social structure of England.** There's so much to discover, so let's get started!

76. **The Norman Conquest was a very important event in English history,** taking place between 1066 and 1075.

77. **Prior to 1066, there weren't any large-scale battles fought between the English and armies from what is now France.**

78. **The Norman Conquest was a gradual process,** not just one single event.

79. **It started with the Battle of Hastings** on October 14th, 1066, when **Duke William of Normandy** (part of modern-day France) **invaded England.**

80. **William defeated King Harold II of England at the Battle of Hastings** and became the **first Norman king of England.**

81. Not long **before King Harold was defeated by William I,** his **Anglo-Saxon army fought and defeated the last great Viking army at the Battle of Stamford Bridge.** Many historians believe **Harold** might have won **Hastings** if **the Vikings had not invaded.**

82. **"Norman"** is a variation of the word **"Northmen."** The **Normans were originally Vikings who were given the land by the king of France** to protect the region from other Vikings.

83. **After winning the battle, William marched to London,** where **he was crowned king on Christmas Day in 1066 at Westminster Abbey by Archbishop Aldred of York.**

84. **William then established his court at Winchester Castle in Hampshire,** which became his main base for ruling England until his death in September 1087.

85. **Though William became king of England**, he spent most of the rest of his life in his homeland of **Normandy.**

86. **William I built many castles as a way of showing his strength to the people of England. Windsor Castle,** near **London**, was built during his reign.

87. **Many monasteries and abbeys were built in the years following the Norman Conquest.**

88. **The Normans are credited with introducing several buildings that were not previously seen in Britain, such as windmills, stone castles, and many Romanesque-style churches and cathedrals.** Some of them still stand today!

89. **The Normans spoke a French dialect,** which **became the language of the English court** until the 14th century.

90. **The Normans introduced some French elements to Old English,** which helped to evolve the English language we speak today.

91. **The new "Anglo-Norman" culture that developed in England after 1066 marked a new beginning in English history**. The people of England who united under the Norman kings can be recognized as the start of the modern-day **"English" culture**.

92. **Much Norman literature had to do with romance**. These romantic legends later influenced courtly culture in England, like **the famous stories of knights and damsels** in distress.

93. **The famous legend of Robin Hood is a story of the Anglo-Saxon resistance** to the Norman occupation of England.

94. **The Domesday Book, which was commissioned by William I,** is an important record that details life during this time. **The book includes information about landholdings, population numbers, and more.** The book was meant **to help William with taxation.**

95. **The most well-known piece of art about the Normans of England is the Bayeux Tapestry,** which tells the story of **the Norman Conquest**, including **the Battle of Hastings.**

96. **After the conquest, nobles who supported William became wealthy and powerful,** while those who opposed him had their lands taken away. Some even had to flee Britain!

97. During this period, **there were three main classes: the king and his family, nobles/lords/high clergy** (who owned most of the land), and the common people, most of whom did not own land.

98. **The Normans introduced feudalism into England**, meaning people worked for nobles in exchange for protection and the use of their land.

99. **Many of the new laws introduced by William were based on Roman law and French customs,** creating a hybrid system with elements from all cultures living in England at the time.

100. **William introduced a new form of punishment for rebellions called the Harrying**, which involved destroying villages or crops as retribution for crimes committed against him or his officials.

101. **Because William and his successors controlled Normandy in continental Europe, trade between England and Europe increased at this time.**

102. **Normans eventually established kingdoms in Sicily and the Holy Land**. This meant that at one time, **Normans ruled places from the North Sea to the Middle East.**

103. **William was very sick for five weeks before he died.** He died in September 1087, and his body was transported many miles to his **capital, Rouen, Normandy**. At the funeral, his abdomen exploded, covering the mourners with his insides. His body was quickly thrown into a hole and covered up.

104. In 1087, William's son, **William II, took control after his death**. William II ruled for a little over a decade before **Henry I** succeeded him. William II is also known as **William II Rufus** because of his flaming red hair. **"Rufus"** means **"red-haired"** in Latin.

105. **The Norman Conquest was the last time that England was invaded.** Though **Napoleon** and **Hitler** planned and prepared for their own **invasions of England**, they were defeated before these attacks could happen.

Plantagenet Dynasty
(1154–1485)

Now we will take a closer look at one of **the most famous English families and dynasties.** We'll discover thirty facts about how the Plantagenet family and its rule affected this period of England's history. You'll learn **interesting facts about how they established an empire**, reformed the legal system, and built universities.

106. **The Plantagenet dynasty ruled England from 1154 to 1485** and included many famous kings like **Henry II, Richard I** (the Lionheart), **John** (Lackland), and **Edward III.**

107. **"Plantagenet" comes from the Latin name** *planta genista*, the yellow broom flower, which is the symbol of the ruling family of **the French province of Anjou**. The Plantagenets were originally from Anjou. The Plantagenet kings are often referred to as the Angevin kings of England. **An Angevin is someone from Anjou.**

108. One of the most powerful members of this dynasty was **Eleanor of Aquitaine**, who brought her vast lands in France with her when **she married Henry II in 1152.**

109. Before Eleanor married Henry II, **she had been the wife of King Louis VII of France**, but the marriage was annulled in 1152.

 110. **While she was married to Louis, Eleanor actually joined the Christian armies on the Third Crusade and traveled to the Holy Land** to try to regain Christian control from the Muslims.

111. In 1173, **Henry II's son, called "Young Henry," revolted against his father. Eleanor was arrested and imprisoned for thirteen years** because she supported her stepson instead of her husband, whom she had grown to hate.

112. **Richard I, sometimes known as Richard the Lionheart** or Lionhearted, **ruled from 1189 to 1199. He fought against the Muslim ruler Saladin in the Third Crusade** and was one of the most influential figures of his time.

113. **King John ruled from 1199 to 1216. The Magna Carta was signed by King John** in 1215, **which limited his power to rule** without consulting a council of nobles first.

114. **Magna Carta means "great charter" in Latin** and is thought to have inspired the **US Constitution.**

115. **King John was forced to sign the Magna Carta after many English nobles vowed to revolt if he didn't.** Many nobles rebelled against John anyway in an attempt to reduce his power and replace his family on the throne.

116. **John's son, Henry III, became king, but he did have slightly less power** than English kings before John.

117. **King Edward I ruled from 1272 to 1307.** In 1290, **he issued a decree expelling all Jews from England.** They weren't allowed back into the country until 1656 under **Oliver Cromwell's** rule.

118. **During Edward I's reign, he enacted laws that punished those found guilty with death by hanging or drawing and quartering**, one of the cruelest forms of execution ever used.

119. In 1274, **Edward I ordered a census and a study of the government in various areas of England called the "Hundred Rolls."** A variety of legal reforms were introduced because of this study.

120. **Edward I added Wales to his realm** between 1277 and 1283. The Welsh still consider themselves the only remaining Britons.

121. During this period, **there were battles between England and Scotland** known as the Wars of **Scottish Independence**, which lasted for over thirty years in the late 13th and 14th centuries.

122. **The famous Scottish hero William Wallace fought King Edward I** at the beginning of the First Scottish War of Independence, which took place from 1296 to 1328.

123. **Edward III ruled from 1327 to 1377.** He created a special order of knights known as **the Knights of the Garter**, which still exists today.

124. In 1337, **King Edward III declared war on France**, which would later become known as **the Hundred Years' War**. It ended in 1453 when **Henry V signed the Treaty of Troyes**, giving up English claims over French lands.

125. **One famous Plantagenet king was Richard III,** who ruled from 1483 to 1485. **He was made famous in Shakespeare's play of the same name**, which was about **the famous Wars of the Roses** that you will read about shortly.

126. **Traveling minstrels or troubadours became popular during this period**. They often sang songs in the royal courts. Their songs were mostly about love or chivalry.

127. **Chivalry flourished among knights at tournaments during this time**. They proved their skill with weapons or jousted on horseback.

128. One of the most famous books in English history was **Thomas Malory's *Le Morte d'Arthur*** (*The Death of Arthur*). The book was written in the mid-15th century. It was the first comprehensive work on the stories of **the mythical King Arthur**.

129. One of the most important pieces of English literature written during this period was **Geoffrey Chaucer's** *Canterbury Tales*, a collection of stories about pilgrims on their way to Canterbury Cathedral.

130. **During the Plantagenet dynasty, schools were founded all over England.** Some even taught Latin, Hebrew, and Greek. **These schools were not for everyone. Only the royals**, nobles, their families, and those destined for the clergy could attend.

131. **Oxford University, which is thought to have been founded in 1096 during Norman times,** became the largest university in England under the Plantagenets. The dynasty banned English students from studying in France. **Cambridge was founded in 1209 and was given a royal charter in 1231 by Henry III.**

132. **The number of fortified castles in England grew at this time.** The wars with the Scots, occasional rebellions, and the possibility of a French invasion caused the Plantagenets to fortify their realm.

133. **The Plantagenet dynasty saw an increase in trade with other countries in Europe,** which led to greater cultural exchange between England and its neighbors.

134. **The Plantagenets created a new system of taxation called lay subsidies**, which required people to pay taxes based on their income or assets. This system had rarely been used in Europe before this time.

135. **The English language continued to evolve during this era** due to the influence of the French after the Norman invasion and the rise of the Plantagenets.

The Hundred Years' War
(1337–1453)

The Hundred Years' War was fought between England and France. The war lasted from **1337 to 1453** and was a time of turmoil that had deep, lasting effects on England and its people. Let's look at thirty **captivating facts about the battles, weapons, and strategies** used on both sides. We will also discover how this very long war impacted both countries.

136. **The Hundred Years' War was a conflict between England and France** that lasted for 116 years.

137. **It began when King Edward III of England, who had a weak claim to the French throne,** invaded France in 1337, which led to a series of battles. The fighting did not end until 1453.

138. Many famous figures from both sides took part in this war, including **King Henry V** on the English side and **Joan of Arc, King Charles VII**, and **Bertrand du Guesclin** on the French side.

139. **It is estimated that over three million people were killed during the war**, making it one of **the deadliest conflicts in European history at that time**. Many of these deaths came from disease, which people contracted because of poor sanitation. The arrival of **the Black Death** from Asia also occurred during this period.

140. **The Black Death killed off a third of Europe's population** and drastically reduced the number of soldiers available for both sides in this prolonged war. **The pandemic might have been one of the factors that led to the war's eventual end.**

141. **The Battle of Auberoche in 1345 is considered one of Edward III's first major successes** during this conflict. His victory enabled him to capture many territories in southwestern France.

142. **In 1346, Edward III scored a decisive victory against Philip VI at Crécy** with his longbowmen, who defeated an army twice their size.

143. **In 1355, Edward III granted his son, Edward "the Black Prince," command over an army.** He used the army to raid French territories during what became known as the **Chevauchée**, meaning "promenade" or "horse charge." **The Black Prince** raided behind enemy lines on horseback.

144. **During this war, both sides used a variety of tactics**, such as siege warfare, mass use of the longbow by the English, ambush, and heavy cavalry charges.

145. **One key strategy used by both sides was to build huge castles as defensive fortifications** along their borders with each other. Many of them are ruins today.

146. **During this war, both sides used spies to gather information** on their enemy's tactics and plans. Some **historians believe that espionage played an important role** in determining who won certain battles!

147. In 1360, **the Treaty of Brétigny led to temporary peace between England and France**. The peace lasted until 1369, when hostilities resumed after **Charles V rejected its terms**.

148. **The Battle of Agincourt** in 1415 saw the English, led by **Henry V,** emerge victorious, even though the enemy outnumbered them six to one.

149. One key moment during the war was when **Henry V captured Harfleur (1415)** on his way to **the Battle of Agincourt**. This was a major victory for the English, and it gave them access to a much-needed port.

150. **The English first used cannons at the siege of Harfleur**, which helped them knock down some of the city's defenses.

151. **During the Hundred Years' War, the English forces managed to capture large parts of France, including Normandy, Aquitaine, and Poitou**. However, they eventually lost control over these territories by 1453 when peace was agreed upon.

152. In 1394, **John Hawkwood, one of the most famous commanders in English history, managed to break through French defenses at Meaux** using innovative siege tactics, such as mining and counter-mining tunnels beneath walls.

153. **Joan of Arc, known as the "Maid of Orléans,"** was a teenage peasant girl who led an army against the English in 1429 after hearing voices from God telling her to do so. **She correctly proclaimed victories before they happened.** People believed she had a personal connection with God.

154. **One reason England ultimately lost was that Charles VII reunited a very divided France under his rule**, giving him a huge advantage in terms of resources.

155. **This long-running conflict had a huge economic impact on Europe** at that time, draining resources and disrupting trade routes, which caused food shortages across Europe.

156. **One key battle from the later stages of this conflict was fought at Formigny in 1450.** French forces under Jean de Villiers defeated an army led by Thomas Kyriell.

157. **De Villiers combined new tactics, like cannon fire, with traditional strategies**, like cavalry charges. This battle marked a turning point in the war. **France would eventually win in 1453.**

158. **Toward the end of the war, the English were suffering from heavy losses and difficulty in supplying their troops across the English Channel**. Disease also took its toll.

159. **The last battle of the Hundred Years' War was fought at Castillon (1453).** This ended with **a decisive French victory** which effectively marked the end of the English claim on the French throne.

160. **This conflict also saw the first use of guns on European battlefields**, although these firearms were much less effective than traditional medieval weaponry like swords and arrows.

161. **The Hundred Years' War led to the creation of new technologies, such as improved crossbows,** which could fire more powerful arrows at longer distances. **Crossbows helped both sides gain an advantage** over each other during certain battles.

162. **This war marked a transition from traditional medieval warfare toward modern tactics,** which included standing armies, better use of **artillery weapons** (like cannons) combined with infantry forces, and siege engines.

163. **The Hundred Years' War marked the dawn of the age of chivalry. Knights** began using **armored horses wearing** full plate armor. **Soldiers** were no longer just mounted archers or light cavalrymen. **"Chivalry"** is an English word with French roots. *Cheval* **is French for "horse."**

164. **Tales of chivalry became quite popular at this time.** People loved to read stories about mounted knights fighting one another and courtly love **between knights and "damsels in distress."**

165. **This long and bloody war was a major cultural event in European history**, with many contemporary writers and poets writing about it in their works.

Wars of the Roses
(1455–1487)

This chapter will explore the fascinating history of **the Wars of the Roses, a civil war in England** that lasted from 1455 to 1487. **It was fought between two branches of the royal house of Plantagenet.** We'll take a look at thirty interesting facts about the people, battles, politics, and legacy of this major turning point in English history.

166. **The Wars of the Roses was a civil war in England** that was fought between 1455 and 1487.

167. **England has had more than one civil war, although there is only one conflict called *the* English Civil War.** That war took place between 1642 and 1652. We'll tell you more about that war in another section.

168. **The war was fought between two branches of the House of Plantagenet,** known as **the House of Lancaster** (symbolized by a red rose) and the **House of York** (symbolized by a white rose).

169. **These wars had an impact on fashion, with people wearing their house colors to show support.** They wore red or white roses at events like tournaments or festivals, which were popular during this time.

170. **These two sides fought for control over England until Henry Tudor of Lancaster won the Battle of Bosworth Field in 1485,** where he defeated Richard III of York.

171. **During these wars, many powerful families supported either side, such as the Nevilles, Percys, Stanleys, Greys, and Talbots.** They all fought for control over England's throne.

172. **Many famous people were involved in the Wars of the Roses**, like **Margaret Beaufort**, who helped her son, **Henry Tudor**, gain power through alliances with other noble families. **John Neville** acted as commander-in-chief for his brother, known as **Warwick the Kingmaker.**

173. **The Battle of Towton in 1461** is considered to be one of **the bloodiest battles ever fought on English soil**. No one knows for sure, but it is said that an estimated twenty-eight thousand people were killed during the battle, which took place in a heavy snowstorm.

174. **Edward IV won many battles for York during these wars,** allowing him to **become king in 1461.** He ruled for twelve years, although he had to flee the country for a short period of time.

175. **Richard III is remembered as a tyrant king because he usurped power from Edward V, Edward IV's son.**

176. **Richard was also thought to have kidnapped and killed the young princes,** his nephews, to prevent them from claiming the throne.

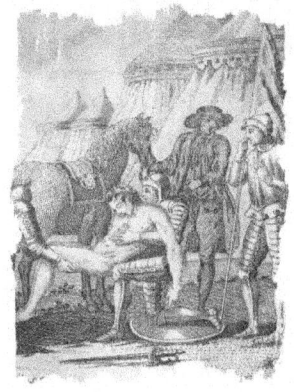

177. **Richard III was later immortalized by William Shakespeare as an evil tyrant in his play *Richard III,*** which helped shape people's opinions of him. Today, historians believe he might not have been as bad as originally thought.

178. **Richard was the last English king to die in battle,** doing so at Bosworth Field, the final battle of **the Wars of the Roses.**

179. **Richard III's body was found in 2012 in the Grey Friars site in Leicester County in an open area** that once was a car park. In 2015, **Richard III was given a royal burial in Leicester Cathedral.**

180. **Margaret Beaufort played an important role in bringing about peace between both sides through her marriage negotiations with Lord Stanley,** who then helped her son **Henry Tudor** obtain victory at **Bosworth Field** against **Richard III.**

181. Women played an important role during this period, like **Elizabeth Woodville,** the non-noble wife of **Edward IV,** whose unpopularity helped bring about **the Wars of the Roses. Margaret of Anjou, wife of Henry VI,** played a large role behind the scenes and was a key figure in the outbreak of the war.

182. **Margaret of Anjou** is another important female figure from this time period. She was **the queen consort of Henry VI** and a powerful leader in her own right, leading troops into battle at the Battle of Tewkesbury, where she was defeated by **Edward IV**.

183. **When the war ended, Henry VII married Elizabeth of York, daughter of Edward IV. Henry and Elizabeth were the parents of Henry VIII** and the grandparents of **Elizabeth I. Henry VII was the first Tudor monarch,** and **Elizabeth I was the last.**

184. At the end of the war, **the symbols of Lancaster and York were united into the Tudor Rose,** a rose with both white and red petals.

185. **One of the major reasons why these wars lasted so long was because both sides were evenly matched,** with neither side having a long-lasting clear advantage over the other until **Richard III's defeat at Bosworth Field**

186. **During this period, England also underwent many changes, including using more gunpowder weapons,** which made battles more destructive. New laws were created, and taxes were increased because the military campaigns took up so many resources.

187. **These wars had a major impact on English politics, with nobles becoming less powerful while Parliament began playing a slightly larger role in national decisions**.

188. **Many towns that were destroyed during this conflict never fully recovered**, leading to lasting economic decline in some areas. It also caused mistrust between different regions. Some of the regional rivalries in soccer, for instance, date back to **the Wars of the Roses.**

189. **This conflict caused much suffering throughout England, with people fleeing their homes or being killed due to battles taking place nearby**. Famine, disease, and poverty spread across many regions, making life difficult for those who survived.

190. **It has been estimated that up to 100,000 men were killed during the Wars of the Roses,** making it one of the bloodiest conflicts ever fought on British soil.

191. **The Wars of the Roses had an impact on literature,** with writers like **William Shakespeare** writing about it in their works. To this day, **the Wars of the Roses** are a popular topic in historical novels.

192. **Music was also influenced by these wars**, with many songs written about it, such as **"Rose of England,"** which was very popular back in the day.

193. Despite everything that happened during these wars, **they ultimately helped to unify England. One king was recognized by everyone**, creating more stability and increasing trade between England and mainland Europe.

194. **The Wars of the Roses helped create a sense of national identity in England,** as people began to feel more connected and loyal toward their country.

195. **It has been over five hundred years since these wars ended,** but they are still remembered today at historical sites around Britain, such as **Bosworth Battlefield Heritage Centre** and **Richard III Visitor's Centre**, both located near **Leicester**.

The English Reformation

This chapter will explore **the momentous English Reformation**, a period of **religious and political revolution** that was affected by **the greater Protestant Reformation**. The Reformation **changed the course of history**; let's see how as we cruise through thirty interesting facts **about this important time in European history.**

196. **The Protestant Reformation was a religious and political movement that changed Europe in the 1500s.**

197. **It started when Martin Luther wrote his *Ninety-five Theses*,** criticizing the Catholic Church for its practices of selling indulgences and other corrupt activities.

198. **Luther was later excommunicated from the Catholic Church by Pope Leo X** in 1521, which officially began the Protestant Reformation throughout Europe.

199. **The Reformation led to the creation of many different forms of Protestantism, such as Calvinism, Lutheranism, and Anabaptists,** which later developed into denominations like **Baptists, Presbyterians, Methodists, and Congregationalists.**

200. **The English form of Protestantism is called Anglicanism.** In some places, it is referred to as Episcopalian.

201. **The Reformation had a huge influence on the English language since the Bible was translated into vernacular** (regional language). **Before, the Bible was printed in Latin.**

202. **William Tyndale was responsible for translating the Bible into English using the original Greek and Hebrew texts.** The first published edition came out in 1526, although revised versions were released posthumously **after Tyndale's execution.**

203. **Tyndale was executed in 1536** on charges of heresy. **He opposed Henry VIII's** annulment of Catherine of Aragon.

204. There were many influential theologians who interpreted the Bible differently. **John Calvin, Huldrych Zwingli, and Philip Melanchthon** are just some examples.

205. **In England, Thomas Cranmer helped Henry VIII with his infamous separation from Catherine of Aragon**. Henry VIII wanted a male heir, and Catherine had been unable to provide him with one. **Henry wanted to annul his marriage and marry a new wife, Anne Boleyn.**

206. **The pope refused to grant Henry a divorce since he didn't want to anger the Holy Roman emperor**. So, Henry decided to split from the Catholic Church, granting himself the separation he so greatly desired.

207. **King Henry VIII's Act of Supremacy was passed in 1534**. The act declared him the head of **the Church of England**. He no longer had to follow what the pope said.

208. **The pope was so upset by Henry's actions that he excommunicated the English king!**

209. **Henry's marriage to Anne Boleyn produced a child**, but he did not get the male heir that he wanted. **Anne Boleyn would eventually be executed on the grounds of treason.**

210. **Although Henry created a new church, he still kept many Catholic practices**.

211. **Though the archbishop of Canterbury ran the everyday business of the Church of England,** Henry VIII was ultimately in charge of the clergy and was considered "responsible" for the souls of his subjects.

212. **Church law, which had once rivaled the Crown's power**, was made subordinate to the laws of the country (aka the king).

213. **Henry VIII seized the land and riches of the Catholic monasteries and religious orders in England** to fund the new church and make himself richer.

214. **Thomas More, author of the classic book *Utopia*, was a government official and a staunch Catholic.** He was executed because he would not accept Henry VIII as the head of the Church of England. More is considered a saint by the Catholic Church.

215. **For at least two centuries after Henry VIII, Catholics in England were persecuted at times,** though the Stuart kings of England in the 17th century were Catholic.

216. **The Church of England changed more drastically during Edward VI's reign.** Edward VI was very young, so he relied on his advisors. These men desired more changes to the Church of England.

217. **In 1549, the Anglican Church introduced the *Book of Common Prayer*** in an effort to give further structure to the church and to unify its followers. A modern version of the book is still used in the Anglican Church today.

218. **Thomas Cranmer was largely responsible for the *Book of Common Prayer*,** although he did borrow heavily from other sources.

219. **After Edward VI died, his sister, Mary, took the throne. Mary was a Catholic, and she wanted to reinstate the religion.**

220. **At first, Mary promoted tolerance, but she eventually began to crack down on Protestants.**

221. **Mary killed over three hundred people during her reign for not adhering to Catholicism.** One of those people was **Thomas Cranmer**.

222. **When Mary died, Elizabeth I took the throne. She reinstated the Church of England but took a more moderate approach.**

223. **In 1559, the Act of Uniformity was passed**, which authorized a revised version of the ***Book of Common Prayer***.

224. **As time passed, groups like the Puritans rose up.** They wanted to strip or "purify" the Church of England of any Roman Catholic practices.

225. **Though the English Reformation radically reduced the power of the Catholic Church in England,** the beliefs and rituals of the Church of England are similar to those of the Catholic Church in many ways.

Elizabethan Era
(1558–1603)

Immerse yourself in the intriguing history of **the Elizabethan era**. Uncover thirty interesting facts about **the culture and events of this period**. Explore the works of one of **the most influential writers in history: William Shakespeare**. Discover **how Queen Elizabeth I's reign impacted English society**, the English language, and science.

226. **The Elizabethan era** was a time when **the population of England and Wales grew** from three million to four million people.

227. **Most people lived in small villages made up of mostly wooden houses with straw roofs.** Some even lived in homes built into the ground. These homes were known as half-timbered houses.

228. **People ate very simple meals** consisting mainly of bread dipped in sauces, boiled eggs, and vegetables like carrots, onions, or cabbage cooked over an open hearth inside their house.

229. **No forks were used during meals**. Food was eaten with spoons or fingers. Knives were used to help cut food into smaller pieces.

230. **Young children didn't go to school** but were instead taught at home by their parents or tutors until around the age of seven. **Boys could attend grammar schools**, though most did not. **Most girls remained uneducated** unless they came from wealthy families who could afford teachers for them at home.

231. **There were no street lights**, so people carried oil lanterns while they walked around at night.

232. **Bathhouses were in England before Elizabeth's reign**. For a small price, people could cleanse themselves and socialize. **In the Elizabethan era, many bathhouses closed** because people began to believe that infection and disease could enter the body through scrubbed skin.

233. **People believed strongly in the power of herbs, plants, and stones as remedies for illnesses.** Leeches were also used to treat various forms of diseases, such as smallpox or scarlet fever. **Leeches were thought to suck out the "bad blood"** caused by these diseases.

234. **Due to poor sanitation and overcrowding in the cities, infectious diseases spread quickly through towns and villages**, resulting in outbreaks of the plague known as the **Great Pestilence**. Thousands died across England!

235. The same disease had afflicted Europe before in the 14th century. That name might sound more familiar; it was called **the Black Death.**

236. **People who practiced any religion other than Anglicanism were often punished because Elizabeth wanted to keep religious unity within her kingdom**. Her religious policies are known collectively as **the Elizabethan Religious Settlement**.

237. **Sir Francis Drake became one of the first English explorers to circumnavigate the globe in 1580** aboard his ship called the *Golden Hind* (a female deer).

238. **Explorers like Sir Walter Raleigh** went on expeditions to explore new lands and brought back exotic plants, animals, spices, and even tobacco to England.

239. **The Royal Navy was established by Elizabeth's father**, Henry VIII, in 1546. In 1588, the loosely organized navy defeated the more numerous Spanish Armada. **Spain wanted to land troops in England and put a Catholic on the English throne.**

240. **The most popular sport during this era was a game called bowls**, which involved rolling wooden balls toward a target on grass or dirt.

241. **People enjoyed watching theater performances**, which often included acrobatics, juggling, sword fighting tricks, and bull and bear baiting (where dogs were used to attack bulls and bears).

242. **Audiences for plays were often quite rowdy, yelling and making comments during the show.** Often, the audience near the stage stood and made up more of the common people. Rich or important people sat in the back or in primitive balconies to watch the show.

243. **Women were not allowed to be actors** but sometimes played the roles of male characters in plays by wearing masks and costumes. Young boys and younger men played female roles.

244. During this era, **William Shakespeare** wrote some of his most famous plays, such as *Romeo and Juliet* and *Hamlet*.

245. **Toward the end of Elizabeth's reign, Shakespeare and others built the famous Globe Theatre**, where many of Shakespeare's plays were performed. Today, you can visit a replica of the theater, which was erected in 1997.

246. **Music was an important part of life in Elizabethan England.** Musicians played **instruments like lutes and violins**. They also sang folk songs together.

247. During this period, **Elizabethan fashion was all about bright colors**, ruffles, and lace trimmings for both men's and women's clothing.

248. **Upper-class men often sported fanciful beards, while the women preferred to have long hair** curled up high or braided down low, with colorful ribbons and flowers woven throughout.

249. **Queen Elizabeth I had dozens of wigs made for her out of human hair or horsehair** so she could change styles frequently. Wigs also allowed her to hide her greying hair when she got older.

250. **Elizabeth's famous white makeup was lead-based**. Many historians believe that lead poisoning was a factor in Elizabeth's death.

251. **Elizabeth reputedly had tremendously bad breath**. She invented a paste that was thought to prevent breathing in "diseased air." It was supposed to smell good, but it was made of sugar and honey. **The paste likely rotted the queen's teeth**, which made her bad breath worse.

252. **In the first part of Elizabeth's reign, she was a much sought-after match.** Many kingdoms sent their princes to England to secure her hand in marriage. They knew England would be a powerful ally. **Elizabeth refused them all.**

253. **Queen Elizabeth I never married, but she did have favorites like Robert Dudley, who she referred to as "her sweet Robin."** There was also **Robert Devereux**, the Earl of Essex, who eventually rebelled against Elizabeth and was executed for treason.

254. One of Queen Elizabeth I's most famous quotes is, **"I know I have the body but of a weak and feeble woman; but I have the heart and stomach of a lion."**

255. **Elizabeth died without having children, making the question of her succession a very important and critical issue in her later life**. She never named a successor, but her chief minister, Robert Cecil, negotiated with **James VI of Scotland**, who had a claim to the throne since he was Elizabeth's cousin through Henry VI. **He became James I of England** in 1603.

The Age of Discovery
(1487–1800)

While England began to explore the world before **the Elizabethan era**, its **Age of Discovery didn't really hit its stride until Elizabeth's reign**. But don't worry; we have included facts about **England's earliest voyages**, as well as what happened during its peak of exploration.

These voyages played a crucial role in **expanding geographical knowledge**, establishing colonies, and shaping the course of history. From **John Cabot's exploration of North America to Captain James Cook's expeditions in the Pacific**, these voyages propelled England to the forefront of exploration, colonization, and maritime dominance.

256. **In 1497, Italian explorer John Cabot set sail on his first voyage to North America, sailing under the English flag**. He reached Newfoundland and became the first recorded European since the Vikings to explore mainland North America.

257. **In 1564, English pilot William Adams washed ashore in Japan** after the Dutch ship he was guiding was damaged in a storm. Japan had relations with Spain and Portugal already, but **Adams became the first Englishman in Japan**. His story was made famous in the novel and TV mini-series *Shogun*.

258. **Sir Francis Drake embarked on his famous journey in 1577**. He became the first Englishman to circumnavigate the globe, returning to England in 1580.

259. **In 1579, Drake landed on the Pacific coast of North America and claimed the area for England**, naming it Nova Albion (New Albion).

260. **In 1589, Drake embarked on what is known as the Drake-Norris Expedition**, which aimed to disrupt Spanish shipping and raid Spanish colonies in the Americas. This expedition was not successful.

261. Sir Walter Raleigh sponsored the first English colony in the New World, known as Roanoke Colony, in present-day North Carolina in 1585. However, the colony mysteriously disappeared, giving rise to the legend of **the "Lost Colony."**

262. In 1607, the English established the colony of Jamestown in Virginia. Jamestown became the first successful permanent English settlement in North America, **marking the beginning of English colonization** in the region.

263. In 1609, Henry Hudson, an English explorer sailing for the Dutch, embarked on an exploration of North America's northeastern coast, resulting in **the discovery of the Hudson River** and Hudson Bay.

264. In 1610, Hudson, now sailing under the English flag, embarked on his final voyage in search of a Northwest Passage that people believed led to the Pacific Ocean. Though he did not find the passage, the voyage laid the groundwork for subsequent English exploration in the area.

265. In 1642, English explorer Abel Tasman, sailing for the Dutch East India Company, **discovered Tasmania** and explored parts of present-day **Australia, New Zealand,** and other **Pacific islands.**

266. The English established the Hudson's Bay Company in 1670. This company played a significant role in the exploration and fur trade in **the Canadian Arctic region.**

267. In 1768, Captain James Cook, an English explorer, embarked on his first voyage on the HMS *Endeavour*. This journey took him to **the Pacific,** where he made significant scientific and geographical discoveries.

268. In 1772, Captain James Cook set out on his second voyage on the *Resolution*. This expedition resulted in the discovery and mapping of various Pacific islands, including Easter Island.

269. Captain James Cook died on February 14th, 1779. He was killed in a violent encounter **with Hawaiian natives during his third voyage** of exploration in the Pacific. Cook and his crew had been attempting to resolve a tense situation with the local population when a fight broke out.

270. In 1788, the English established the first permanent European settlement in Australia with the arrival of **the First Fleet at Port Jackson** (Sydney). This marked the beginning of the colonization and development **of Australia as a British territory.**

The English Civil War
(1642–1651)

Now we'll explore **the English Civil War**. During this time, **the Royalists** (those supporting the monarchy) were pitted against **the Parliamentarians** (those who supported Parliament). The civil war involved important figures such as **Oliver Cromwell and Charles I. Learn** who fought on the side of **the Royalists** and the Parliamentarians' **New Model Army**.

For a time, **England had no king and was called the Commonwealth**. This war spurred significant political and **religious changes in England, Scotland, and Ireland**, like the adoption of **the English Bill of Rights** (similar to America's but over a hundred years older) and the rise of **the Puritans**.

271. **The English Civil War lasted from 1642 to 1651**. It was a conflict between supporters of **the monarchy (Royalists)** and supporters of **Parliament (Parliamentarians)**.

272. **Parliament was the legislature of England** (and all of Great Britain today).

273. There were (and still are) two parts of Parliament: **the House of Commons**, made up of elected officials, and **the House of Lords**, made up of men (and now women) who came from the nobility.

274. **The House of Lords had much more power than it does today** and was banned by the Roundheads for a time after the war.

275. **Many Parliamentarians were concerned about King Charles I's** increasing movement to revitalize **the Catholic Church in England**.

276. **Oliver Cromwell, a leader of the Parliamentarians, was a key figure in the war**. He led England for a time after it ended as **"Lord Protector."**

277. **The Parliamentarians wanted to limit the king's powers**. They believed Parliament should have more power.

278. **Many leading Parliamentarians were Puritans**. The Puritans were a fundamentalist sect. **They believed everyone should read the Bible,** but they also believed their church elders were better equipped to interpret it. **Many Puritan groups grew to be less tolerant** of other Protestant belief systems.

279. **After the restoration of the monarchy, there was a crackdown on the Puritans**. They eventually fled to Holland and North America.

280. **The Royalists were led by King Charles I,** who many believed was Anglican in name only. **Charles was also married to a Catholic princess from France.**

281. **Many Protestants feared that he would restore Catholic influence**, though the war was mostly about **Charles trying to grab more power than the Parliamentarians** were comfortable with.

282. **The Royalists were commonly called Cavaliers**, a word that comes from the French word for **"cavalry" or "horse." The Parliamentarians were called Roundheads** due to their bowl-shaped haircuts.

283. **The Royalists were supported by most Irish people**, as Ireland remained a strongly Catholic part of Britain.

284. **The Scots supported both sides of the conflict**, with one powerful Scottish lord, **Lord Leven,** switching sides from the Crown to Parliament during the war.

285. **Welsh soldiers fought on both sides**, though no battles took place in Wales.

286. **Many Welshmen were Catholic and supported the king**, but many others supported Parliament, where they were also represented.

287. **The war was fought in many parts of England, Scotland, and Ireland**.

288. **The first battle of the English Civil War was the Battle of Edgehill in 1642.**

289. **Oliver Cromwell was one of the chief generals of the Roundheads** and led the New Model Army.

290. **The New Model Army** was made up of people who made the military their profession rather than the levies, or draftees, that had been used before.

291. Many of the leaders of **the New Model Army were nobles** with combat experience who brought their own private armies with them and merged them into **the larger Roundhead army.**

292. **King Charles I was said to have been quite brave**, but he was not a good military leader.

293. **The Roundheads were better organized and better equipped than the Cavaliers.**

294. **The Royalists had more money,** but **the Parliamentarians had a larger number of troops.**

295. **The Parliamentarians defeated the Royalists at the important Battle of Naseby in June 1645.** This battle was the turning point in **the English Civil War.**

296. About a month later, **the New Model Army destroyed the last effective Royalist fighting force** in **the Battle of Langport.**

297. **Charles was put on trial in London's Westminster Hall in January 1649.** This was the first time in history that a king was put on trial for crimes against his people.

298. **The Parliamentarians executed King Charles I for high treason in 1649,** though his supporters continued the war for another two years.

299. **Charles was the only English king in history to be executed.**

300. **At the beginning of the war, many Scottish nobles supported Parliament** instead of Charles because they sought more power for themselves. However, when he was executed, many turned against Parliament, but this ended in the defeat of the Royalist cause in 1651.

301. **The English Civil War, along with the later Glorious Revolution,** put an end to the absolute monarchy in England.

302. **Oliver Cromwell's military successes made him a powerful political figure in England.**

303. **Despite being a Parliamentarian during the war, Cromwell dissolved Parliament** in 1653 because of the many quarrels among the Parliamentarians. He ruled England as a virtual dictator from 1653 to 1658, when he passed away.

304. **Power struggles between different factions within Parliament and an ineffective government after the death of Cromwell** in 1658 **led to negotiations with the House of Stuart** and to the restoration of the monarchy in the form of **Charles II,** son of the executed king.

305. **Charles II had to promise not to restore Catholicism** as the national religion and follow laws that limited the power of the monarchy.

306. **Charles II had been king of Scotland for over ten years by the time he retook the English throne in 1660.**

307. **Both Charles I and II were members of the Stuart family**, a powerful Scottish clan with ties to the royal families in both England and Scotland.

308. From the beginning of **the Commonwealth** until **the Restoration** in 1660, **Great Britain was governed as a republic.**

309. **Though the Commonwealth had many flaws,** including putting too much power in the hands of the executive, this period was the first time Britain had ever been governed by anything other than a monarch.

310. **The changes that began after the death of Charles I** and during the Commonwealth resulted in **the English Bill of Rights in 1689.**

The Restoration
(1660–1688)

After the English Civil War, **the Restoration happened**. This period saw **the monarchy come back to England,** although it was more limited than before. Let's look at thirty interesting facts about England's culture during this era, including **the scientific discoveries of Isaac Newton.**

311. **The Restoration was a period of time in British history from 1660 to 1688.** The name of the period comes from **King Charles II** being restored to the English throne after the end of the English Civil War.

312. **The Age of Reason** began during this period. Many scientific discoveries based on logic, evidence, and the new **scientific method** replaced guesswork, superstition, and religious belief as the basis of scientific research.

313. **Isaac Newton**, **Robert Boyle**, **Edmond Halley**, and many others made important contributions to many fields of science at this time.

314. **The Restoration** was a time of growing religious tolerance and freedom of speech.

315. The period saw **the rise of coffee houses, playhouses**, and **newspapers**.

316. **The first English newspapers were published during this period.**

317. The first women's magazine, called **"The Ladies Mercury,"** was published in 1693.

318. The period saw a flowering of the arts, with writers such as **John Dryden and William Congreve** penning works.

319. **John Locke** was one of the foremost writers of the time. Although he lived before the period historians call **the Enlightenment**, he is often considered one of the first "enlightened" writers because of his call for **individual liberty** and **democratic ideals**.

320. **When Charles II** came to the throne, he had **Oliver Cromwell's** body dug up and hung for everyone to see. Cromwell had been instrumental in the sentence and execution of **Charles II's** father, **Charles I**.

321. **The Bank of England was established** in 1694. It was the first real attempt to centralize power over the economy and provide unified rules about currency, interest, and more.

322. **The population of England and Wales doubled during this period.**

323. **The slave trade began to expand during the Restoration.**

324. **The East India Company** was founded in 1600 and began trading with India. During the Restoration, it expanded its reach in India.

325. **The Navigation Acts were passed** in 1651, 1660, and 1663. These acts imposed trade restrictions on the English colonies in America.

326. **The Whigs and Tories were two political parties** that developed during this period. Generally speaking, **Whigs** tended to oppose the monarchy, and **Tories** tended to support it.

327. **The Restoration** gave its name to a whole genre of drama and comedy, with styles starting to shift away from the "looser" language and style of **Shakespeare** toward a more formal and structured writing style.

328. **The Royal Society was established** in 1660 and was dedicated to promoting scientific research.

329. **The Great Fire of London** in 1666 destroyed much of the city.

330. **Charles II** and his close friends, who had spent time in France during the Commonwealth period, valued French clothing, writing, and drama. In Charles II's court, a more **"French" style**, which was much more formalized than what the English were used to, became popular.

331. **The first police forces were established in Scotland and England** in the 1600s, though these were far different than the police as we know them today.

332. Many critics of **the Stuart court** saw it as decadent, meaning that the king and his followers enjoyed a little too much wine, women, and song. They were more concerned with their own pleasures than ruling the country.

333. **In 1685, James II took the throne**. He was Charles II's younger brother.

334. At first, **James had widespread support** from people in England, Ireland, and Scotland.

335. As time passed, people became dissatisfied with his rule. **James II was interested in restoring the Catholic Church** to its former position within England. The people did not want Catholicism to be forced on them.

336. **When he gave birth to a son, the people were worried that he would begin a Catholic dynasty.** They revolted against his rule.

337. **The Glorious Revolution of 1688 saw the overthrow of King James II** and the establishment of a constitutional monarchy.

338. **The Glorious Revolution** inspired later acts. For instance, **the Act of Toleration** in 1689 granted freedom of worship to **Protestant Nonconformists**. Nonconformists were Protestants that had different beliefs than the predominant Church of England.

339. **The Act of Union in 1707** established the United Kingdom. **This act "united" Scotland and England.** Queen Anne, James II's daughter, was on the throne at this time.

340. **Ireland had been invaded by the English** in the 1500s and would become part of **the United Kingdom** in 1801.

The Glorious Revolution
(1688–1689)

And now we have the remarkable events of **the Glorious Revolution**, which happened between 1688 and 1689. Here are thirty interesting facts about this **revolutionary period,** including its **causes and consequences**. We'll discover **how the power of the monarchy was limited** and how a strong, **unified nation was established**. Furthermore, we will learn how **the Glorious Revolution** helped to spread the ideas of limited government throughout Europe.

341. **The Glorious Revolution** was a peaceful event in which **Catholic King James II** of England was **replaced by William III and Mary II,** who were **Protestant rulers**.

342. **The Glorious Revolution** is also known as **the Bloodless Revolution** because no fighting between armies took place.

343. Although most accounts describe **the Glorious Revolution** as **peaceful with little bloodshed,** some historians argue there were still casualties due to riots or revenge attacks. It's estimated that around **five thousand people died** in the months leading up to this event.

344. **England had experienced religious turmoil under King James II, who tried to bring back Catholicism as the official religion**. His reign ended when he fled to France after losing support from most nobles and clergymen.

345. **Queen Mary II was the daughter of James II** and **his first wife**. She was also **the niece of Charles II.**

346. **William III was Mary's husband**. He arrived **from Holland to take over the English throne** in 1688 with fifteen thousand soldiers at his side.

347. One important figure during **the Glorious Revolution** was **John Locke**. He wrote about **natural rights** like life, liberty, health, and property. His ideas were influential in the making of **the Bill of Rights** and also influenced **the American Revolution**.

348. Another important figure during **the Glorious Revolution** was **John Churchill**, later known as **Duke of Marlborough**. Churchill defeated forces loyal to James II at battles like **the Battle of Sedgemoor** and **the Battle of Dunkeld**, which helped **secure victory for Protestants in England**. He later defeated the armies of **Louis XIV at Blenheim**. John Churchill was Winston Churchill's 6x-great-grandfather.

349. This event saw many **Protestants from different backgrounds come together** to support the cause **against James II's rule.**

350. **The Glorious Revolution** saw the rise of **the Whig Party in England**, which was a **political party that supported Protestantism** and limited government power.

351. **After James II fled England**, his supporters (known as **Jacobites**) tried several times to put him back on the throne. Their efforts were unsuccessful each time due to strong opposition from **William III's** forces and most of **the English people**.

352. **William and Mary were crowned the monarchs of England and Ireland** on January 22nd, 1689. This is called **the Convention** Parliament, where those in Parliament were asked to **publicly vote yes or no for the new king and queen**.

353. On April 11th, 1689, **the Convention Parliament** proclaimed **William and Mary the king and queen of Scotland as well.**

354. Even though **Mary was queen alongside her husband**, she had less political influence than him because **women weren't seen as equals to men** during this period.

355. **The Glorious Revolution** also helped to end **the absolute monarchy in England** since **William III and Mary II shared power with Parliament**. This is one reason why **modern Britain has a constitutional monarchy** instead of an absolute one.

356. **This event marked the end of Catholicism** as the official religion in England and Scotland. It ended with an agreement called **the Bill of Rights of 1689**, which established more **freedom for citizens.**

357. **In 1689, William and Mary issued a joint declaration known as the Declaration of Rights,** which stated that all citizens should have certain rights like freedom of speech or trial by jury. These are still fundamental liberties for people living in Britain today.

358. **Parliament passed several laws that limited royal power**, such as forbidding the monarch from suspending laws or raising an army without consent from Parliament. **The monarch also could not set taxes without Parliament's approval.** These limits on government power still exist today.

359. **The Glorious Revolution worried rulers around Europe**. They feared similar revolutions might happen in their countries.

360. **At first, many people were scared that taking away royal power would lead to anarchy,** but surprisingly, it didn't cause any major problems. Instead, it made England more stable than ever before.

361. **After the Glorious Revolution, William III increased English naval power by building new ships** and creating a stronger navy, **which helped England in its wars against France and Spain.**

362. **William allied England with Holland** in an effort to limit the rise of French power.

363. **The king of France from 1643 to 1715 was Louis XIV**. He was perhaps the greatest absolute monarch of all. He was worried that the reforms in England would become popular in his country and **worked hard to destabilize England**. He also created a system of censorship that was aimed at preventing **"dangerous ideas"** (to him) from spreading to his country.

364. **Parliament abolished some taxes** on trading goods and granted more freedoms to merchants, causing economic growth throughout England.

365. **After the Glorious Revolution, William III made some changes to how taxes were collected,** which meant that more money could be raised for the government. These reforms helped make sure there was enough money available for the general welfare if it was needed.

366. **Many historians argue that the Glorious Revolution was one of the most important moments in history** because it **established many basic human rights** like religious tolerance and liberty under the law. These ideas spread throughout the world and are still important today.

367. **The Glorious Revolution period saw England become a worldwide empire**, competing with France for dominance in Europe and the New World.

368. **The freedoms that developed in Britain** during this time were largely responsible for a new political and social movement called **the Enlightenment**, which **inspired the American revolutionaries** and many others.

369. **Before William became king of England, he was known as William of Orange.** Orange refers to a territory his family had controlled for a long time.

370. **Because of his popularity in Holland, the color orange became the national color of that country.**

Age of Enlightenment
(1715–1790)

The **Age of Enlightenment** was a period of intellectual growth and change in Europe that lasted through most of **the 18th century**. In this section, you'll read about thirty noteworthy facts revealing the development of **new ideas and the invention of new technologies**. We will also explore how people began to think of themselves as **individuals with rights and freedoms**.

371. **The Age of Enlightenment** was a period in history when people started to think more about **science, philosophy, and freedom**.

372. **The Age of Enlightenment** began around 1715 and ended around 1790 when the **French Revolution began.**

373. During this time, some very famous thinkers **like Voltaire and Jean-Jacques Rosseau** wrote books that changed how people thought about **government**, **society**, and **religion**.

374. During this period, **British and French writers and philosophers** greatly affected each other's countries and societies.

375. In **France**, a group of men known as the **Philosophes**, which included **Jean-Jacques Rousseau,** wrote popular books on **politics** and **philosophy** during this period.

376. The ideas of **French and British Enlightenment** thinkers had a profound effect on the **American Founding Fathers** and played a crucial role in starting **the American Revolution.**

377. Many important inventions were made during **the Age of Enlightenment**, such as steam engine technology by **James Watt,** a Scottish inventor. **The steam engine revolutionized transportation in Europe.**

378. **Isaac Newton**, an **English mathematician** who developed **calculus**, was the head of **the Royal Society** from 1703 until his death in 1727. **The Royal Society** still exists today; it is the oldest scientific academic institution in the world!

379. **The Constitution of the United States** was largely based on ideas discussed during **the Age of Enlightenment**, including the new belief that natural rights were held at birth regardless of an individual's class or status in life.

380. **People began questioning traditional ideas about religion during the Age of Enlightenment, which led to new religious movements, such as Deism.** Deism is the idea that there is a higher power that created the universe, but this power does not interfere in human affairs and is not affected by a belief in **organized religion.**

381. **The idea of human rights** was **popularized by John Locke**, who wrote *Two Treatises of Government* **in 1690,** which argued for a government based on protecting **individual rights** instead of on power or divine right, the belief that **God puts kings on the throne** and allows them to govern as they see fit.

382. **People also began to think differently about education** during this period. They started believing that **education should be accessible to everyone**, not just the wealthy.

383. **Newspapers gained popularity** due to increased literacy rates, **allowing people to learn more** about what was happening in their countries.

384. **David Hume** was an important **Scottish Enlightenment** writer who **believed that all human knowledge came from experience**, not religious beliefs or God.

385. **Slavery existed in the British colonies until 1833.** Slavery was challenged by a group of people called **abolitionists**, who used arguments from **Enlightenment** philosophers to make a **strong case against slavery.**

386. **Women in England and France** began to slowly gain more rights. This was due to influential women and their works, such as **Mary Wollstonecraft's** 1792 work *A Vindication of the Rights of Woman.*

387. **Musical styles changed**. Two of the most famous composers of all time, **Mozart and Beethoven, were from this period.**

388. **The Enlightenment** and **the French revolutionary** period that immediately followed it are considered by most historians to **mark the beginning of the modern era.**

389. **This era also saw advances in medicine**. For instance, **English doctor Edward Jenner** invented a **vaccine** for smallpox.

390. **English chemist Joseph Priestley** discovered **oxygen**, which changed how we thought about air!

391. **A new era of European exploration began**. Explorers like **James Cook** mapped out **new lands** and cultures previously unknown to Europeans.

392. **Many Enlightenment philosophers wrote books advocating for democracy**, arguing it would be a better form of government than a monarchy or a government ruled only by the upper classes.

393. **New ideas about economics emerged** from thinkers like **Adam Smith**, a Scottish economist who wrote *The Wealth of Nations*, which examined **free-market capitalism.**

394. **In France and England**, people in the upper or the rising upper middle class could subscribe to get book series before they were printed. The most famous example is the immensely popular *Encyclopédie* by **Frenchman Denis Diderot**, though many English authors and journals began offering subscriptions.

395. **Coffee houses were popular places** for discussing new ideas about politics, society, and the events of the day.

396. **Coffee houses became so popular that laws were passed to limit how long people could stay in them!**

397. **The first public parks and zoos opened up during this time,** allowing more people access to nature than ever before.

398. **Italian philosopher Cesare Beccaria** wrote about **reforming the criminal justice system in Europe.** Torture was still used in England at this time, and its jails were horrible dungeon-like places.

399. **This era saw an increase in urbanization.** Factories, canals, and other infrastructure projects caused cities to spread out and more people to move to them.

400. Lastly, many European governments, mostly in **western and northern Europe, started giving their citizens greater freedoms**, such as freedom of speech or freedom of the press, which had previously been restricted.

The American Revolution
(1765–1783)

In this section, you'll discover thirty important facts about **the American Revolution from the British point of view.** Learn how the British felt about **the rebellious colonists** and the rights that **King George III** and his government believed they had in the **American colonies**. You'll also learn about the might of the **British armed forces** and why overconfidence was one of the reasons **the British were defeated in the war.**

401. **The British initially viewed the conflict with the American colonies as a minor disturbance rather than a full-scale rebellion.**

402. **The British government believed it had the right to tax the American colonies** to help pay for the cost of defending them during **the French and Indian War** (1754–1763).

403. **King George III** and many British officials saw **the American Revolution** as a betrayal by the colonists, who were considered British subjects.

404. **The British military**, with its highly trained and experienced troops, initially had the upper hand in the early battles of **the American Revolution**.

405. British soldiers, called **Redcoats** (or "Lobsterbacks" by rebels in New England), were often better equipped and more disciplined than **their American counterparts**.

406. **The British strategy focused on capturing major cities** and defeating the Continental Army to force the Americans into submission.

407. **Many British officers and soldiers viewed the American rebels as undisciplined and lacking proper military training**. However, many Americans had to hunt to stay alive and generally were much better shots than British recruits.

408. Most Americans lived in the countryside at this time and were familiar with living in the wild, while many British soldiers were not.

409. The British hired German mercenaries, known as **Hessians**, to bolster their forces during the war.

410. Most of the troops defeated by **George Washington** and his men at the famous **Battle of Trenton** (1776) **were Hessians, not British**.

411. **The British military** faced significant challenges in transporting troops and supplies **across the Atlantic Ocean**. By the time the men, ships, and supplies were gathered in England and transported across the sea, the situation they faced was different from the message they had received from **British officers asking for help in America**.

412. **The British government struggled to effectively communicate and coordinate with their commanders in America** due to the long distance and slow communication methods.

413. **The British navy, the most powerful in the world at the time,** maintained control of important coastal areas and waterways for most of the war.

414. **General William Howe**, the first British commander-in-chief, believed in a more conciliatory approach toward the colonists and was criticized for not being aggressive enough. **He resigned in 1778, saying the reason was lack of support at home**.

415. **The British underestimated the resolve and determination of the American rebels**, who were fighting for their independence.

416. **The British army faced logistical difficulties in supplying their troops**, especially during the harsh winter months.

417. **British generals often had to contend with conflicting orders from the British government** and disagreements among their own officers.

418. **The British hoped to gain support from Loyalists** (colonists who remained loyal to Britain), but this support was not as widespread as they had anticipated.

419. **The American Revolution exposed divisions** within the British government, with some officials advocating for a more conciliatory approach while others pushed for a harsher military response.

420. **The British faced challenges in recruiting enough troops to fight the war**, leading them to rely on hired mercenaries and colonial Loyalists.

421. **The British government struggled to finance the costly war**, leading to increased taxes and borrowing.

422. **The British army employed scorched-earth tactics** and confiscated property to weaken the rebels' support base. Scorched-earth tactics means burning crops, houses, farms, and businesses to weaken the enemy.

423. **Many American Loyalists fled to Canada during the war and after**. Some historians called **the American Revolution a civil war** because there was much fighting between rebels and Loyalists during the conflict.

424. The American rebels' use of guerrilla warfare tactics, including hit-and-run attacks, disrupted British operations and wore down their morale.

425. The British attempted to implement a blockade of American ports to restrict trade and weaken the colonial economy.

426. The Battle of Saratoga in 1777 was a major turning point in the war, as the British suffered a significant defeat.

427. **France, Britain's enemy in Europe, saw that the Americans might win** the war and began sending massive amounts of aid.

428. **The British public grew increasingly weary of the costly and prolonged war**, which ultimately influenced the government's decision to seek a negotiated peace with the United States.

429. **The Treaty of Paris of 1783 ended the American Revolution** in favor of the colonists.

430. **Britain recognized America's independence, and in time**, relations between the two would be repaired. Today, they have a strong and healthy relationship.

The Napoleonic Wars

From 1789 to 1815, **Britain became involved in a great struggle against France**. In 1789, the French people, who had been kept down for centuries by the absolute rule of the French kings and the aristocracy, revolted. **The French Revolution sent shockwaves through Europe, especially England,** which was only miles away from France across the English Channel. After years of chaos and violence in France, **General Napoleon Bonaparte took power and conquered most of Europe.** Though Napoleon had many foes, **his arch-enemy was England.**

Let's take a look at twenty exciting facts about **the Napoleonic Wars.**

431. **The French Revolution** began in the summer of **1789. The people of France decided to fight for the rights they had been denied for centuries**, such as the freedom of speech, freedom of the press, and freedom of religion.

432. Though **England** had gone through many similar changes over the years, the aristocracy and the **king still held most of the power.** They were threatened by the ideas of **the French Revolution.**

433. **The French revolutionaries** spread the **ideas of the revolution** to other countries, including England.

434. From 1792 to 1797, **England was part of the First Coalition**, which included other European countries seeking to defeat revolutionary France.

435. From 1798 to 1802, **England was part of another alliance called the Second Coalition,** which attempted to defeat a more successful France and its newest military hero, **General Napoleon Bonaparte.**

436. **Bonaparte rose to fame in France because of his defeat of the British** at the French Mediterranean port of Toulon in 1793 during the War of the First Coalition.

437. Between 1793 and 1804, **Napoleon kept gaining power and support**. By 1800, he was *the* power in France. In 1804, **he was proclaimed emperor of the French.**

438. **Because Britain would not agree to Napoleon's terms for peace, he began what's known as the Continental System.** France and its conquered countries could not trade with Great Britain.

439. **The Continental System eventually backfired on Napoleon** because England traded with many other parts of the world.

440. **The Royal Navy was powerful enough** to ensure that France could not trade with others.

441. **One of England's greatest victories came during the Battle of Trafalgar. English Admiral Nelson,** who was killed in the battle, led the British home fleet against the French Navy. The French were soundly defeated.

442. **Napoleon vowed to conquer England.** He gathered an invasion force of men, ships, landing craft, and even hot air balloons on the French side of the English Channel.

443. However, other events and the money it cost to gather and supply the invasion force while waiting for the right time **made Napoleon give up on the idea of invading England.**

444. **The British had far fewer men in their army than the French, so they were limited in what they could do against Napoleon in Europe.** The British allied themselves with other nations and chose their battles carefully.

445. **In 1808, Napoleon invaded Spain,** which resulted in a long and violent guerrilla war. **England was allied with Portugal,** Spain's neighbor, and landed troops there to fight the French in Spain. **Spain threw Napoleon out in 1814 with England's help.**

446. **In 1812, Napoleon invaded Russia** but was **ultimately defeated by Russia** and the other countries of central Europe that had been previously conquered by Napoleon. In June 1815, **Napoleon's armies were defeated, and he gave up the throne.**

447. **He was exiled to the small island of Elba** in the Mediterranean under British guard.

448. **In February 1815, Napoleon escaped from Elba,** landed in France, and gathered another army. He took over France once again **and launched a war against the Third Coalition.**

449. **At Waterloo in Belgium, Napoleon was defeated for the final time.**

450. **British troops played a central role in Napoleon's final defeat at Waterloo.**

Industrial Revolution
(1760—1850)

The Industrial Revolution was a time **of great change and technological advancement for Britain.** Here are forty interesting facts about that time, though there is much more to learn about this incredible time. **We will explore the invention of new transportation and communication methods,** how the factory system developed, and the positive effects of the railroad. The impacts of **the Industrial Revolution** are still felt worldwide, so let's dig in to find out why!

451. **The Industrial Revolution** was a period of time between **1760 and 1850**, during which **new machines and technologies were developed** to help make production faster and more efficient.

452. **The Industrial Revolution brought about a huge change in how people lived,** worked, ate, traveled, dressed, thought, and communicated with each other.

453. **It also changed where people lived**. Many moved from rural areas into cities to look for factory jobs or better opportunities. **Cities became crowded**. People lived close together in small homes without modern amenities like running water or electricity.

454. **The Enclosure Movement caused a shift in land ownership from small farmers to large landowners**, allowing for increased production of goods on farms using new technologies. Many small farmers were forced to move to cities to make a living.

455. **Inventions like the reaper** allowed farmers to harvest crops much faster than before. The increased crop yields meant lower prices for consumers across Europe.

456. **Improved agricultural techniques** helped increase yields from farmers' fields during this period, leading to greater food security across Europe.

457. **Inventors such as Joseph Priestley, Humphry Davy, Michael Faraday, and Charles Babbage developed new technologies** that spurred industrial growth during this period.

458. During this period, inventions like **the steam engine helped power factories**. Factories made things like cloth and steel on an industrial scale for the first time in history.

459. **New technologies allowed factories**, particularly those located near rivers or canals, **to increase the production of goods.**

460. **In 1764, James Watt, a Scottish inventor, improved the steam engine.** It could produce more power than earlier models, which allowed for more efficient production of goods like textiles and iron products.

461. **Inventors like James Watt developed machines that could harness energy sources in new ways.** Unfortunately, **steam engines used a lot of coal**. By the end of the 19th century, pollution was taking a toll on the health of people, animals, trees, and water. It also **created an almost permanent grey sky over many British cities.**

462. One type of **power unit is called a watt,** as in a 60-watt lightbulb. Watt discovered many things we take for granted today.

463. **Coal mining was transformed due to inventions like hydraulic props,** which supported tunnels underground, and the steam engine, which allowed for deeper, more efficient mines.

464. **Inventions like the cotton gin increased the production of textiles** by allowing larger quantities to be produced at once in factories rather than handcrafted by workers at home. **This had a big impact on employment rates and prices of goods.**

465. **The spinning jenny was invented in 1764 by James Hargreaves**, an English weaver. The spinning jenny could simultaneously spin eight threads instead of just one, making it much faster to produce cloth.

466. **The invention of the power loom in 1785 helped reduce the cost and time it took to produce cloth**, which led to cheaper clothing in stores all over Britain and beyond. **Power looms** were automated machines that could weave faster than humans!

467. **The invention of the Jacquard loom in 1801 made it possible to produce fabrics** with intricate patterns by using punch cards. This was a major advancement over previous **handweaving** methods.

468. **The invention of interchangeable parts made mass production possible as early as 1798.** These components could be assembled into a product without being custom-made each time they were used.

469. **The invention of machine tools like lathes** made precision engineering possible, leading to improved accuracy when producing parts or products.

470. **The new methods of production allowed for the greater production of tools** and consumer goods, as well as weapons for the army and navy.

471. **Improvements in manufacturing processes like mass production allowed for lower prices on items,** such as furniture or clothing, giving consumers access to goods that were previously too expensive.

472. **Early factories were often organized by gender**, with women doing certain tasks like spinning cotton while men operated heavy machinery.

473. **Many changes took place in the workplace during this time**, with workers beginning to push for better working conditions and shorter hours. However, owners pushed back on many of the workers' ideas.

474. **The Factory Acts of 1802 and 1833** set limits on **how many hours children under nine years old could work in factories.** Before then, there were no restrictions!

475. Eventually, owners built things like guard rails around machinery to keep workers safe while they worked. **Miners would gradually start to use metal helmets to protect themselves** from falling rocks and other dangers.
476. **Many people were injured in the new factories**, but there was no unemployment or medical insurance. Many people were reduced to begging and crime to survive.

477. **In England, the murder rate increased because of overcrowded** conditions and because **many crimes were punishable by death**. Since that was the case, many criminals killed witnesses to their crimes.

478. **The Industrial Revolution saw gradual improvements in sanitation**, which helped reduce disease rates. Things like **public water systems**, sewers, and better waste disposal methods were developed during this period.

479. **Gas lighting was invented in 1792**. Over the years, it became more widespread, allowing people to work or travel after dark without having to rely on candles or oil lamps.
480. **The development of more accurate clocks** enabled people to keep track of their working hours, which was important when calculating wages since many jobs were paid by the hour.
481. **Improved banking systems**, such as new investment schemes, encouraged entrepreneurs to pursue many **new business opportunities** during this period.

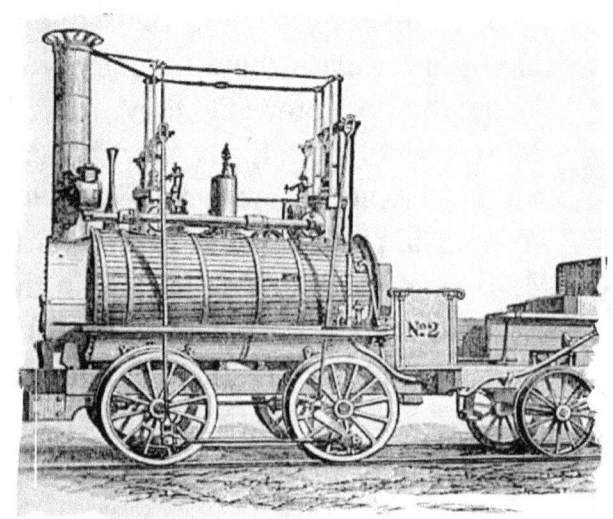

482. **In 1807, Robert Fulton, an American engineer, invented the first commercially successful steamboat**, allowing large numbers of goods to be shipped up and down rivers quickly.

483. **The development of canals allowed for the more efficient transportation of raw materials** from mines or ports directly into cities where factories could use them. These waterways also provided jobs for many people who worked on building them or navigated boats through them.

484. **The first entirely steam-powered trans-Atlantic voyage was made by the Canadian vessel, the SS *Royal William*, in 1833.**

485. Ships that depended on sails would often stop or slow down when there was little to no wind. **The steamship** eliminated this problem and **made sea travel faster and more reliable.**

486. **The first successful steam locomotive was built by George Stephenson, an English engineer, in 1814. The locomotive revolutionized the transportation** of goods and people across greater distances more quickly.

487. **The construction of railways across Europe enabled goods and people to travel long distances quickly and cheaply**. Railways helped spread ideas from one place to another, leading to greater innovations in other fields, such as **medicine, engineering, and architecture.**

488. **The invention of the telegraph** allowed information to travel rapidly across long distances. **The telegraph was used commercially** as early as 1845.

489. **Improved communication networks, including postal systems and the telegraph**, enabled people from different parts of a country or even from different countries to communicate with each other in ways never seen before.

490. **The Industrial Revolution**, which did not happen outside Europe and North America until much later, marked the beginning of a period of **Western economic and military supremacy throughout the world.**

Slavery and Its Abolition
(1807–1838)

The abolition of the slave trade greatly impacted the lives of the British and those who were enslaved. We'll look at **forty interesting facts about slavery in Britain and its colonies,** including the people who campaigned for abolition and the legacy of the slave trade today.

491. **The slave trade saw English ships travel to West Africa** with goods like guns and clothes, which they used to trade for Africans. **These Africans became enslaved.**

492. **Africans were taken on board ships and then sold in Europe, the Americas, or India. Slaves cost around £20 to £30** per person at this time, which is equivalent to hundreds or even thousands of dollars today.

493. **In 2007, a group of scientists from Liverpool University identified human remains found on board ships that were used for transporting enslaved** Africans across the Atlantic Ocean. This research helped uncover evidence about what life must have been like for those taken away from their homes so long ago.

494. **In 1772, a court in England ruled that slavery was not legal**, but this decision did not stop the slave trade.

495. **In 1807, the British government made a law that said it was illegal to buy or sell people as slaves in Britain and its colonies**. The new law was called the Abolition of the Slave Trade Act. It ended the slave trade but did not end slavery itself.

496. **Before 1807, around one million enslaved Africans lived in Britain's colonies worldwide. Olaudah Equiano** had been enslaved and wrote about his experiences. He helped persuade many people to support **abolition.**

497. **Ignatius Sancho was an enslaved man in England**. He escaped and found refuge with a powerful noble who educated him. **Sancho eventually became a shopkeeper, an abolitionist, and a well-known writer and composer**. He died before the abolition of the slave trade, but his life and writing had a profound effect on attitudes in England.

498. **Many brave campaigners worked** hard to make the abolition of the slave trade happen, including **Thomas Clarkson** and **Granville Sharp. They established the Society for the Abolition of the Slave Trade.**

499. **Many campaigns against the slave trade were done by churches,** such as **Quakers, Methodists,** and **Baptists,** whose members actively worked together on pamphlets, petitions, and protests.

500. **Women played an important role in the anti-slavery movement** too, such as **Mary Prince, Elizabeth Heyrick, and Anne Knight**. These women wrote pamphlets or gave speeches encouraging people to stop buying things made with slave labor.

501. **Some campaigners used boycotts to stop businesses from using goods produced with slave labor**. They stopped buying sugar, tobacco, or other items made with slave labor in a process known as **"moral suasion."**

502. **During their campaign against slavery, abolitionists adopted vivid imagery, such as coffins and nooses**, in their publications and demonstrations to help draw attention to the cruelty that slaves endured from the moment they were captured.

503. **William Wilberforce, a prominent abolitionist** MP (member of Parliament), and others campaigned for ten years. They thought the act was the first step toward the abolition of slavery.

504. Even though **the Abolition of the Slave Trade Act** passed, there were still thousands of slaves living in British colonies after 1807.

505. **Between 1796 and 1806, before the end of the British slave trade, it's estimated that about 400,000 slaves were taken captive and sent to work in the West Indies.**

506. One British sailor on a ship assigned to catch slave traders wrote, **"They were in the most dreadful condition that human beings could be in … I should never have believed that anything could have been so horrible … Some of them mere walking skeletons."**

507. **The Slave Trade Act also stated that any ships carrying enslaved Africans after this date would be confiscated by the British government**. Their crews would be arrested.

508. **The British Royal Navy formed the West Africa Squadron to intercept slave ships coming from regions where slave ships often departed**. They also formed other squadrons that patrolled other parts of the Atlantic.

509. **The Royal Navy stopped over 1,600 ships carrying an estimated 150,000 enslaved Africans.**

510. **Many of the people freed from slave ships had nowhere to go**. Many areas of Africa did not have officially recognized borders at the time, and most people didn't know where they were from other than in a very general way. **Many people were left in settlements of freed slaves in the West Indies** or formed communities themselves.

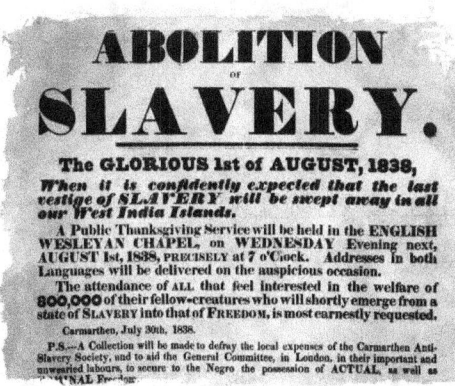

511. **After Britain abolished its slave trade, some African territories started forming their own anti-slavery societies**, campaigning against further enslavement by European countries.

512. **It wasn't until 1833 that another law, the Slavery Abolition Act, finally made it illegal for any person or business to own slaves within Britain's colonies**. This act set all enslaved people free in the British Empire, with the exception of a few of its colonies.

513. **The number of slaves freed in the United Kingdom and its territories was anywhere from 800,000 to a million people**.

514. **It took a very long time for all enslaved Africans living within Britain's colonies to be freed.** Even after 1833, many slaves were simply called "apprentices" and given a small wage to get around the law.

515. **Some people didn't believe slavery was wrong and kept slaves even though it was illegal.** These people were called "illegal traders" and could be jailed if they were caught.

516. **This act also provided compensation for those who lost money when they had to free their slaves.**

517. **Britain paid over twenty million pounds to former slave owners**, which was about 40 percent of the British budget.

518. **Some former plantation owners turned their land into sugar refining factories using new technologies,** and other former slave traders tried new ways of making money, such as investing in cotton mills or setting up trading companies that dealt with goods from Africa, like palm oil.

519. **Some sugar plantations replaced enslaved Africans with indentured laborers from India or China.** These workers signed contracts lasting five to seven years. Almost all of them were paid less than half of what freemen earned.

520. **Indentured servants came from all over the British Empire, including Ireland.**

521. **In the 18th and 19th centuries, many British prisoners were sent to the sugarcane fields in the Caribbean**, where many perished from the climate, disease, and mistreatment.

522. **Though the United Kingdom was one of the first countries to ban slavery, Denmark and Norway banned the slave trade in 1803.**

523. **Even after 1833, many countries worldwide still allowed slavery, such as France, which abolished slavery in 1848. The United States didn't abolish it until 1865.**

524. **Many Africans welcomed Britain's decision to abolish slavery.** They saw it as an opportunity for freedom and self-determination.

525. **Today, monuments and museums throughout Britain and other countries worldwide are dedicated to remembering those affected by the slave trade** and celebrating freedom from slavery, such as **the International Slavery Museum in Liverpool**, England, a port city and the center of the slave trade before abolition.

526. **In 1833, there was a huge celebratory march through London's streets** when news spread that slavery had been abolished in Britain and its colonies. Thousands joined together for this event, now known as the Abolition Parade.

527. **In 2007, Britain celebrated two hundred years since abolition** with various events held throughout the country, including special exhibitions in museums, plays, and concerts for people to learn more about this important moment in history.

528. **Though slavery was abolished in the UK in 1833, African Britons faced considerable discrimination and prejudice,** which is still an issue in much of the UK.

529. **There were still discriminatory laws on the books in Britain** until the middle of the 20th century. Even after laws were passed, many black English people were discriminated against in housing and the job market.

530. **In more recent times, British prime ministers and the government have issued apologies for the era of slavery**.

Reform Acts
(1832–1867)

The Reform Acts were a series of laws passed in Britain with the aim of bringing about a more equal and representative government for its people. Let's look at thirty facts about **how the Reform Acts affected the country**, including how voting and parliamentary representation changed.

531. **People had been protesting for reform since the 1640s,** but it wasn't until the 1830s that the government started listening.

532. **This period from 1832 to 1867 is sometimes called the Age of Reform** because so many laws were passed during this time to improve how government worked and how people voted.

533. **The Reform Act of 1832 was the first law passed in Britain that allowed small property holders to vote for representatives in Parliament.**

534. **Before the Reform Act, only 2 percent of British citizens could vote**. They were mostly wealthy landowners.

535. Before this reform bill, **Britain's political system had been largely based on a patronage system,** where MPs were elected by rich landowners who held most of the power.

536. **Most of the power had rested with the aristocracy,** but as the changes of the Industrial Revolution progressed, a new, more numerous and wealthy middle class began to gain power and influence.

537. **The Reform Act of 1832 created a new set of qualified voters known as "forty-shilling freeholders,"** who could vote if they paid more than forty shillings in rent or taxes each year.

538. **The Reform Act extended voting rights from just a few hundred thousand people to over 600,000 people**. These people could now elect members of Parliament (MPs).

539. **The Reform Act also changed how seats were allocated in Parliament** by making regions or constituencies more equal based on population size and wealth.

540. **It also gave some representation to cities and industrial areas** that had previously been underrepresented or not represented at all.

541. **The act allowed for some of the larger cities, such as Birmingham and Manchester, to gain representation in Parliament**, ending rules that had kept them from being represented.

542. **As part of this act, small borough constituencies with fewer than one thousand voters lost their seats**. Larger borough constituencies gained or absorbed them. As a result, more MPs began representing urban areas instead of rural ones.

543. **The Reform Act was designed to stop "rotten boroughs"** from having undue influence over Parliament. Rotten boroughs were constituencies with very few voters that still had representation in Parliament.

544. **By reducing the number of "rotten boroughs,"** the country saw more fairness and made voting easier for many citizens.

545. **In addition, it defined how constituencies would be redrawn every ten years in case of population shifts.**

546. **This law ensured that each constituency had enough people registered to vote** so their voices would be heard and represented fairly, though it was a slow process.

547. **Limits began to be put on the upper house of Parliament, the House of Lords,** which was made up of men from old aristocratic, titled families.

548. **The Reform Act also gave the government some responsibility** for ensuring that elections were fair and free from corruption or bribery.

549. **Many new industries, or rather their owners, were better represented in Parliament.** Previously, they had no voice whatsoever in Parliament.

550. **While this act increased voting rights considerably, certain groups were still excluded, including women** and those who did not own property or pay sufficient taxes.

551. It's important to remember that **the movement toward equality, complete representation, and openness in government was a slow process**. Change didn't happen overnight. It wasn't **until after World War One** that men and women from social groups other than the aristocracy had meaningful representation and power.

552. **This legislation is often called the *Great* Reform** Act because it was an incredibly important piece of legislation that **changed British politics forever.**

553. **The laws in the Reform Act of 1832** were perhaps the most radical legal and political changes since the Magna Carta (1215) and the Glorious Revolution of 1689.

554. One of the things that happened during this time was that **many districts were recreated to include roughly the same amount of people**, with only one member representing each district. This was the main focus of the Third Reform Act of 1884.

555. In addition, **due to complicated registration processes, some eligible voters were discouraged and did not take part**, which is what some people had hoped would happen.

556. **When the Third Reform Act was passed, about 40 percent of men had the right to vote.** Women could not vote at this time. Many districts and regions had their own rules about who could vote, mainly based on old, out-of-date laws and traditions.

557. **The Representation of the People Acts that were passed between 1918 and 1928 allowed even more people to vote, including women.**

558. **After the Reform Act of 1832 passed, Britain's two-party system began forming,** which is essentially how the British political landscape looks today.

559. **Separate acts were passed in Ireland and Scotland called the Irish and Scottish Reform Acts.** They made similar changes in those areas, though not completely, especially in Ireland, where many people were hostile to British rule. **In many places, the Irish could not vote. Others refused to vote, as they saw the British as an occupying force.**

560. **Although there were some limitations on who could actually vote due to property requirements,** overall, **the Reform Act led Britain toward a more democratic system** where citizens had a say in their government.

SECTION 2: Uncovering Britain Beginning with the Victorian Era

Victorian Era
(1837–1901)

We have arrived **at the Victorian era, a period of great social, political, and technological change. Queen Victoria was on the throne. The Industrial Revolution** changed the way people worked and lived. And **Great Britain was one of the world's most powerful countries.** So much happened during these **sixty-four years.** Let's look at thirty fascinating facts about **this famous era** in history.

561. **The Victorian era was named after Queen Victoria.** She had a powerful influence on British society during this time.

562. Until **Queen Elizabeth II's** death in 2022, **Queen Victoria** had been the longest reigning monarch in British history, ruling for **sixty-three years and seven months**, from 1837 to 1901.

563. **During the Victorian era, Britain became one of the most powerful countries in the world. Its vast empire included India, Canada, and parts of Africa and Asia.**

564. One of the many **titles Queen Victoria** held was **Empress of India**. The United Kingdom controlled much of the Indian subcontinent.

565. **Great Britain and France almost went to war with each other in 1898 over a territorial dispute in East Africa**, where they both claimed colonies.

566. The Victorian era did see war, though. **The Crimean War** (1853–1856) was a conflict between **Russia and an alliance of Britain, France, the Ottoman Empire** (Turkey), and **Sardinia**.

567. **Queen Victoria's husband, Prince Albert, co-organized the Great Exhibition of 1851 with Henry Cole, the inventor of the Christmas card**. The exhibition showcased products from around the world, including new inventions like **steam engines, sewing machines,** and much more.

568. **The telephone, typewriter, and phonograph were all developed during this era.**

569. **Newspapers, phonographs, photos, and much else all helped to bring more common threads to the people of Britain**, which became more united at this time.

570. **Photography was developed in the second part of the 19th century**. This allowed people to record personal and public events like weddings and wars.

571. **Queen Victoria popularized wearing white wedding dresses, which became the standard for brides around the world.**

572. **Scottish-born American Alexander Graham Bell invented the telephone**, allowing people to quickly communicate over large distances and get emergency help. The telephone was expensive for many years. Only wealthier people owned one.

573. **The Penny Black stamp went into circulation in 1840,** allowing people to send letters across long distances quickly for a penny.

574. **Railways linked most parts of Britain together**, which made traveling easier than ever. **Trains became the preferred mode of transport** for people traveling between cities.

575. **Expanding railways** and the growth of cities meant that large groups of people were meeting and interacting with people from distant parts of the country for the first time.

576. **The underground rail system opened in London in 1863**, revolutionizing transportation around cities and making it more efficient than ever before.

577. **Electric lighting was introduced**, which made it easier to work at night without having to use gas lamps or candles.

578. **Street lighting became common throughout Europe**, allowing people to move around safely at night with less fear of being mugged or attacked by criminals.

579. **Despite street lights and the development of a professional police force**, many English cities suffered from increased crime rates during this period.

580. **The changes brought by the Industrial Revolution made some men and families incredibly wealthy**. Many of these people were not aristocrats. They were members of the rising middle class, which would play a greater role in Britain from this point on.

581. **Agricultural production increased due to mechanization**, resulting in much higher yields.

582. **Laws were passed that limited child labor**, with factories having specific laws about how old a child had to be before they could work. **More children gradually began attending grade school for free.**

583. **The sewing machine was invented**, making it easier for women at home or working in factories to make clothing.

584. **Women's rights advanced significantly during the Victorian era**. They gained more access to education opportunities and some legal rights like **owning property or inheriting land without permission from a male relative.**

585. **Life expectancy increased significantly** due to better sanitation standards and advances in medicine, though the inner cities of England, especially in bigger cities like London, were dangerous, unhealthy, and crowded places for a long time.

586. **Advances in science, such as pasteurization, were made during this time**, which led to improved sanitation standards around Europe and America.

587. **Charles Darwin published his famous book** *On the Origin of Species* **in 1859**, which proposed evolution by natural selection.

588. **The Victorian era was called the Golden Age of English Literature. Charles Dickens, George Eliot, Thomas Hardy,** and many other famous authors wrote novels during this time.

589. **Three of Victoria's grandchildren were kings in Europe when WWI began: George V of England, Wilhelm II of Germany**, and **Nicholas II of Russia**, who were all cousins.

590. **By the time of Victoria's death in 1901, Britain had colonies or territories around the globe. Around 25 percent of the world was controlled by Great Britain**. Many of the world's oceans were dominated by the British Royal Navy. A popular saying was, **"The sun never sets on the British Empire."**

The Great Exhibition
(1851)

The Great Exhibition of 1851 was a fascinating event that showed off the wealth and power of Great Britain. People could see **the Crystal Palace** or the thousands of exciting objects on display. **This event had an incredible impact on people across the world;** let's see how.

591. **The Great Exhibition of 1851 was the world's first international exhibition. It was held in London.**

592. **It took place in a building called the Crystal Palace,** which had over 990,000 square feet of display space!

593. **Over one hundred countries sent items to be displayed at the Great Exhibition.** The exhibition showcased art and items from all around the world!

594. **The exhibition was a reflection of a more interconnected world with Britain** at its center.

595. **A grand opening ceremony marked the start of the Great Exhibition. Queen Victoria arrived on horseback accompanied by her husband, Prince Albert,** as well as their seven children. They were all dressed in white.

596. **Over six million people visited it during its six-month run.** That was about one-third of Britain's population at that time.

597. **The Great Exhibition became "the place to be" for members of British society.**

598. Many famous figures attended the exhibition, including **Charles Dickens** and **Michael Faraday**, both of whom gave lectures while they were there.

599. **Special steam engines were set up outside so visitors could travel easily by train directly into Hyde Park,** where the exhibition was located.

600. **To make sure visitors didn't get lost while they explored all the wonders, special maps were made of the Crystal Palace's** interior, complete with street names like Regent Street or Oxford Street after famous London locations.

601. **Interpreters from different countries were hired so visitors could ask questions** about items in their own native tongue.

602. **The Great Exhibition was the first time many people got to experience international cuisine.** A variety of food from around the world was available, including **Indian curries, Chinese noodles**, and **Turkish delights**.

603. **It was also the first time that most people saw exotic items like ostrich feathers, Japanese lacquers, and kangaroo leather products.**

604. **Thirteen thousand items were displayed at the Great Exhibition**, including the famous **Koh-i-Noor diamond**, which weighed **186 carats**. The diamond was just under one pound!

605. **One popular attraction at the exhibition was life-sized dolls that could move their eyes and mouths.** These mechanical marvels were surprisingly lifelike for the time.

606. One of the most famous attractions **at the Great Exhibition was a giant water fountain** that could shoot jets up to forty feet in the air!

607. **To show off Britain's industrial might, different areas of the Great Exhibition showcased items like steam engines and heavy machinery produced by British companies.** These objects were found in an area called the Machinery Hall.

608. **As well as having displays inside on topics like engineering and industry, the Crystal Palace also boasted a huge garden area** outside featuring exotic plants imported for the event.

609. **Every evening during the Great Exhibition, performances would be put on by bands that played traditional music from different countries.**

610. **The Great Exhibition is seen by many historians as a kind of "coming-out party" for Great Britain.** The exhibition made it clear that Britain was the preeminent economic and cultural capital of the world, as well as a great military power.

Crimean War
(1853–1856)

The Crimean War was fought between Britain, Russia, Turkey, France, and Sardinia. Why did they fight? For control of **the Crimean Peninsula, the Caucasus region, and the Baltic Sea.** There are so many interesting facts about this war, including **the daring Charge of the Light Brigade**, the introduction of **new military tactics**, the use of new technologies, and so much more.

611. **The Crimean War was fought between Russia and an alliance of France, Britain, the Ottoman Empire (Turkey), and the Kingdom of Sardinia (in modern Italy).**

612. **One of the reasons Britain and France allied with Turkey was because they were afraid that Russia would dominate the region since** Turkey was not as strong as it once had been.

613. **Although France had mainly entered into this conflict because of its alliance with Britain,** it also wanted control over Syria, which Russia had been trying to gain access to.

614. **The war lasted from October 1853 to February 1856.**

615. The most important battle of the war was **the Siege of Sevastopol (1854–1855).**

616. During a battle near **Sevastopol**, an entire regiment of **elite French Zouaves** ("zwah-vays") charged into Russian lines while singing the French anthem, **"La Marseillaise."** They inspired other troops with their bravery, despite suffering terrible losses themselves.

617. Another famous engagement took place at **Inkerman in 1854**. A small force of **British soldiers** held off nearly ten times their number for several hours before reinforcements arrived, earning them recognition for their courage under fire.

618. **During the Battle of Balaclava in October 1854**, a group of British soldiers held off an entire Russian division for over three hours. They became known as the **"Thin Red Line."** **Their bravery was honored with six Victoria Crosses**, the highest military decoration in Great Britain.

619. **At Balaclava, Lord Cardigan led his cavalry on what is called the "Charge of the Light Brigade,"** which became the subject of songs and stories, even though it was a British defeat.

620. **When the Crimean War first began, British soldiers wore elaborate uniforms, similar in many ways to what the queen's or king's guards at Buckingham Palace** wear today. They looked great on the parade ground but were incredibly hot, too colorful, and not tough enough to withstand conditions on the battlefield. Many British troops took what they could from dead Russian soldiers or traded with their allies for better uniforms.

621. **The use of the telegraph allowed the British to move their troops rapidly** to where they were needed most.

622. **The British Navy blockaded Russian ports**, preventing ships carrying supplies or reinforcements from entering or leaving, leading to shortages and **weakening Russia's position.**

623. **The Crimean War was the first major conflict where railways were used for military purposes.** Trains transported troops, ammunition, and supplies across vast distances quickly, allowing for more efficient movements of armies around Europe.

624. **In March 1855, the autocratic Russian emperor, Nicholas I, died and was replaced by the more liberal Alexander II.**

625. **In November 1855, Russia agreed to peace negotiations**. But before any treaty could be signed, hostilities broke out again, lasting until **March 1856** when both sides finally reached a compromise.

626. **Before the war, most armies used older weapons, such as muskets, which took a long time to load and fire.** During this conflict, some forces started using new weapons that could shoot much faster.

627. **British inventor Henry Bessemer developed a new kind of artillery shell,** but the cannons couldn't handle it well. After the war, Bessemer developed what's known as the **Bessemer process**, which allowed for the mass production of higher-quality steel.

628. **This conflict saw some advances in military engineering,** like trench-building techniques and the large-scale use of mobile artillery. Both of these innovations would **later become integral parts of WWI battlefield strategies.**

629. **During this conflict, soldiers from all countries wrote letters home describing their experiences.** Many of these correspondences were later published in books and newspapers, giving us valuable insight into what life on the front line was really like.

630. **This war was the first time that photography was used** to document a conflict. **Roger Fenton famously took photographs of the battlefields** and armies during his visits there in 1855 and again in 1856.

631. **The Crimean War was the first major international conflict** to be covered by newspapers, providing an unprecedented level of public awareness about this war's events.

632. **Several important inventions came out of this conflict,** such as improved **ambulance wagons**, which were designed specifically for transporting wounded soldiers from battlefields. **Medical tents** were also set up near the front lines so injured men could receive treatment quickly.

633. **The Crimean War saw some advances in medical science too**. **Anesthetics** were used for surgery for the first time during combat operations by British surgeons working in the field.

634. **Improvements in medical hygiene made during the Crimean War would later influence the Union Army's hospitals during the American Civil War.**

635. **Florence Nightingale** became famous for her work as **a nurse during this war**. She helped improve hospital conditions for wounded soldiers on both sides of the conflict.

636. **Americans were deeply interested in the Crimean War** for many reasons. One of the groups most interested were doctors, some of whom journeyed to Crimea **to study battlefield medicine** and ways it could be improved. **Many of these changes were implemented in the US during the Civil War.**

637. **In total, there were over 600,000 casualties from all sides during this conflict.** Around **250,000 of those died due to disease** or other causes unrelated to the fighting, such as cold weather or poor sanitation practices.

638. **The Treaty of Paris of 1856 ended this war. It regulated trade between Russia and other European countries** and established a neutral zone in the Black Sea and its coastline. No one could build ships or fortifications there without permission from the nations who signed the treaty.

639. **The terms of the peace treaty were largely drawn up by Britain and France. Since Turkey was the weakest partner, it benefited the least.**

640. **The official language used in negotiations between Russia and Britain at one point was French,** even though both nations had representatives present who could speak English or Russian fluently!

641. **The Treaty of Paris ended more than just hostilities between Russia and the Allied forces.** It also redrew many borders across Europe, including those separating **Austria and Hungary along the Danube River.**

642. **Though the war was fought in the Crimean Peninsula,** Russia lost land on its western border in the treaty that ended the war.

643. **Although Britain had entered the war mainly due to concerns about Russian expansion into Ottoman territories,** it increased its influence over those same lands after the conflict.

644. **The British and Russians struggled with each other over control of Afghanistan in the 1870s and 1880s.**

645. **Because of British domination, its increased power in Ottoman territories, and its disputes with France in Africa, many foreigners called England "Perfidious Albion."** **"Albion"** is an old name for England, and **"perfidious"** means **"untrustworthy."**

646. **In the second part of the 19th century, Britain greatly expanded its power and influence**. Some historians view the Crimean War as one of the major reasons to its rise in power.

647. **After the war ended, a number of monuments were erected to commemorate those who had lost their lives**. One of the most famous is **the Valley of Death in Sevastopol,** where over ten thousand soldiers from both sides are buried together as brothers-in-arms.

648. **One of the Russian soldiers involved in the war was a young Leo Tolstoy,** who is arguably **the greatest Russian writer**. The observations he made while serving as an artillery officer during the Siege of Sebastopol became key parts of his most famous work, *War and Peace.*

649. **Florence Nightingale was the most famous woman of the war**, but others came to help, including a biracial woman from Jamaica named **Mary Jane Seacole**, who became known as **the "Creole with the tea mug"** for supplying tired and wounded troops with some of the comforts of home. **"Creole"** is an old term for someone of Caucasian and African descent in the Western Hemisphere.

650. **When the war ended, Russia was almost broke and needed cash and gold badly.** This was one reason **the Russians sold Alaska to the United States** in 1854.

Irish Potato Famine
(1845–1850)

The Irish Potato Famine, also called the Great Famine, was a period of **great suffering and loss of life in Ireland.** Many **Irish families migrated to America** because of it. What caused this massive famine? How did it shape Irish culture and the culture of the countries those immigrants landed in? **How could a potato blight spread so quickly and destroy so much more than the plants in the ground?** Why was the British government so slow to respond?

This famine is still remembered today and has been used as a symbol of resilience and determination in the face of adversity. Let's explore forty facts about this terrible event in history and **the relationship between the Irish and the English.**

651. **Contact between England and Ireland went back centuries before the 19th century.** Christianity spread more quickly in Ireland than in England, and many **early evangelists in England were Irish monks.**

652. **Ireland had the same issues as England when it came to the Vikings.** The Vikings took over much of Ireland's coastline but could not spread inland due to fierce resistance.

653. **Over time, a new culture, a mix of Irish and Norse, spread in coastal Ireland called Hiberno-Norse. Hibernia** was the Roman name for Ireland.

654. **The English began their domination of Ireland in 1169 when a revolt against Henry II by his sons and ex-wife, Eleanor of Aquitaine, broke out there.** Henry's family allied themselves with powerful Irish chieftains against Henry but were defeated.

655. From the mid-16th century until 1625, **English and Scottish lords were granted huge areas of Ireland by the English monarchy,** forcing the Irish out.

656. **In 1601, a Spanish force landed in Ireland, hoping to rally their fellow Catholics against English and Scottish Protestant rule.** The English defeated the Spanish and took formal control of Ireland from 1603 until 1921. **In 1921, the southern part of Ireland (the Republic of Ireland) gained independence.**

657. Much of what is Northern Ireland today was settled by Scottish and English Protestants, along with a number of local Irish Protestants. Today, **Northern Ireland is still part of the UK.**

658. **In 1798, the Irish Rebellion occurred. It spread from Dublin into the countryside and then throughout the country**. The rebels wanted an end to English rule, and many attacks on Protestants took place, resulting in a cycle of revenge. **The rebellion was forcibly ended in October 1798, six months after it began.**

659. **During the late 18th century and into the 19th century, the English began a concerted campaign to destroy the Irish language**. The language was a key part of Irish identity and reminded the Irish of their history.

660. **As a result of English and Scottish lords claiming much of Ireland as their own, many Irish were forced off their farms and into factories**. Many went to England and the United States in search of opportunities but faced discrimination.

661. **Large Irish communities exist in many cities in England,** especially in the northwest.

662. **In 1845, the Irish Potato Famine began**. It lasted until 1850 and changed Ireland forever.

663. **The Irish Potato Famine had a major impact on the population of Ireland**. The population decreased by over 20 percent between 1841 and 1851 due to death or emigration.

664. **Over one million people died during this time**, while **another two million left their homes and emigrated to other countries,** such as Canada, Australia, New Zealand, the United States, and England.

665. The US has more people of Irish descent than Ireland does. This is largely because of the Potato Famine.

666. The famine was caused by a fungus known as *Phytophthora infestans*, which attacked potatoes all over Europe. **The fungus impacted Ireland the most due to the country's high dependence on potatoes as its main food source.**

667. It is believed that one of the main factors behind why the blight spread so quickly across Ireland was **that many farmers planted only one type of potato, which made them more susceptible to disease.**

668. **One-third to one-half of all potatoes grown during this period were diseased.** Even if farmers managed to save some crops, they often ended up having rotten potatoes instead.

669. **Poor nutrition levels combined with poor sanitation meant that people not only died of hunger but also suffered from diseases.**

670. **The British government didn't do enough to help those affected** by the famine or provide relief efforts even though they knew what was going on since reports started coming out about it soon after it started.

671. **In 1845, Ireland exported more than three million tons of grain,** yet the British colonial government still failed to provide relief efforts or put an end to grain exports, which further contributed to **the suffering and starvation of the Irish.**

672. **In 1847, an act was passed by the British government to provide relief efforts to those affected by the famine.** However, this relief came too late and had little effect on reducing deaths or stopping emigration out of Ireland.

673. **In 1845, the British Whig government created 700,000 jobs for Irishmen.** They were poorly paid but made enough to keep them and a small family from starvation. Unfortunately, this program was cut when **the conservative Tory Party came back into power, costing the lives of many Irish.**

674. **During the famine, charity organizations, such as Quakers, provided much-needed relief efforts,** including soup kitchens, medical care, and temporary housing for displaced people.

675. **In some areas, potato stocks were buried underground so they could be used later on,** but many of them ended up rotting because there weren't enough people left to eat them.

676. **Much of the best land in Ireland was held by British aristocrats and their Protestant Irish compatriots.** What land was left over was held by the common people, but plots were often so small that the only crop that would grow in sufficient numbers was potatoes.

677. **Due to an increase in poverty levels after the famine, many children were forced into workhouses** where they worked long hours under harsh conditions for little or no pay.

678. **Many people turned toward crime or prostitution to survive,** which led to an increase in crime rates across Ireland.

679. **In order to survive, people turned toward crime or prostitution, while others joined militias such as Ribbonmen and Whiteboys,** who used violence against landlords due to their harsh evictions and waged a small-scale guerrilla war against Irish Protestants. This war would grow throughout the rest of the century until Ireland won its independence in 1921.

680. **Irish painter Daniel Macdonald (1821–1853) recorded the misery of the famine in his many paintings.** In 1847, his paintings were exhibited in London, bringing increased attention to the suffering in Ireland.

681. **The Great Potato Famine not only impacted those who lived through it but has been used as an example in history books ever since to illustrate how important food security is.**

682. **To try to prevent other famines from occurring, governments in Europe began introducing laws that restricted grain exports and imposed heavy taxes on landowners** so that they could not keep food from those who needed it.

683. **After the potato blight had passed, new crop strains were developed that allowed for greater yields.**

684. **The potato blight has been known to reoccur sporadically** ever since its initial outbreak, most recently in the 1970s. Potatoes were affected again, but luckily, no large-scale famines have occurred since then.

685. **Despite the Irish Potato Famine's tragic consequences, there have been some positive effects** from it, such as increased economic opportunities abroad for many Irish immigrants who often couldn't find work or a decent wage at home.

686. **The Irish Potato Famine greatly contributed to a rise in Irish nationalism,** with many people wanting independence from British rule after seeing how little help was provided to them.

687. **The Great Hunger Memorial, located at Battery Park in New York City, is dedicated to all those lost during this tragedy** and serves as a reminder of how important it is to offer aid when disasters occur.

688. **One of the institutions the English installed in Ireland to "discourage" poverty and unemployment was the workhouse.** The workhouse was a place with a bed, enough food to survive, and a little pay for a lot of work.

689. **Many Irish families sold what little they owned and tried to get into the few workhouses in the country.** However, the workhouses filled quickly, and the government refused to build more since they didn't want the Irish to get used to British "welfare."

690. **The Irish Potato Famine has been recorded in many books over the years** and is still remembered today as a major tragedy.

The Boer Wars
(1880–1881 and 1899–1902)

Now we'll explore **the late 19th-century Boer Wars**, which were two conflicts fought between **the British Empire and the two independent Boer republics: the Orange Free State and the South African Republic.** Learn thirty interesting facts about the military tactics used and the aftermath of the conflicts. **Modern South Africa was shaped by these wars.** Let's learn how!

691. **The Boer Wars were fought between the British Empire and the Dutch settlers in South Africa who called themselves the Boers.**

692. **The Boers were descendants of the original Dutch colonists** who settled in South Africa in 1652.

693. **The British began to settle in southern Africa in the early 19th century**. The Dutch and the British fought costly wars against the dominant tribe in the area, **the Zulu**, who fought other tribes for control of much of **eastern and southeastern South Africa**.

694. **In 1879, the British and the Boers were allied against the Zulu**. The British and the Boers were successful, marking the start of a long policy that eventually ended in a racially segregated country for most of the 20th century: **the Republic of South Africa.**

695. **The Boer Wars were part of a larger program of British expansion in Africa** during the second half of the 19th century. **By 1900, most of Africa was controlled by Britain and France. Germany, Belgium, Italy, and Portugal** controlled smaller parts.

696. **The First Boer War was between Great Britain and two independent South African republics:** the **Transvaal Republic** (Zuid-Afrikaansche Republiek or ZAR, meaning South African Republic) and **the Orange Free State** (OFS). The war lasted from 1880 to 1881.

697. **There were many causes for the war, including British immigration**, a belief that **the British were pushing the Boers** out of the territory they considered their own, and unfair taxation on the Boers by the British government.

698. **The Boer Wars saw the use of new tactics, such as trench warfare**. Soldiers would dig deep trenches to protect themselves from incoming fire. **Trench warfare** wasn't as effective as it could be since soldiers often had to rebuild the trenches after each battle.

699. **Many historians argue that the use of trenches greatly increased civilian suffering** since anyone found near these fortifications could be arrested without trial.

700. **The standard British uniform consisted of a red jacket, blue pants with a red stripe, and a white safari or pith helmet**, which made them stand out in the African landscape. **The Boers, most of whom were hunters and very good shots**, were able to easily spot the British.

701. **In 1899, the Second Anglo-Boer War or the South African War began** when three separate Boer governments declared independence from Great Britain: **the Transvaal Republic, the Orange Free State, and Goshen**, the latter of which was a short-lived republic near modern-day Botswana.

702. **Paul Kruger served as president of the Transvaal Republic** during the Second Anglo-Boer War. He refused to surrender even when his own people started running out of resources.

703. **One of the most influential people in the Second Boer War was Cecil Rhodes**, who provided financial support to Britain's military forces. **He even formed his own paramilitary organization known as the Rhodesia Regiment**, which fought alongside regular troops. **The Rhodes Scholarship is named after Cecil Rhodes.**

704. **Another famous man from the Second Boer War was Winston Churchill**. Churchill was a former **soldier in South Africa** who became a journalist. He was captured after an intense battle. **Churchill escaped the prisoner-of-war camp** he was in and traveled hundreds of miles to freedom. When he was finally free, he was greeted with a huge hero's welcome in London.

705. **The man who took Churchill prisoner was P. W. Botha**, who later became **the leader of South Africa's Imperial Army** and an ally of England during WWII. **Botha eventually became South Africa's first independent president.**

706. **Another recognizable figure of the Boer Wars was Mahatma Gandhi**. He worked as an ambulance driver for British forces. **He also spread his philosophy of nonviolence** and civil disobedience through his writings at this time.

707. Many women fought alongside men during the Boer Wars, including **Emily Hobhouse,** who ran supplies between different camps while dodging enemy fire. **She also wrote several books** discussing her experiences there before becoming a famous British suffragette later in life.

708. During these wars, several secret societies sprung up with the goal of gaining independence for **the Transvaal Republic (ZAR)** and **Orange Free State** (OFS). Two examples are **the Afrikanerbond and Het Volk**, whose members included future president **Paul Kruger**. They would later take part in a successful revolt against British rule known as **the Rebellion of 1914**.

709. **During the Second Boer War, many women and children were placed in internment camps by British forces**, which caused a lot of suffering and claimed many lives. **The internment of Boer civilians put pressure on the Boers to make peace with Britain.**

710. **To gain support from other countries, both sides sent diplomats overseas**. Boer diplomats spread tales about their own people's suffering under British rule in an attempt **to win sympathy for their cause**.

711. **African tribes living close by took part in some engagements against British forces during both wars**. They were often hired by local chiefs who wanted revenge on their former oppressors.

712. **After failing to defeat the Boers directly, British forces decided to use a scorched-earth policy**, which involved destroying crops and farms owned by Dutch settlers so they wouldn't have enough supplies.

713. **The British sent messages to as many Boer farms and areas as they could to cause slaves to flee and fight for Britain**, which had outlawed slavery. The Boers still held slaves in the territories under their control.

714. **In 1900, some towns, such as Mafeking, were declared independent from Great Britain** when they refused to accept surrender terms offered by General Frederick Roberts at that time. **The townspeople eventually gave in after 217 days because of the lack of food supplies** caused by the siege.

715. **Many British people were horrified by what happened during the siege of Mafeking and put pressure on their government to end the war.**

716. In 1901, a group of Africans that called themselves **"the Peaceful Revolution" started peaceful protests throughout the Transvaal Republic** (ZAR) and **Orange Free State** (OFS) in hopes of gaining independence from Great Britain. Although they failed to achieve their goal due to the lack of support from other countries, many historians believe **their actions inspired later civil rights movements around the world.**

717. **In 1902, just three years after Queen Victoria's death, Britain signed a treaty with the Transvaal Republic** (ZAR) and **the Orange Free State** (OFS), ending the Second Boer War.

718. **After the war ended in 1902, both sides signed a treaty that granted the Transvaal Republic (ZAR) and the Orange Free State (OFS) independence from Great Britain.** However, they were still part of the Union of South Africa. **The Union of South Africa ended in 1961 when the union became a republic.**

719. **Britain gained control over what is now known as the Union of South Africa**, which included **the modern-day countries of Lesotho, Botswana, Namibia, and Zimbabwe.**

720. **After the war ended in 1902, an estimated fifty thousand Boers died either due to combat or disease**. Twenty-two thousand British soldiers were killed during the conflict.

World War I
(1914–1918)

World War I was a global conflict between the Allied Powers and the Central Powers. More than **sixty-five million soldiers from thirty countries fought in the war**. The war saw **the first major use of tanks, airplanes, submarines, and chemical weapons**, resulting in about **forty million casualties**, with anywhere from **fifteen to twenty million dead.** This chapter will explore forty sobering facts about the conflict, including the **weapons used, the battles fought, and the war's impact on society**.

721. **The Triple Alliance of Germany, Austria-Hungary, and Turkey** faced off **against the Triple Entente of Britain, France, and Russia in World War I.** Later, **Italy** and **the United States joined the Allies** (the Triple Entente).

722. **The reasons for the war are many, but the immediate cause was the assassination of Austrian Archduke Franz Ferdinand by Serbian nationalists in Bosnia**. Once that happened, **Serbia and Austria mobilized their armies**, leading their allies to do the same. War was declared in 1914.

723. **Britain and France were interested in stopping the ever-more powerful Germany from dominating Europe.**

724. **European nations used propaganda to try and win the hearts and minds of their citizens to gain support for the war effort**. They used posters, newspapers, radio broadcasts, and even movies.

725. **Many British women served near the front lines as nurses during the war.** Like it did for many men, the intensity of the first major war of the 20th century stunned and horrified them.

726. **At home, many women worked in factories, making weapons and supplies. WWI provided many employment opportunities for women,** who filled roles vacated by men who had gone off to fight overseas. **Women built tanks and aircraft. They drove buses and trains.** They also handled administrative duties within army units, giving them greater freedom than ever before.

727. **On Christmas Day, 1914, British and German soldiers laid down their arms in some areas along the Western Front so they could celebrate together peacefully**. This event became known as **"the Christmas Truce"** or **"the Silent Night Truce."**

728. **The British, along with many Australian, New Zealand, and French troops, attempted to knock Turkey out of the war** by invading the Gallipoli Peninsula near the Turkish capital in 1915. The effort was a total failure.

729. **Winston Churchill came up with the idea and was blamed for what happened**. Later studies have shown that though the Allies likely would have lost the battle, **Churchill was not the only one who deserved blame** for it.

730. **During most of the war, the British supreme army commander was General Douglas Haig,** who came to represent all that was wrong about the British officer corps. **Haig and his staff did not seem to care about the number of casualties and kept using the same tactics** almost until the war's end.

731. **One of the officers opposing the Allies at Gallipoli was Mustafa Kemal,** who became **the first president of the Turkish Republic in 1918** when the Ottoman Empire fell. He is known as **Ataturk, "Father of the Turks."**

732. **Submarines had been used in the US Civil War**, but they were often more dangerous to the men in them than to anyone else. **WWI saw the use of the first "modern" and deadly submarines in warfare.**

733. **German U-boats attempted to disrupt Allied supply lines** carrying raw materials needed for industrial production. This caused shortages that affected civilians in Britain, France, and other nations. **Britain was particularly vulnerable since much of its food came from overseas.**

734. **In 1915, a German U-boat sunk the passenger ship *Lusitania*, which killed almost 1,200 passengers aboard. Over a hundred of them were American citizens.** Germany claimed the British liner was carrying weapons and war supplies, which the English denied. **Decades later, it was proved that over 170 tons of shells and bullets were on board.**

735. **British naval forces implemented a blockade on German ports** that lasted throughout WWI. **This almost completely halted Germany's imports and exports**, causing severe shortages and leading to famine and malnutrition among its civilians.
736. **In 1916, British forces launched the Battle of Jutland**, a massive naval confrontation that was both tactically inconclusive and strategically indecisive. **The battle led to significant losses on both sides.**

737. **Though the Battle of Jutland was a stalemate, the British lost more ships than the Germans.** However, the British had more to lose. The German surface fleet did not engage in any other important battles during the war.
738. **In 1916, the British lost over thirty thousand men killed and wounded *in one day* at the Battle of the Somme**, which has been memorialized in English poems and stories.

739. Many famous works came from WWI. **Siegfried Sassoon is known for his sarcastic view on patriotism.** Perhaps the most famous work was **"In Flanders Fields" by Canadian army surgeon John McCrae.**
740. **In 1917, Russia was forced out of World War I after a bloody revolution led by Vladimir Lenin** overthrew **Tsar Nicholas II's government**.
741. **On April 6th, 1917, America declared war on Germany,** joining the Allied war effort.

742. **Great Britain had to borrow enormous sums of money from the United States to keep fighting the war,** which was one of the many things that contributed to the Great Depression.

743. **The British army was the first to use mass formations of tanks**. This happened near **the French town of Cambrai** in late 1917. Tanks broke through enemy lines without taking heavy losses from artillery fire.

744. **WWI brought about significant advancements in technology, such as tanks, airplanes, machine guns, and chemical weapons**. The effects of chemical weapons were horrible, causing external and internal burns and internal fluid buildup in the lungs that could drown a person. **After the war, most nations signed various agreements, promising not to use chemical weapons ever again.**

745. **Because both sides dug strong defensive trenches and fortifications on the Western Front,** specific weapons were created to help attackers. One was **the submachine gun**, and the other was **the terrifying flamethrower**.

746. **Depending on the model, flamethrowers could squirt a hot jet of flame many yards**. Men were so terrified of being set on fire that the men who carried the flamethrowers were "high-value targets" in any assault.

747. The RFC, **the "Royal Flying Corps," was the British air force during WWI.** Planes were used in combat for the first time during the war.

748. **English cities were bombed by German bombers and Zeppelins during the war.** Though these raids did far less damage than what occurred in WWII, they made **the English realize they were vulnerable to foreign attacks from the skies.**

749. **WWI saw the first use of aircraft carriers**, but their use was very limited. It would not be **until WWII that aircraft carriers would become critical at sea.**

750. **In 1917, Allied forces led by General Edmund Allenby captured Jerusalem from Turkish forces**. Jerusalem had been under Muslim rule for four centuries. This event marked an **important milestone in WWI's Middle Eastern campaign**. It also had a **profound effect on the Middle East** since much of the area was controlled by Europeans after the war.

751. **In January 1918, US President Woodrow Wilson issued his famous Fourteen Points speech,** outlining his vision for peace following the Great War. His speech would eventually lead to the establishment of **the League of Nations in 1920.** This organization wanted to promote international cooperation and prevent further wars.

752. **The fighting ended at 11 a.m. on November 11ᵗʰ, 1918.** This was due to the armistice or ceasefire that both sides agreed to. However, it was clear to most people on both sides that the Central Powers, specifically **Germany, had lost the war.**

753. **WWI saw some major advances in medical science. Antibiotics were used** to treat wounded soldiers and **help prevent infections from spreading.** These drugs would eventually become essential components of modern healthcare, saving countless lives worldwide.

754. **In 1918, the Spanish flu epidemic killed an estimated fifty million people** around the world. **More people died of the Spanish flu than from the war!**

755. **The Treaty of Versailles was signed on June 28ᵗʰ, 1919, marking the official end of WWI.**

756. **The Treaty of Versailles severely weakened Germany by forcing it to surrender its colonies and pay huge reparations.** The Germans resented the treaty. They would later lend their support to a group that promised to bring back the Germany of old. **This group was the Nazi Party.**

757. **The British prime minister at the end of the war was David Lloyd-George,** the first of four Welsh-born prime ministers in British history and one of the authors of the Treaty of Versailles.

758. **Millions of people died during WWI. British losses are estimated at over 700,000 men from the British Isles.** That number rises to around one million when Britain's possessions are taken into account.

759. **The Britons, especially the Englishmen, killed during the war came to be known as the "Lost Generation."**

760. **Because of the almost unending shelling on the Western Front, many men, including thousands of British soldiers, developed PTSD** (post-traumatic stress disorder). Back then, it was called **"shell shock"** and often showed itself through uncontrollable shaking, spasms, and panic.

The Women's Suffrage Movement

Today, many women take it for granted that they can vote in important elections and have a voice in their government, but **the right to vote in Britain did not come easy**. Another name for voting is **"suffrage,"** and the **women and men who fought for the women's right to vote were subjected to harassment, jail, beatings**, and other mistreatment at the hands of authorities and conservative forces. Let's examine twenty important facts about this movement.

761. **The women's suffrage movement in Great Britain aimed to secure voting rights for women,** allowing them to participate in the democratic process.

762. **The movement began in the mid-19ᵗʰ century with the formation of various organizations, such as the National Society for Women's Suffrage** (1867) and **the Women's Social and Political Union** (1903).

763. One of the prominent figures in the suffrage movement was **Emmeline Pankhurst**, who, along **with her daughters Christabel and Sylvia**, founded **the Women's Social and Political Union** (WSPU).

764. **The WSPU adopted more militant and aggressive tactics in their fight for suffrage.**

765. **The suffrage movement faced opposition from men and women who believed that a woman's place was in the home** and that they were unfit to participate in politics.

766. **Various methods were employed by suffragettes to gain attention** and advocate for their cause. These methods included **protests, hunger strikes, and acts of civil disobedience like blocking the entrances to important government buildings.**

767. **The suffrage movement faced significant setbacks**. Many suffragettes were arrested and imprisoned for their actions. They were often subjected to harsh treatment while in prison.

768. **One of the most famous tactics the suffragettes used in prison was the hunger strike,** in which they refused to eat.

769. **Rather than be blamed for allowing these women to die from hunger, the authorities often force-fed them, which was painful and torturous.**

770. **The suffrage movement gained momentum during World War I when women took on roles traditionally held by men,** such as **working in factories and serving in the armed forces.** This helped to change public opinion regarding women's capabilities.

771. **The Representation of the People Act of 1918 granted voting rights to women over the age of thirty** who met certain property qualifications. This marked a significant milestone for the suffrage movement.

772. **The 1918 act was also the first time almost all adult men were able to vote.**

773. **The Equal Franchise Act of 1928 extended voting rights to all women over the age of twenty-one**, putting them on equal footing with men.

774. **The suffrage movement in Great Britain inspired similar movements in other countries around the world,** including the United States, Canada, Australia, and New Zealand.

775. **Many suffragettes faced public ridicule and were labeled as radicals** or troublemakers for their involvement in the movement.

776. **Many also questioned their sexuality** at a time when same-sex relationships were severely looked down on and sometimes prosecuted.

777. **The suffrage movement brought together women from various social and economic backgrounds**, including working-class women, middle-class women, and even some members of the aristocracy.

778. **One of the men who opposed women's suffrage but later admitted he was wrong was Winston Churchill.** He was a member of Parliament and a member of the Cabinet at times during the suffragettes' struggle.

779. **Notable suffragettes like Emily Davison sacrificed their lives for the cause. Emily Davison died after throwing herself in front of the king's horse during the 1913 Epsom Derby**. Like many other suffragettes, she had gone on numerous hunger strikes and had been arrested a number of times for her beliefs.

780. **The suffrage movement in Great Britain paved the way for future advancements in women's rights,** leading to greater gender equality in various aspects of society today.

The General Strike
(1926)

The UK General Strike of 1926 was a nine-day work strike. Over 1.7 million workers took part in it. This strike aimed at forcing the government to intervene in preventing wage reductions and worsening conditions for coal miners. The strike had many supporters, including labor activists, the Labour Party, and even the Communist Party of Great Britain. The strike is remembered as a significant example of workers' actions to secure better working conditions. Let's look at ten interesting facts about the General Strike.

781. **The General Strike of 1926 was a nine-day event that started on May 4th and occurred in much of the United Kingdom.**

782. **It was organized by coal miner unions to protest** wage cuts and poor working conditions.

783. **The coal miners had support from many different industrial sectors,** including miners, transport workers, printers, and dockworkers.

784. **More than three million people participated,** making it one of the largest strikes in history and the first of its kind in England.

785. **Prime Minister Stanley Baldwin called an emergency meeting of Parliament,** where he made proposals like raising wages. However, the proposals did not pass, as his ideas did not go far enough for the strikers.

786. **After nine days of striking, the government brought in troops to break up picket lines so they could get supplies into some cities like London.** Some of the strikers were dockworkers and people who worked on the canals and railways. These people were needed to supply the city.

787. **Despite its large size, only minimal violence occurred during the strike**. Most of the **violence was caused by police action against protesters** or strikers attacking property or businesses deemed as **"scab" operations** (those who continued to operate despite being asked not to).

788. Oddly enough, **King George V agreed with many of the miners' demands**, but he did not have the power to do anything about the strike. He famously said to anti-strike politicians, **"Try living on their wages before you judge them."**

789. **Chancellor of the Exchequer Winston Churchill was very much against the strike** and urged **Prime Minister Stanley Baldwin** to take forceful action. **Baldwin refused,** and the strike ended in a relatively peaceful manner.

790. **Eventually, negotiations between employers and union leaders led to both sides agreeing on some improvements,** such as setting minimum wages and reducing the number of hours worked per week. The union leaders made little progress on pay increases.

The Great Depression
(1929–1939)

The Great Depression was a worldwide economic collapse that hit the industrialized countries of Europe and North America particularly hard. The Depression had many causes, some of which were rooted in WWI and rampant speculation of stocks. The spark that set off the Great Depression began in New York and spread quickly through the industrialized world, causing untold suffering and the rise of authoritarianism in Europe. Let's look at twenty facts about this important moment in history.

791. **The Depression began when the New York Stock Exchange began a series of steep drops from October 24th to October 29th**. October 29th is generally considered the day of **the Great Wall Street Crash of 1929**. The stock market lost more than half its value.

792. **In both the UK and the US, people could buy stocks "on margin," meaning they would be loaned money to buy stocks**. They would have to pay the loan when the stock went up. When the stock went down, they would have to pay their loan and any loss taken.

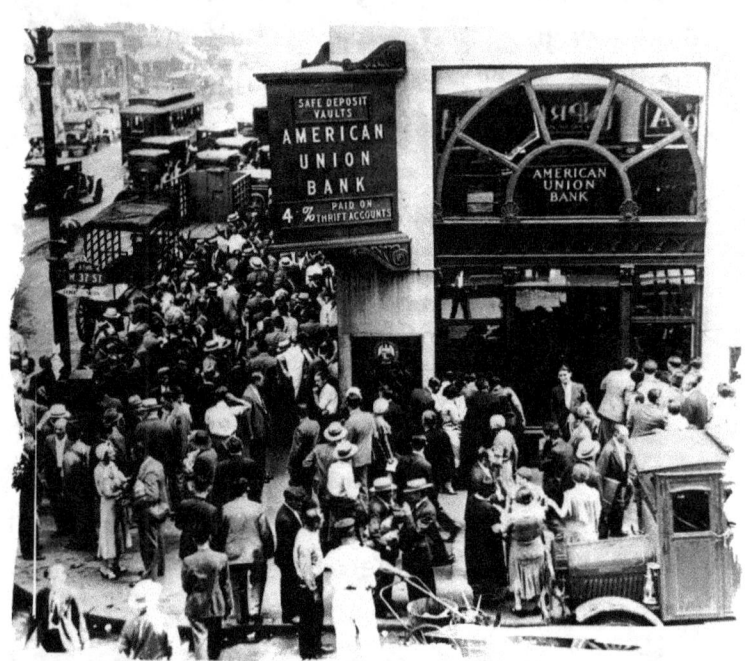

793. **Many people bought stocks on margin**. But when banks called in their margins, very few people could pay them back, leading to bank failures.

794. **Many company shares became worthless**. Many owners owned stock in their businesses. **Thousands of companies went out of business in the US, the UK**, and throughout the world.

795. **Since so many people lost money**, there was little money left over to invest. **Many companies that depended on investments could no longer afford to keep paying all their workers.** The industrial areas, such as **coal mining and transportation**, were hit the hardest.

796. **The slowdown in the economy meant people were eating less, which affected farming**. The disappearance of farms contributed to hunger around the globe, including in **Great Britain**.

797. Though **the Great Depression** began with **the New York Wall Street Crash, the Depression in Great Britain** didn't get bad until some months later.

798. **Though there had been economic depressions in Britain and the US before**, they were mild and short-lived in comparison to **the Great Depression**.

799. Before the Depression began, **Britain and much of Europe had begun to import many American goods.** Britain was a **net exporter**, meaning it sold more than it bought overseas.

800. **During the Depression, American exports to Europe greatly decreased**, which affected the economy. Britain also sold its goods around the world, but people couldn't afford to buy them, **which caused the British economy to worsen.**

801. **Twenty percent of the working population in the UK was unemployed in 1933**, the highest it had ever been. **More than three million people did not have a job.**

802. **The UK had unemployment insurance in 1911**, long before the US, which introduced it in 1932.

803. **Big industrial areas like Liverpool and southern Wales experienced higher unemployment than the rest of the country**, reaching close to one in three people over eighteen years old (around 33 percent).

804. **Crime in Great Britain increased during the Depression.**

805. **The aristocracy and upper middle class in England were worried that the lingering Depression might cause a revolution**. In Germany, **Hitler took power in early 1933**. In other European countries, extreme left- and right-wing movements began.

806. **Oswald Mosley, an upper-class former member of Parliament, started the British Union of Fascists in 1932**. He visited **fascist Italy and Nazi Germany** to look for support.

807. **Mosley's party never enjoyed great popularity**, but many supporters lived in London, making the party seem larger than it was. **Mosley was jailed in 1940 for treason and spent all of WWII in prison.**

808. **In 1931, the government began a series of banking, business, and economic reforms that would slowly begin the nation's recovery from the Depression.**

809. **Unfortunately for the UK, the Depression was not fully over when WWII began in September 1939.**

810. **After WWII, a variety of factors, including the immense debt Great Britain gained from borrowing billions from the US during the war**, caused the 1940s to be a time of continued economic suffering for many people.

World War II
(1939–1945)

World War II was a global conflict that resulted in more than eighty million deaths worldwide. We'll learn forty interesting facts about the people and events that shaped the war, from **the Allied Powers** (led by the United States, the United Kingdom, the Soviet Union, France, and China) to **the Axis Powers** (led by Germany, Italy, and Japan). **Strategies and advanced weapons were key to winning the war**. We will also explore the losses suffered by each side and **the important role women played in the war** effort.

811. **Adolf Hitler became the leader of Germany in 1933.**

812. **Nazi Germany was responsible for starting World War II in Europe** when it invaded Poland on September 1st, 1939.

813. **In May 1940, Hitler invaded western Europe, conquering France, Belgium, and Holland.** British troops were forced to retreat into a pocket around the French port of Dunkirk.

814. **Around 850 private boats sailed to Dunkirk to help rescue the soldiers trapped there.** The navy also arrived to help in the rescue

effort. **Dunkirk is one of the greatest stories of the war.**

815. **The Royal Navy still dominated the waters, especially near Europe and the Middle East.** Part of **the reason Italy joined Hitler was because it wanted to gain control of the Mediterranean and the Suez Canal**. On paper, Italy had a very strong navy.

816. **At the same time Hitler was invading France, Winston Churchill became prime minister of Britain**.

817. Many people doubted that anyone could handle the prime minister's job during this intense time in history. However, **Churchill rose to the occasion, creating the position of minister of defense.**

818. **Churchill had the idea for commando troops** (what we call "special forces" today) because **he had been captured by a special Boer unit called *Kommandos*.**

819. **The commandos staged raids along the coasts of Europe, hoping to cause Hitler to spread his forces to defend the long coastline.** They also worked to gain intelligence and give hope to people in the UK and Europe.

820. **The Battle of Britain in 1940 was Germany's attempt to dominate the skies over the English Channel** and the southern coast of England. Germany wanted to invade the country.

821. **Despite the greater number of German planes, the British RAF ("Royal Air Force") enjoyed many advantages**, like the earlier development of radar. British planes were also able to use less fuel than the Germans because they were flying over their homeland.

822. **The famous fighter pilot heroes of the RAF were known as "the Few" from a speech by Churchill**, where he thanked them for their service and sacrifice.

823. **During the war, women took over jobs that had previously been done by men**. Many men fought in the war, leaving jobs open that needed to be filled. Women produced weapons or other necessities for the country's war effort.

824. **During World War II, many countries experienced food shortages due to rationing**. Rationing meant people had limited access to certain items, such as sugar, butter, and coffee. However, the people could still get enough sustenance thanks to programs like **Britain's "Dig for Victory" campaign**, which encouraged citizens to grow their own vegetables at home.

825. **Britain depended on oil from Asia and the Middle East** for its war effort. Therefore, they sent large armies, planes, and many ships to those areas to defend them. **There were more British soldiers overseas than there were defending Britain itself.**

826. **Italian troops in North Africa were defeated by the British, forcing Hitler to intervene there. In 1941**, he sent one of his best **generals, Erwin Rommel**, with tanks and infantry to face the British. **Rommel's force was called the Afrika Korps.**

827. For almost two years, **the British and Germans fought across much of North Africa**. The turning point in the battle was **the British victory at El-Alamein in Egypt.**

828. **In June 1941, Hitler invaded the Soviet Union** (the USSR). This was the largest invasion in history. **Overnight, the USSR went from being a nation that Britain treated with suspicion to an ally.** While the UK was experiencing its own troubles, the British sent many war supplies to the USSR.

829. **The Germans had developed a complex code machine in 1926 that they believed was unbreakable. The Enigma machine** allowed German commanders to communicate without fear of enemies translating their messages, leading to some significant victories.

830. **To combat the Enigma machine, British codebreakers deciphered its secrets in 1941, using an advanced machine developed at Bletchley Park in England known as Colossus.** This machine could decode messages quickly enough to give valuable intelligence about troop or submarine movements so England could plan for an attack ahead of time!

831. **Hitler was an ally of Japan**. When the **Japanese attacked the US Navy at Pearl Harbor,** Hawaii, in late 1941, **Hitler declared war on the US.**

832. **At the same time Japan was attacking Pearl Harbor, the Japanese attacked British, American, and Dutch colonies in Asia. Singapore, Malaya, Hong Kong, and Burma** were all attacked. Only part of Burma remained British.

833. **The Dutch East Indies were conquered by the Japanese** as well. **The Philippines** and **the islands of Wake and Guam** were also taken by the Japanese.

834. **By the time the US entered the war, the US had been supplying Britain with war equipment, food, and much else**. The Americans helped the British defend their supply routes at sea and **fought the Germans in Africa**.

835. **In November 1942, US troops landed in western North Africa, pushing the Germans and their allies eastward**. Meanwhile, the British pushed the Germans westward. In the summer of 1943, the Germans and Italians retreated from North Africa to defend Italy.

836. **In 1943, US and British forces conquered the Italian island of Sicily and then invaded Italy itself.** Generally speaking, the British moved up the east coast of Italy while the Americans moved up the west coast.

837. **The Italian campaign was Churchill's idea**. He hoped Allied troops could move through Italy into southern Germany. **It was a bad idea** for many reasons. At the end of the war, Allied troops were still fighting in Italy.

838. **The Battle of Monte Cassino** took place from January 17th to May 18th, 1944. Allied forces **managed to break through German lines** after a months-long siege. **This battle is considered to be one of the bloodiest battles during WWII,** with over fifty-five thousand Allied casualties and an estimated twenty thousand for the Germans.

839. **By the time Rome was conquered in June 1944, it was clear that Britain was taking a backseat in the war.** The US was supplying more men, equipment, and money to the war effort than Britain. With some exceptions, the British had to go along with the Americans' ideas for the rest of the war.

840. On June 6th, 1944, **Allied troops traveled from England to Normandy, France, in the D-Day invasion.** D-Day was the beginning of the Allied attempt to liberate northwestern Europe.

841. **At about the same time as D-Day, the British were fighting off Japanese attacks in Burma** and the eastern border of India.

842. **Though British and Imperial forces** (mostly Australia, New Zealand, and India) fought in the Pacific, **the larger British effort was against the Nazis in Europe**. The Nazis presented a greater threat to England itself.

843. **Many refugees from Nazi-dominated Europe fled to England**. Many of them formed army, commando, and air force units to help regain their homelands. **Many of the Imperial troops fighting in Europe were New Zealanders, Canadians, and Indians.**

844. *Another group of refugees, some of them German Jews,* knew what life was like in Germany and occupied Europe. **They became spies or intelligence agents during the war.**

845. The most famous of **the resistance movements based in England was the French Resistance**, led by future French president and WWI hero **Charles de Gaulle**.

846. **By the spring of 1945, Hitler had been defeated**. Germany and Berlin, its capital, were divided into four zones of control. **The US, the UK, France, and the USSR took control of the four zones. The British sector was in the northeast**, and the British sector of Berlin was between the French in the north and the Americans in the south.

847. **British territories were restored to British control with the surrender of Japan in the late summer of 1945**. Within a few short years, many of these territories would be fighting against the British to achieve their independence.

848. **Over eighty million people died during WWII, making it one of the deadliest wars in history.** While Britain suffered economic and personal losses, **it suffered only around 450,000 deaths in the war.** Other countries had a much higher death count.

849. **Though WWI had weakened Great Britain, it was still considered one of the strongest countries on Earth.** When WWII ended, everyone knew that **Britain's time as a world superpower was over.**

850. **Most historians agree that had Britain not held out against Hitler in 1940, the war might have ended in a negotiated peace** that left Hitler in command of all of Europe. It is also plausible the war would have continued for many more years.

The Welfare State
(1946–1979)

Before WWII ended, the British people voted Winston Churchill out of office, despite having great respect for him. They saw him as a great war leader, but they believed he was too conservative to deal with the changes many people wanted to take place in the UK. After WWII, the British government implemented social reforms that came to collectively be called the Welfare State. This system's goal was to provide economic security and social welfare services to citizens in England, Scotland, Wales, and Northern Ireland.

Despite a sharp shift away from the Welfare State in 1979, the changes implemented within this new system were seen as a major step forward for social justice. The changes provided a safety net for people in need, reduced poverty and inequality, and improved living standards for the citizens. Let's look at twenty interesting facts about the Welfare State.

851. The Welfare State was a period of social reform in the United Kingdom between 1946 and 1979. It started under Labour Prime Minister Clement Attlee in 1946.

852. During this period, the government created measures to improve public services and social security, such as the National Health Service (NHS).

853. Under the Welfare State, unemployment benefits were expanded. National insurance was introduced to provide protection against illness and poverty in old age.

854. Government subsidies for food, fuel, and rent were also introduced during this period. Other reforms included measures to tackle discrimination based on race and gender.

855. The government gradually increased spending on public services, such as health care, education, and housing.

856. Public education became free at all levels up to the university level under the 1944 Education Act. Don't be confused, though. To this day, private schools and academies in Great Britain are called "public schools."

857. **The 1944 Education Act** made it easier for girls and children of working-class families to attend school.

858. **Housing subsidy schemes were set up to help people buy their own homes** or rent properties at affordable rates. **Construction of housing projects called "council homes"** or **"council tenancies"** began in most British cities as a way to provide affordable housing.

859. **Many famous British rock bands** in the 1960s and 1970s sang about how bad life in council projects really was.

860. In 1948, **Britain launched the National Health Service** (NHS), which provided universal healthcare. Medical treatments were funded by taxation rather than individual payments.

861. For a time **after the war, prescriptions were free of charge**, but for a variety of reasons, including a change of government, **fees began to be charged** for most prescription drugs.

862. In 1952, **London was affected by the Great Smog, a cloud of thick pollution**. The 1956 **Clean Air Act regulated smoke emissions** from industrial buildings. New laws regarding clean water supplies were introduced in 1961.

863. **The 1959 Mental Health Act provided more rights to people with mental health problems.** The 1967 Abortion Act made abortion legal under certain conditions.

864. **The 1968 Trade Union Reform Bill** allowed trade unions greater freedom from state control, allowing them to negotiate pay raises for their members.

865. **From 1969 onward, comprehensive education was implemented across Britain,** which provided equal access to education for all children regardless of their ability or racial or economic background.

866. **The 1971 Industrial Relations Act protected workers' rights** by providing legal recognition for trade unions and introducing guidelines about working hours and severance pay.

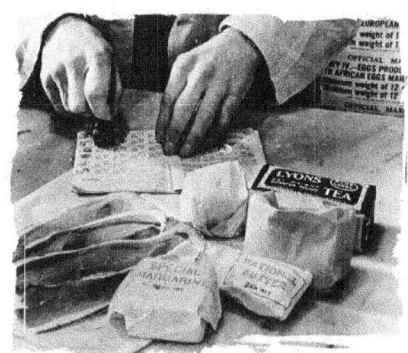

867. **During this time, British people developed a reputation for bad teeth**. This was partially due to the fact that two of the cheapest commodities in post-war Britain were sugar and flour. **Lots of bread, jam, and sugar meant lots of cavities.**

868. During this period, **there were also measures taken to reduce poverty**, including the introduction of a national minimum wage.

869. **Many of these laws and schemes were more effective on paper than in reality**. Bureaucratic **"red tape"** (meaning unnecessary rules, paperwork, and lack of direction) slowed progress or made the changes ineffective.

870. Despite expanding the government's role in everyday life, **it was difficult for the British to recover from WWII.** They owed a great deal of money. Many men had been killed or injured. **And there was great damage from German bombing raids**. For many in Britain, the post-war years were harder economically than the war years.

The Suez Crisis
(1956)

The Suez Crisis was a major international event that shaped global politics for decades to come. We'll discover **the political and military actions** of the major players involved and **the UN's role in resolving some of the event's** lasting economic and political impacts. Discover ten capitating facts about this moment in history.

871. **The Suez Canal was built in 1869 by French engineer Ferdinand de Lesseps**. It was completed in 1875.

872. **The Suez Crisis happened in 1956**. It was a conflict between **Egypt and Israel**, the latter of which had just become a new country.

873. **At the time of the crisis, the canal was owned by the Suez Canal Company, a private company based in Britain and France.**

874. **The Suez Crisis was a major international issue that involved many different countries, including the United States, the United Kingdom, France, and the Soviet Union.**

875. **Problems began when Egypt nationalized the Suez Canal,** which was a vital shipping route between the Mediterranean and the Red Sea.

876. This move was seen as an act of aggression by Israel. **Israel invaded Egypt because of it.**

877. **British and French forces took control of the Suez Canal**, which both nations depended on for supplies from the Middle East and Asia.

878. **The crisis had far-reaching effects, including strengthening the United Nations as a peacekeeping force**, the rise of Arab nationalism, and the weakening of European powers. It also led to **the United States and the Soviet Union becoming more involved in the affairs of the Middle East.**

879. For a variety of reasons, including **serious threats made by the Soviet Union over British and French** possession of the canal, **the US put pressure on both countries to remove their troops from the canal zone.** Many historians see Britain's and France's agreement with American demands as yet another sign of these nations' decline in power and influence.

880. **The Suez Canal is still a major waterway today**. It is one of the busiest shipping routes in the world.

Decolonization
(1947–1966)

Britain's complex process of decolonization took place in the mid-20th century. Many countries that had been **ruled by Great Britain gained independence**. Discover how **decolonization ultimately changed** the face of the world with these fifteen interesting facts.

881. **Decolonization is the process of freeing countries from the control of colonial powers.** It occurred mainly in the mid-20th century, although some countries were freed later. For instance, **Britain finally gave control of Hong Kong back to China in 1997.**

882. **Though imperialism/colonization meant that people were often treated as second-class citizens**, it also meant the people were protected by a stronger power.

883. **Decolonization took place mainly in Asia and Africa.**

884. **Many countries experienced civil unrest during decolonization.** Violent protests and revolts occurred in some areas.

885. **The most prominent country to gain independence during decolonization was India** in 1947.

886. **India was the largest country to gain independence from Britain during decolonization,** though it was later divided into two countries: **India and Pakistan.** Pakistan later split in two, with a new country called **Bangladesh** emerging in 1971.

887. Probably the most famous figure of the decolonization period was **Mahatma Gandhi, an Indian lawyer** who preached a policy of non-violent protest that likely prevented much bloodshed before **India gained independence**. Gandhi influenced many other activists, including **Martin Luther King Jr**. in the United States.

888. **The Mau Mau Rebellion took place in Kenya** from 1952 to 1960. Though the rebellion was eventually defeated and resulted in widespread brutality on both sides, Kenya became an independent nation in 1963.

889. Some of the other African countries that gained **independence from Britain include Zimbabwe, Namibia, Gambia, and Cameroon.**

890. In 1956, the first big wave of decolonization began with **the independence of Sudan and Malaysia from Great Britain.**

891. By the early 1970s, the British Empire was a shell of what it had been. The British Commonwealth was formed. **The British Commonwealth contains the former British colonies and territories closely linked with the United Kingdom.**

892. Between 1979 and 1990, the **UK gave independence to Belize, Dominica, Kiribati, the Solomon Islands, St. Lucia, St. Vincent and the Grenadines, and Vanuatu.**

893. **At the British Empire's height in the early 20th century, it consisted of fifty-seven territories**. Most of them are now independent. Today, there are **fourteen overseas territories that are British possessions,** though most of them have a great deal of independence.

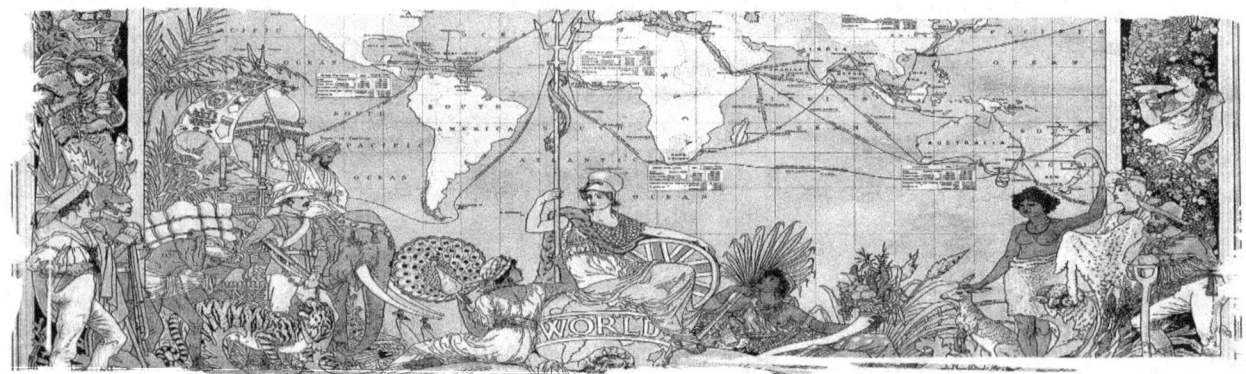

894. **Though European and British imperialism was unfair and oppressive in many ways, there were a number of developments that benefited the people**, such as modern infrastructure and modern educational systems.

895. **In 2023, there are still fourteen British Overseas Territories**. Most are small islands in the Atlantic, but there are two in the Pacific and the British Antarctic Territory.

British Culture after WWII: Music, Movies, and More

Throughout WWI and into the 1940s, American culture had a great impact on British popular culture. In this section, you'll learn more about how it spread and how the **British made rock music their own in the 1960s**. You'll also find out about famous British actors, movies, and TV shows!

896. **With the invention of the radio and the worldwide distribution of newspapers, the world became closer than ever**. For Britain, that meant new ideas in fashion, music, and other art forms.

897. **Before WWI, much of the entertainment in the UK had originated there**, but with radio and **the huge numbers of American** troops in **England** and **France** during **WWI, American music** and culture **spread throughout western Europe**.

898. **The first wave of American music to capture the hearts of the English was jazz.** Many British jazz bands emerged during this time. They toured the country, mostly **playing American songs** and using American slang in their lyrics.

899. **Jazz music has roots in African American culture**, giving the British their first real taste of African American culture.

900. **Many African American musicians moved to England** and other parts of western Europe, where discrimination against them was much less common. However, it still existed.

901. **In the 1930s and 1940s, a new kind of music called swing became popular**. Swing music was faster and more organized. It was very fun to dance to.

117

902. **American music and movies ushered in a new age of fashion in Britain**, especially in England. Not all Britons approved of the changes. **Just like in America, many older and conservative people believed jazz and swing music led to sexual activity, drug use,** excessive drinking, revealing fashion, and more.

903. **By the late 1920s, England had its own thriving movie industry**. British movies were shown around the world, especially in the territories **of the British Empire**.

904. **Many British actors became famous in the United States**. Some were regarded as better actors than Americans. **Many British actors had trained on the stage**, performing **Shakespeare** and **other classic plays**.

905. **Laurence Olivier is considered by many to be the best actor of the 20th century**. He starred in British and American productions.

906. **One of the first popular color movies was the American Civil War epic,** *Gone with the Wind,* which was released in December 1939. Many people don't know that three of its main actors were British: Vivien Leigh, Leslie Howard, and Olivia de Havilland.

907. **Before WWII, some of the most popular plays on Broadway were written by English playwright Noel Coward**.

908. **During WWII, millions of Americans came to England to prepare for the invasion of France.** They influenced many young people with their dress, **chewing gum** (which was new to England), **music, and slang.**

909. **In the early 1950s, rock and roll came to Britain from America, causing a craze among the British youth who listened to it on the radio.** They bought albums imported from America.

910. **Four Englishman who fell in love with American music at this time were John Lennon, Paul McCartney, George Harrison, and Richard Starkey** (better known as Ringo Starr). These men would be part of **the Beatles**, which is perhaps the most popular rock band of all time.

911. **Music from Jamaica, a British territory, also became popular at this time**. Rock steady, ska, and reggae music became very popular in the UK, especially among many British ethnic groups.

912. **In 1962 and 1963, Beatlemania took over England and Scotland and then spread to Europe,** British Overseas Territories, Canada, Australia, and the United States. **Hundreds of thousands of people clogged the streets and arrived at airports to see the Beatles.**

913. **The Beatles set off a frenzy for any rock music coming from England. The Rolling Stones, the Who, the Kinks, and Led Zeppelin** were just four of the many groups and artists that were part of what people in America called the British Invasion.

914. **Rock musicians protested a lot of what they saw going on around them in the 1960s and early 1970s.** By the mid-1970s, it seemed like popular music ignored the problems of suburban life and life in the inner cities, especially in the English-speaking world.

915. **Because of this, punk rock began in the late 1970s in both the UK and the US.** Punk rock music and fashion and the outrageous behavior that went with the genre shocked many people. Though there were many influential British punk rock groups, the most famous was the Sex Pistols.

916. **One of the Sex Pistols' most popular songs was "God Save the Queen."** This song **heavily criticized Queen Elizabeth and the British government and aristocracy.** The song and the album it was on were banned from the radio. However, **the record sold more than any other in England that year.**

917. **New wave began in the UK and the US out of some of the changes happening in music and technology.** Many British new wave groups, like **Depeche Mode, Echo and the Bunnymen, and the Cure,** became immensely popular in Britain and the US.

918. **In the 1990s and 2000s, many English movies became popular around the world.** Some of these include *About a Boy, Notting Hill, Bridget Jones's Diary,* and *Snatch.*

919. **The depictions of aristocratic life in Britain became popular in the 1990s and 2010s with movies and television shows like** *Remains of the Day* and *Downton Abbey.*

920. In the 1970s, **popular British comedies, like the low-brow** *Benny Hill Show* or the hilarious but strange *Monty Python's Flying Circus*, became huge hits in the US.

The Thatcher Years
(1979–1990)

The Thatcher Years were a time of great change and reform in Great Britain. This period of time is named **for Prime Minister Margaret Thatcher**, the first female prime minister. Her nickname was the **"Iron Lady"** for her toughness and determination. **"Thatcherism" sought to reduce the role of the state, privatize nationalized industries, and deregulate the economy**. Let's learn twenty facts about the many changes during Thatcher's time as prime minister.

921. **Margaret Thatcher came from the Conservative Party**. She became **the first female prime minister of Great Britain** on May 4th, 1979.

922. **Thatcher and the Conservative Party were determined to roll back many of the state-funded programs that had begun in the post-WWII years**. They believed these programs stifled free enterprise and cost the government too much money.

923. **In 1981, Americans had a conservative in charge, Ronald Reagan. Reagan and Thatcher believed in many of the same things**, including the need to stand up more strongly to **the Soviet Union**. The Soviet Union had become more active by 1980, attempting to spread communist ideology.

924. During this period, **British and American governments worked to weaken Soviet control of Eastern Europe,** beginning with Poland.

925. **The British Nationality Act of 1981** was passed during the Thatcher Years, which allowed citizens of British Commonwealth countries to have the same rights as British citizens.

926. **The Thatcher Years saw an increase in immigration to the UK**, with people from Asia, Africa, and the Caribbean coming to live and work in the UK.

927. **On April 2nd, 1982, Argentina invaded the Falkland Islands, a British possession off the coast of Argentina**. The Argentines believed the islands belonged to them, but Britain disagreed. From April to June, Argentina and the UK fought a war over the islands. The British won.

928. **The Thatcher Years saw the signing of the Anglo-Irish Agreement in 1985**, which established a relationship between **the UK and the Republic of Ireland**, the southern independent part of the island.

929. **The Thatcher Years saw the beginning of the building of the Channel Tunnel,** a rail tunnel connecting England with France.

930. **The Thatcher Years also saw the introduction of the Environment Act**, which set out regulations to protect the environment.

931. **The Thatcher Years saw the introduction of the national curriculum,** which standardized education across the UK.

932. During the Thatcher Years, **the UK helped to create the Single European Act**, which aimed to create a single European currency by 1997. The euro came about because of this act.

933. **The Thatcher Years saw the privatization of many public services and industries,** including British Rail and British Telecom.

934. **The Thatcher Years saw the introduction of the poll tax,** which was a flat-rate tax on each person in the UK.

935. The Thatcher Years also saw the introduction of the right to buy council houses, which were apartment and housing project units people could rent relatively cheaply. These changes allowed people to buy homes with generally favorable terms.

936. In 1984, the Police and Criminal Evidence Act was passed. It set out regulations for the police to follow when dealing with criminal matters.

937. By the end of the Thatcher Years, the UK saw a decrease in unemployment and a rise in living standards. However, for much of the Thatcher era, unemployment, poverty, and crime were high in the inner cities.

938. Younger people in Britain were divided on Thatcher's leadership. Many in the cities believed she did not care for the poor. The upper-middle class and the people living outside the cities saw her as the person who could restore Britain's economic power and influence.

939. After eleven years in power, Margaret Thatcher lost a vote of support in the Conservative Party, leading to her resignation and the eventual election of the next prime minister, **Conservative Party member John Major.**

940. Thatcher and her legacy are still hated by many in the UK, especially among the poor, minorities, and liberals.

The Falklands War
(1982)

The Falklands War was a conflict between Argentina and the United Kingdom, lasting from April to June of 1982. Why did Argentina invade the British-controlled Falkland Islands? How did a British naval force retake the islands? Learn about the battles fought during the war and the long-term effects on Britain and Argentina with these twenty enthralling facts.

941. **The Falklands War was a conflict between Argentina and the United Kingdom** that took place from April to June of 1982. It was the first war fought in **the South Atlantic** since World War II.

942. **The Falkland Islands are a group of islands in the South Atlantic Ocean** located about 930 miles off the east coast of Argentina.

943. **The Falkland Islands had been under British control since 1833.**

944. **Argentina had wanted to take control of the islands** for many years before the war began.

945. **Argentina's invasion of the British-controlled Falkland Islands began on April 2nd, 1982.**

946. **Argentina claimed the islands were theirs and had previously named the islands the Malvinas.**

947. **The British government ordered a naval task force to the South Atlantic Ocean to take back the islands.**

948. Many important battles were fought during the war, including **the Battle of San Carlos Water, the Battle of Goose Green, and the Battle of Mount Harriet.**

949. On May 21st, 1982, a British submarine sank the Argentine cruiser *General Belgrano*. This marked the largest loss of life in a single day of the war.

950. **Argentina surrendered on June 14th, 1982,** and the British regained control of the islands.
951. **The war was the first British victory in an overseas conflict since the end of World War II.**
952. **The British lost 255 men. The Argentinians lost 649.** Three Falkland Islanders and a British civilian also lost their lives during the war.
953. **The British took most of the Argentinian occupation forces prisoner by the end of the war.** They captured over eleven thousand men, all of whom were released when the war ended.

954. **Behind the scenes, the United States, Britain's closest ally, warned other powers, namely the Soviet Union,** from becoming involved in the conflict.
955. **Many people criticized the British government for its decision to send troops to the Falkland Islands instead of trying to find a diplomatic solution.** However, an equal number of people criticized Argentina for invading the islands in the first place.

956. **The war caused tensions between Argentina and the United Kingdom that still exist today.**

957. **The war was an important factor in the British general election of 1983, which returned Thatcher to power.**
958. **The war was expensive for both sides, but Great Britain could afford the cost. Argentina could not.** This was a major factor in **the collapse of the Argentine economy** later in the 1980s and the overthrow of the military government.
959. **In 2013, a non-binding vote or "referendum" was taken in the Falklands.** A large majority of the people voted to remain a British territory.

960. **Today, the Falkland Islands remain under British control.** The population has grown significantly since the war ended.

The Good Friday Agreement
(1998)

This chapter will explore the significance of **the Good Friday Agreement and its lasting impact on Northern Ireland**. Let's discover twenty facts about **the agreement and how it was designed to bring peace to the region**. We'll also discover **how the agreement provided for the release of prisoners** and the establishment of human rights acts and organizations.

961. **Northern Ireland remained part of Great Britain when the rest of Ireland won its independence in 1921**. Most of the people in the south were **Catholic**. A significant minority in Northern Ireland were **Protestant**. They were worried their right to worship freely would be taken away if Northern Ireland became part of Ireland.

962. **From the late 1960s to 1998, Northern Ireland went through a period of time called the Troubles. Catholic and Protestant paramilitary groups fought each other** in the streets of Northern Irish cities, especially the biggest city, **Belfast**.

963. **Cities like Belfast had been unofficially divided along religious lines for decades**. During the Troubles, **it was dangerous for a Catholic to be in Protestant areas** and vice versa.

964. **The British Army had a sizable presence in Northern Ireland during the Troubles**. British forces were accused by Catholics of committing many human rights abuses. Though **the British Army's role was to keep the peace**, it often found itself fighting against paramilitary groups and demonstrations that often included women and children.

965. **The Irish Republican Army or "IRA" was the biggest Catholic paramilitary group in Northern Ireland**. As of 2023, its political wing, **Sinn Fein**, is the largest party in the territory.

966. Many **Protestant paramilitaries existed, including the UDF or Ulster Defence Force**.

967. **The Good Friday Agreement was signed in 1998**. The agreement was named after the holiday it fell on, **Good Friday**. This agreement was a **major breakthrough in the history of Northern Ireland**.

968. **The Good Friday Agreement established the North-South Ministerial Council.** This council allowed for cooperation between the governments of Northern Ireland and Southern Ireland.

969. **Northern Ireland was given its own parliament and ministers, allowing for more independence.**

970. **Under the agreement, citizens of Northern Ireland have the right to hold both British and Irish passports,** though not all do.

971. **The Good Friday Agreement brought about the Single Equality Commission,** which aims to promote equality for all citizens.

972. **Guarantees were made regarding the Irish language and cultural rights.**

973. **Paramilitary prisoners were released, and the Police Service of Northern Ireland was created.** The police force was made up of both Catholics and Protestants.

974. **The Northern Ireland Assembly,** which is responsible for making decisions on issues like health care, education, and transport, was created because of this agreement.

975. **The Independent Commission on Policing was another result of the agreement.** The commission was responsible for reforming the police forces of Northern Ireland.

976. **The Good Friday Agreement was also responsible for establishing a new criminal justice system in Northern Ireland.**

977. Thanks to the Good Friday Agreement, **the Human Rights Commission and the Equality Commission were started.**

978. **Peace was further served by instituting the Northern Ireland Executive,** which is responsible for the day-to-day running of the region.

979. **Despite vast improvements, there are still tensions between the two religious groups in Northern Ireland,** particularly during the so-called **"Marching Season."** During this time, conservative and sometimes extremist Protestant groups hold marches through Catholic areas on religious occasions from April to August.

980. **In 2023, new concerns have been brought up by all sides in Northern Ireland over Britain's exit from the European Union.** Many in Northern Ireland fear their economy will suffer. Most people were against Brexit.

Brexit
(2016–2023)

Now we bring ourselves to the present day. **This section will explore Brexit: Britain's decision to exit the European Union.** We will cover **the referendum, negotiations, political unrest, and anti-immigration sentiment** in twenty facts. These events have **had a great impact on the UK's relationship with other countries**, as well as the lives of its citizens. Let's see how.

981. **The EU, or European Union, is an organization of twenty-seven countries** whose economies, monetary policies, and much else are governed **by the European Commission**, the main governing body of the EU.

982. **Brexit is a word that describes the United Kingdom leaving the European Union (EU).** The name **"Brexit"** is a combination of the words **"British" and "exit."**

983. **The Brexit movement began in the 2010s when many British people began to feel that much of their economic and political independence was being lost to the EU.**

984. **More than seventeen million citizens voted to leave the EU on June 23rd, 2016. About sixteen million voted to stay.** These numbers may have changed since 2016, but the UK is still deeply divided over Brexit.

985. **Those voting to leave the EU said they wanted the UK to be more independent.**

986. **UK Prime Minister David Cameron wanted the UK to stay in the EU.** He resigned after losing the vote.

987. **Prime Minister Theresa May officially triggered the Brexit process on March 29th, 2017,** by way of **Article 50 of the Lisbon Treaty**, which cemented many of the rules and policies of the European Union.

988. **A transition period was agreed upon by both entities**, allowing UK businesses to continue trading with the EU until December 2020.

989. Negotiations between the UK and the EU were difficult and long, but Britain finally left the EU in 2020.

990. The UK had to decide how it would trade with the EU and other countries and how it would protect the rights of people from the EU who lived in the UK.

991. Some people in the UK are worried that leaving the EU will make it harder for them to travel, work, and live in other parts of Europe.

992. The proposed new rules for immigration to Britain included a visa-waiver program for citizens from countries outside the EU.

993. The EU created a financial aid package worth €500 million to help farmers and fishermen absorb the losses they faced if they were unable to trade farm goods easily with **the UK or fish in British waters**.

994. British companies must now pay extra costs (tariffs) to trade with other European countries. People in Britain worry that tariffs will cause a significant increase in prices.

995. The British currency, the pound, suffered a significant loss after the passage of Brexit, primarily because the UK faced the unknown.

996. The UK will no longer be part of the European Union's single currency, which means that the pound will likely be worth less than the euro.

997. The UK will no longer be part of the European Union's political and economic systems, which means it will have to find new ways to work together with other European countries. **This could benefit the UK because it will allow the country to set up its own trade agreements** without having to submit them to the EU for approval.

998. The UK no longer has to follow the same laws as other countries in the EU.

999. Brexit could end up costing the UK economy as much as £66 billion every year, though estimates run from £40 billion to £75 billion or more. This is because of the loss of trade and trade privileges with most of Europe.

1000. Brexit has been a big issue all over the world. Many people are watching to see how it all turns out because **it will affect the world economy**.

Conclusion

Our journey has taken us through centuries of history. We have explored many events that have **shaped the United Kingdom**. Learning about **England's history** is an important and fascinating endeavor. **From the Norman Conquest to the Industrial Revolution** and beyond, the country has been shaped by a rich and complex set of events, figures, and ideas.

Exploring England's past provides invaluable insight into the development of its political, social, and economic systems and its contributions to global culture. Its stories are rich with the drama and intrigue of human experience. It is no wonder that **so many people are captivated by England's past;** it provides so many interesting topics to study!

Thanks for joining us on this amazing, many-faceted trip through England's history. We hope we have encouraged you to learn more about its history.

Part 2: English History Stories

50 True and Fascinating Tales of Major Events and People from England's Past

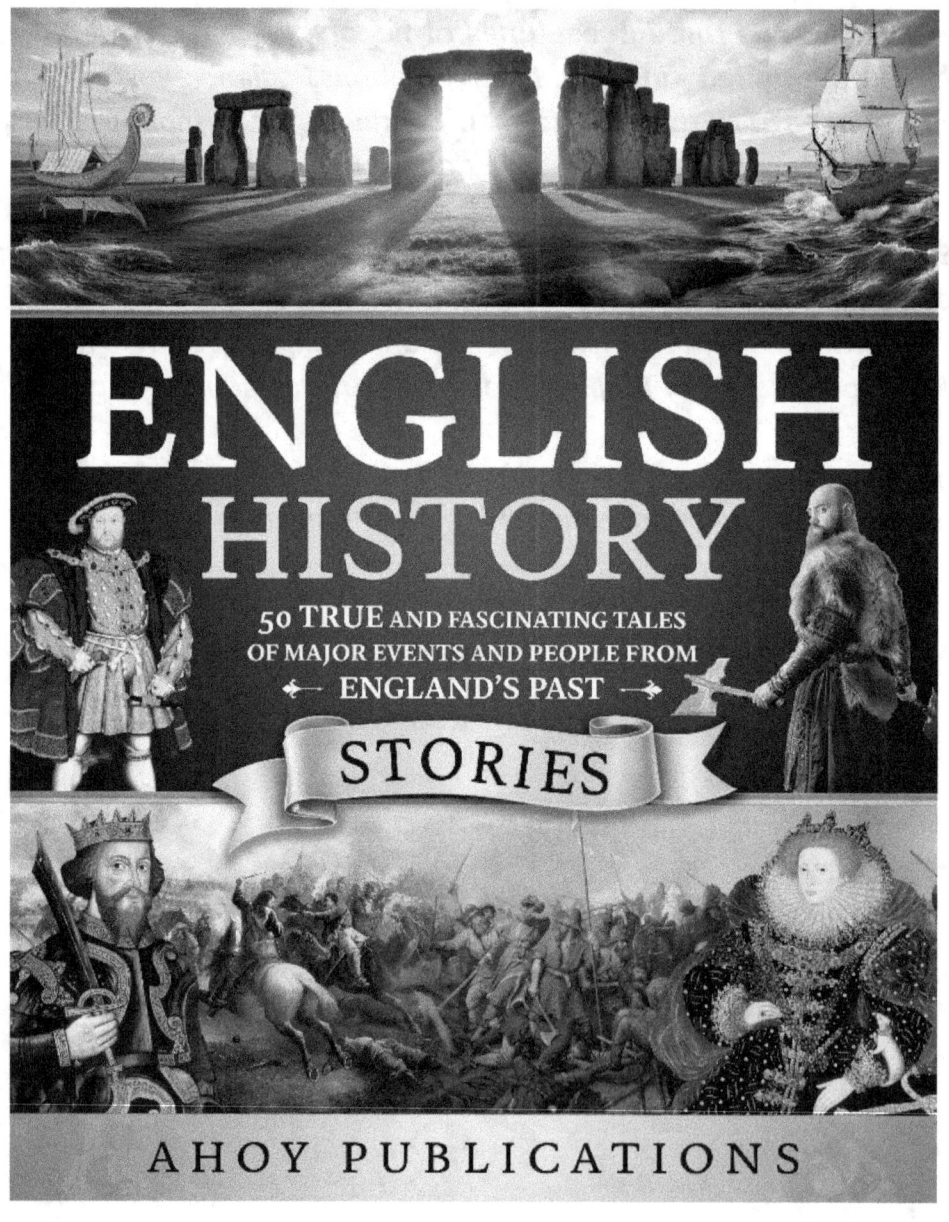

Introduction

History is a fascinating adventure with exciting stories, inspirational people, and decisive moments that shaped the world we know today. It gives you the chance to relive people's journeys, learn from their mistakes, and see the world not only through their eyes but from different vantage points. This book will act as a time machine and take you on a journey to witness Great Britain's history.

This book's journey will first take you back to the intriguing stories of Stonehenge and prehistoric England. You will discover tales of ancient societies and their extraordinary achievements and uncover the mysteries of Stonehenge and how it came to be.

Then, the following chapter will explore the legendary tales of the Vikings. You will learn here about the impact of the Vikings' invasion of the British Isles and the destruction they left behind.

England has gone through various transformations over the years. One of the most influential events in its history was the death of King Edward the Confessor. This set the stage for the Norman Conquests, which included tense and dramatic tales that changed the political landscape of Britain forever.

Another impactful moment in Britain's history was the signing of the Magna Carta and how it changed the political environment in the country. The book presents several stories showing why this document was revolutionary.

The book then takes you to the Hundred Years' War. This was a fascinating and tumultuous period in Britain's history riddled with events, battles, and many remarkable characters about whom people tell stories to this day.

The Tudor era was both captivating and powerful. The stories that took place during this period were filled with love, lust, betrayal, and events that transformed Britain in many ways.

After the Dark Ages, Britain stepped into the Era of Enlightenment, a time of intellectual exploration and cultural evolution. Many of the literary works that you read today wouldn't have been possible without all the events that took place in that era. The book presents you with stories about thinkers, scientists, and authors who revolutionized Britain during this time.

When the British Empire rose to power, it changed the world. The book takes you on a journey to Africa, India, and many other countries to reveal how Britain's ambitions, conflicts, and adventures influenced the growth of this powerful empire.

Britain played a big role in both World Wars. The book tells stories of the experiences and bravery of the British soldiers and the people during these tough times.

The last part of the book focuses on Britain's modern history. You will find stories about significant events in Britain whose influence still echoes in British culture.

History is more than stories about ancient events. Everything that took place in the past is relevant today. So, buckle up and get ready for an adventurous journey back in time that will show you how Britain's past has shaped its present.

Chapter 1: Stories on Stonehenge and Prehistoric England

Stonehenge is an incredible sight to witness. It is one of the most popular monuments in the world, with thousands of tourists visiting it every day. Throughout the centuries, Stonehenge has been linked to mythology and even magic. Many legends and folklore surround this fascinating monument. It was once claimed that Stonehenge was built by none other than the Arthurian wizard Merlin. Others also believe that the stones have healing and magical powers. To this day, Stonehenge still fills people with curiosity and wonder, and they always come up with theories to try and solve its mystery. Some of these theories are interesting, while others may seem far-fetched, almost like a plot for a science fiction movie. For instance, some people believe it is a female fertility symbol. However, others believe it was once a landing area for an alien spacecraft.

Although these are all fun and thought-provoking theories to entertain, Stonehenge isn't magic or a place for extra-terrestrials to park their spacecraft. So why does this monument spark people's imagination? What is its origin and history? This is what you will discover and more in this chapter.

It has been around for thousands of years and took over 1500 years to finish.[1]

1. The Origins and Construction of Stonehenge

Similar to the pyramids of Giza, Stonehenge is filled with secrets and raises more questions than answers. 5,000 years ago, ancient Britons built this monument on Salisbury Plain. Since they didn't have the modern technology that we do today to create a monument of that size, the construction process took about 1500 years and went through multiple phases.

It all started with the Neolithic Britons digging a huge circular ditch on Salisbury Plain. A few centuries later, builders raised 83 bluestones in a circular or horseshoe shape. These stones came to be known as Stonehenge. Sadly, only 43 of them have survived the test of time.

These stones have been standing tall for centuries, piquing people's interest with questions about who built them and why. During the 12th century, the ancient Britons were under the impression that the legend of King Arthur was factual. So, they believed that Merlin created Stonehenge. However, the monument was built centuries before the story of Merlin and King Arthur came to be.

Stonehenge has also been associated with the Celts and their priests, the Druids. However, the stones were built hundreds of years before the arrival of the Celts. So, who built Stonehenge? It was built by a group of tribes, contributing to several phases throughout the centuries to create this work of art.

The purpose of Stonehenge is one of the biggest mysteries in the world. The only way to answer this question is to invent a time machine and ask the ancient Britons themselves. However, many theories hold merit.

Judging from the placement of the stones, it is believed they acted as a solar calendar, and astronomers used them to mark the four seasons. However, recent discoveries suggest that the area was a burial ground for the ancient Britons and a temple to honor their dead and connect with their departed ancestors.

Archeologists also discovered ancient human remains that showed signs of illness and injury. This led them to speculate that ancient Britons believed Stonehenge was a place for treating ailments. When they fell sick, they traveled to Stonehenge, seeking the blue stones' healing powers.

One of the most fascinating and beautiful theories about Stonehenge is that it represents the unity of Great Britain. During the construction, people came from every part of the island to work on creating this masterpiece. This theory makes the most sense for various reasons. The construction of Stonehenge took resources and manpower that required the help of many people on the island. Thousands of people brought the stones from Wales and worked together to place them in the right spot and erect them. Stonehenge serves as a reminder of a time when the British people let go of all their differences to create something that could last until the end of time.

This next theory is pretty entertaining. It is believed that aliens visited Earth, shared their knowledge with the ancient Britons, and helped them create a model of the solar system, which came to be known as Stonehenge.

Stonehenge can have more than one purpose. It has been around for thousands of years and took over 1500 years to finish. It makes sense that people used it for many different reasons.

2. Druid Connection with Stonehenge

The Druids were high priests who lived among the Celts and acted as mediators between the gods and the people. They were educated and well respected by all of Britain. They practiced Druidry, a spiritual belief that revolves around the sacredness of nature. Hence, they performed many of their rituals outdoors in various locations. Was Stonehenge one of these locations?

For centuries, ancient Druids have been associated with Stonehenge. Perhaps the mystery behind Stonehenge and the mystery of the Druids led people to come up with their own theories and believe that these ancient priests built Stonehenge.

It has been established that the Druids didn't build Stonehenge since they weren't around during its construction. There is also no evidence to suggest that they practiced rituals there.

So, how are the Druids connected to Stonehenge? Well, they aren't. The Druids worshiped their gods and practiced rituals in groves. There is no evidence associating the Druids with Stonehenge or any other stone monument.

The misconception could also be related to the modern Druids who feel connected to Stonehenge and often practice their rituals there. However, their practices differ from those of their ancestors since this revival movement took place centuries after the ancient Druids disappeared.

If there is nothing linking the ancient Druids with Stonehenge, why do many people believe they are connected? When it was discovered that prehistoric Britons built Stonehenge, the Druids were ancient pagan priests who lived in Britain, so people assumed that the ancient Druids built it. However, with the advancement of technology, archeologists discovered that Stonehenge predates the Druids.

Some of the modern Druids who brought back Druidry also studied Stonehenge and found it to be the perfect place to practice their new faith. So, the ancient monument is connected to the revived Druidry, not the ancient practices. Since many people don't know the difference between modern and ancient Druids, this led them to believe that all Druids are connected to Stonehenge.

Another reason for this misconception was the book publishers. Authors who wrote about Stonehenge struggled to find publishers for their books. Some writers added the Druids into their books and linked them to Stonehenge to make it more interesting. This tactic worked, and many writers got the chance to publish their work, like William Stukeley, author of "Stonehenge: A Temple Restored to the British Druids." The information in that book and others like it wasn't 100% accurate and contributed to the spread of this misinformation.

Even though Stonehenge isn't associated with any religious movement, it still has a spiritual significance. Pagans from all over the world visit this site every year to connect with nature and practice their beliefs. Thanks to the mystery and mythology surrounding Stonehenge, many people believe that it holds spiritual and magical powers connecting them to their gods and the spirits of their loved ones.

Pagans consider Stonehenge to be a sacred place where they can call on the spirits of their ancestors and become one with nature. Many people believe that these stones have healing powers, and many go there for clarity and guidance. Pagans and non-pagans feel their energy shift after visiting Stonehenge as the place leaves them feeling lighter and motivated.

The shapes and colors of the stones are also meant to honor deities like Thor, the Norse god of thunder. This strengthens the belief that Stonehenge is a temple and a place for worship.

Whatever a person's beliefs are, they usually experience a spiritual awakening at Stonehenge.

3. The Beaker Folk

In 2,500 BC, many people migrated to Great Britain, and they were called "The Beaker Folk." They were given this name because their potter vessels resembled the shape of a beaker. When they first arrived in Britain, their numbers were small; however, the Beaker Folk managed to become landowners in a short time and control many parts of the region. They were archers, farmers, aristocrats, and the first metalsmiths in Britain.

The Beaker Folk had a significant influence on ancient Britain. They were the first people in the country to work with bronze. They introduced alcoholic beverages and woven garments and were famous for making pottery, some of which are still intact and displayed as artifacts in British museums.

Since many of them were farmers, the Beaker Folk paid a lot of attention to agriculture. They cultivated more lands to accommodate the country's growing population and took advantage of marginal lands that many farmers ignored. They also changed the common societal orientation during the Neolithic Era, called for equality, and introduced patriarchies in the Bronze Era, when kings and tribal chiefs were given special treatment.

The Beaker Folk transformed Britain, and it is impossible to imagine what the country would have been like if they hadn't migrated there.

You are probably wondering how the Beaker Folk relates to Stonehenge's history. The Beaker Folk were prehistoric people living in Britain prior to the construction of Stonehenge. It is believed that they were the ones who built the historic monuments. Looking at their history and influence over Britain, it is clear that they had the skills and resources to create such a complex masterpiece.

The Beaker Folk were extremely smart and ahead of their time. They were skilled metalworkers, highly artistic, and exceptional potters, so they were qualified to create something that survived the test of time, like Stonehenge. The Beaker Folk left their mark on Great Britain by leaving behind their metalwork and pottery. However, Stonehenge showed the world their true genius. Even though the Beaker Folk are long gone, their legacy will forever be remembered through Stonehenge.

When the Beaker Folk arrived in Britain during the Stone Age, they considered Stonehenge a sacred place and used it to bury their dead.

Between 2,400 and 2,200 BC, they continued the work of the Neolithic Agrarians, who laid the foundation of the monument in the first phase. The Beaker Folk started the second phase by erecting 82 bluestones in the area. They brought these stones from Wales. Archaeologists discovered that Stonehenge was first built in Wales. The bluestones were considered sacred, and the Welsh highly venerated them. However, the Beaker Folk dismantled the stones and brought them to Salisbury, where they are still standing.

This was a tough journey, and it took the Beaker Folk hundreds of years to finish Stonehenge. It isn't clear why they moved the monument from Wales to Salisbury. Whatever their reasons were, they definitely managed to create a mysterious monument that people still wonder about to this day.

4. Prehistoric Britain Life

Unfortunately, there aren't any written records about the lives of prehistoric Britain and how the people lived their lives. All the information available today comes from archeological findings. They found bits and pieces in various places around Britain and put them together like puzzle pieces, giving them an idea of what the lives of the ancient Britons were like.

The first people in prehistoric Britain were hunters and gatherers. They fed off plants and animals like pigs and cattle but avoided wild animals like wolves and bears. Many of Britain's early visitors led a nomadic lifestyle. However, archaeologists discovered ancient huts that date back to 9,500 BC. This indicates that many of them settled in and made the island their home.

In 4,000 BC, many young farmers migrated to Britain from various parts of Europe. At the time, Britain wasn't familiar with agriculture, so the arrival of these folks changed Britain forever and contributed to increasing its population.

The farmers cultivated land and grew various crops like wheat, barley, and pulses. However, many people had no interest in agriculture and preferred to live a nomadic lifestyle and hunt for animals.

With the rise of agriculture, Britain could offer resources for many individuals looking for a place to settle. More and more people, like the Gauls, Celts, and Belgae, were moving to the island. Britain – which was once empty – was now filled with people from different cultures and ethnicities.

The Celts had the biggest impact on the country. They introduced their own mythology and legends that inspired many of the great literary works you continue to read today. They also created fascinating characters like the banshee and leprechaun, still a part of today's lore and folktales.

In the Bronze Age, ancient Britons were introduced to weaponry, jewelry, and beaker pottery, which came with the arrival of the Beaker Folk. Archaeologists discovered these items in ancient graves as people were buried with many of their belongings so they could use them in the afterlife. This indicates that the prehistoric Britons believed in life after death.

The rich were buried near Stonehenge in fancy graves with luxurious goods. The difference between the graves of the rich and the poor was probably influenced by the Beaker Folk and their patriarchal society.

They used cattle to pull carts during that time because horses weren't domesticated until the Iron Age. They highly relied on dogs for hunting, shepherding, and guarding. They made clothes out of animal leather and learned to sew them using needles made from animal bones. They also lived in rounded houses in villages.

In the Iron Age, the ancient Britons began manufacturing iron tools and weapons. This was a significant time for them that had a huge impact on the country's history. During this time, the Romans invaded Britain, and Julius Caesar provided the world with the first written records of the ancient British. He was the first person to write about the Druids and describe their power and influence over the people. However, one shouldn't take his accounts at face value. The ancient Britons and their kings listened to the Druids and considered them leaders and teachers. This was a problem for the Romans, who wanted to take control of the country. So, Caesar might have provided false accounts to destroy the Druids' reputation.

He also pointed out the difference between the lives of the people of Britain before and after 47 BC. People used to lead a primitive lifestyle and lived on animal flesh and milk, but later became civilized.

Unfortunately, there aren't more written records about prehistoric Britain. Some of the information is based on the accounts of Julius Caesar, which many believe to be exaggerated. Thanks to the discovery of archaeologists, the world has an accurate picture of the lives of the ancient Britons.

5. Stonehenge Astronomical Features

The world will never stop trying to figure out the mystery of Stonehenge. It is fascinating, and archaeologists are constantly discovering more of its secrets. One of the most intriguing aspects of Stonehenge is its astronomical features. It observes moon cycles, eclipses, solstices, and many other astronomical events.

The stones are aligned in such a way that if a person sits at Stonehenge's center, they will see the summer solstice sunrise over its heel stone. During winter, one could see the solstice sunset between the tallest trilithons. However, this would be impossible to witness now since half of the trilithon has fallen.

One of the main purposes behind Stonehenge is to observe the solstices and the sun's movements throughout the day.

It was significant for prehistoric Britons to mark the sun's movements, judging by the effort and time it took to transport the stones and place each one in the right spot. Farmers and herders also needed to keep track of the changing seasons so they could determine the appropriate time to plant their crops.

Ancient Britons focused more on midwinter celebrations than midsummer. Archaeologists found evidence that they held feasts at Stonehenge, and people would gather to eat and celebrate. These festivals often took place during the darkest and coldest days of the year. They were meant to honor the sun to guarantee its return in the spring.

It is understandable why prehistoric Britons wanted to mark the sun's movements, but why were celestial events like the eclipse significant to them? Many ancient cultures, like the Neolithic culture, believed that these occurrences were a sign from their deities that could foretell various events in their lives. For instance, powerful celestial events like the solar and lunar eclipse symbolize chaos. When the sky turned dark in the middle of the day, it meant there was a disruption in the universe's natural order.

Stonehenge is an architectural masterpiece that was ahead of its time. During a period when people didn't have the technology or any of the resources one has today, they managed to design a display of stones and place them in a certain way to mark the movements of the moon and the sun. The monument also acted as a calendar to let them know the beginning of each season and even predict celestial occurrences.

Stonehenge is covered with mystery. It could be a solar calendar, a burial ground, a place to perform rituals and connect with the divine, or maybe the aliens built it. It could be all these things, some of them, or it could be something else entirely.

However, one thing everyone agrees on is that Stonehenge is a spiritual place. Whatever your beliefs, you will always feel something different when you are surrounded by these stones. Could this be its main purpose all along? Did the Beaker Folk build it to give people a unique spiritual experience? Maybe one day, someone will discover a way that could answer all these questions. A time machine, perhaps?

Chapter 2: Stories on the Invasion of the Vikings

At the mention of the word "Vikings," different people give varying reactions based on their knowledge of that culture. The Vikings are heavily depicted in many modern-day documentation, whether poetry, archeology, sagas, or even common proverbs. History buffs usually approach the subject with equal amounts of trepidation and fascination with the enchanting and bloody chronicles of the Norsemen. Motion picture enthusiasts are more lenient when it comes to depicting the ways of the Scandinavian raiders as a direct result of several enticing productions such as Vikings and the 13th Warrior. In all cases, there is no doubt that the Vikings' presence impacted the way we perceive the history of many European nations, most of all modern-day United Kingdom.

Historians identify Vikings as Scandinavian pagans that hail from the North (Denmark, Norway, Sweden). They were famous for their rugged appearance, hostile behavior, and tribal culture. They were skilled sailors who moved swiftly through any body of water and settled in lands yet undiscovered. The Vikings left their mark throughout Europe, yet not always in a positive way. While they were excellent traders, they were equally proficient in raiding, pirating, and pillaging.

The Vikings left their mark throughout Europe.[2]

At the time when the Norsemen set their eyes on Britain near the end of the 8th century, the island wasn't as unified as it is now. In fact, the land was divided into kingdoms separated by the socio-political and economic disturbances that were caused by the Roman departure at the beginning of the 5th century. These kingdoms also included immigrants from Scandinavia and northern Europe and were called the Anglo-Saxon Kingdoms. They included Wessex in the southwest, Mercia in the Midlands, North Umbria in the north (reaching as far as southern Scotland), and finally, East Anglia, currently referred to as Norfolk and Suffolk.

It is safe to say that none of these kingdoms expected the devastation and momentous change that befell them at the hands of the Vikings.

6. The Raid on Lindisfarne

The Vikings set their eyes on the wealthy, easily accessible coastal lands of the Anglo-Saxons and set sail. Anglo-Saxon writers reminisce about the period preceding the assault, saying, "immense whirlwinds, flashes of lightning, and fiery dragons were seen flying in the air," which was considered a dark omen ushering ill fortune. The shores of Wessex were no stranger to the raids of the Vikings. Earlier in 789 AD, three Northern ships landed and killed the king's reeve (a local administrative agent), who had been sent to bring them to the West Saxon court. However, the attack in 793 AD left a deeper impact.

June of 793 AD marked the beginning of the heathens' invasion and settlement in Britain. It was said that three Viking ships approached the shores of Lindisfarne on the northeast coast of England. The abbey's reeve mistakenly believed that they were traders who'd lost their way and made his way to assist them up the coast to the location he thought they were meant to set at. As he got close, the sailors attacked and killed him. They then went on to pillage the abbey and murder all of the island's inhabitants.

This assault varied from its earlier counterparts, as this was no ordinary land they attacked. Lindisfarne was the most sacred heart of North Umbria, the Holy Island, for this is where Christianity laid its roots in the nation. It was where the body of Cuthbert the Bishop was revered as a saint. The Christian monastery was desecrated, the shrine defiled, and the monks were enslaved and put to the sword. It was such a vicious attack that some Medieval writers believed it was God's punishment for their sins.

News of the bloody attack reached Alcuin, a Northumbrian scholar who lived in the Frankish Kingdom and taught King Charlemagne's children. Appalled by the events that had unfolded, Alcuin wrote to the Bishop of Lindisfarne, Higbald, saying,

"Either this is the beginning of greater tribulation, or else the sins of the inhabitants have called it upon them. Truly, it has not happened by chance, but it is a sign that it was well-merited by someone. But now, you who are left, stand manfully, fight bravely, and defend the camp of God."

He pressed on, asking Higbald to look for the reasons why God would allow such a violation of the sacred ground, implying that it was an act of holy vengeance. As the Viking attacks went on targeting holy entities, he continued to press monks and priests not to give in to the pagans.

Following the attack, several religious artifacts, including the body of Cuthbert, were relocated repeatedly to keep them safe from the Vikings.

The attack on North Umbria was a strategic success as the area had been plagued with a five-year period of harrowing tales of betrayal and royal assassinations, and that's when the Norsemen attacked. Economically, it was known for its wealthy monks, and archeological evidence suggests that it was a thriving community with enormous estates littering the mainland, probably housing the biggest Medieval population in the north of York. So, in the eyes of the Vikings, it was an easy treasure to grab.

7. Tale of Ragnar Lothbrok and His Sons

The fable of Ragnar and his sons is a mystical mix of legend and history. The story itself was recited for 350 years long after he was believed to have died. Ragnar had many titles: the whip of England and France, the father of the Great Heathen Army, and the lover of Queen Aslaug. He was one of the main influences that painted the modern archetypal idea of what the Vikings were like.

Ragnar was a Danish royal, son of King Sigurd of Sweden. Two main accounts delve into his life: the Icelandic Sagas and the Danish Gesta Danorum. The Sagas focus more on his domestic life but fail to mention his first wife, Lagertha, who is mentioned in the Danorum. In the latter, it is said that he went to war with the King of Sweden, Froh, who had killed the Norwegian King, Siward, and enslaved the women in his family to work in a brothel. As Ragnar attacked to avenge the murdered king, the enslaved women, clad in men's clothes, fought by his side, taking down King Froh. It is believed that one of these women was Lagertha, his first wife. Impressed by her swordsmanship and courage, he decided to court her, though when he tried to call on her at her home, he found it guarded with a bear and a hound. Undeterred, he slayed the beasts, making quite an impression on Lagertha, who then agreed to be his wife. They had three children together: a son, Fridleif, and two daughters whose names are not mentioned. In the years to come, it is believed that he divorced Lagertha for setting beasts upon him, a notion that greatly angered him. He took a second wife, Thora Borgarhjort, daughter of the king of Sweden, and had several children with her. It was said that he won her hand by fighting two snakes that guarded her house, wearing protective clothes that earned him the name "Hairy Breeches" or "Lodbrok." His third wife, Aslaug, was probably the most renowned, as she gave him three sons who went on to gain more fame and glory than he ever had. His sons, Bjorn Ironside, Ivar the Boneless, and Sigurd Snake-in-the-Eye (and in other recounted tales, he had two others, Halfdan Ragarsson and Ubbe), were master tacticians and warriors with their own tales and adventures.

Driven by his ego and in an effort to prove that he was as good as, if not far better than, his sons, Ragnar decided to go on a conquering voyage to England, which would soon prove to be a horrible tactic on his behalf. In his conquest, Ragnar only sailed with two ships worth of soldiers. When he arrived, he was demolished by the forces of King Aella, who outnumbered him. It is said that he met his doom when he was thrown into a pit of snakes, but not before saying his famous words, "How the little piglets would grunt if they knew how the old boar suffers," foreseeing the arrival of the Great Heathen Army to the shores of England.

Shortly after, the army arrived, led by his sons, Ivar the Boneless, Sigurd, and Ubba (who may or may not have been Ragnar's son). They triumphed and conquered Northumbria, avenging their father's death in the most epic way possible. King Aella was defeated in the battle of York in 867 AD, paving the way for his sons to move further south into the land, eventually killing King Edmund (Edmund the martyr) of East Anglia by 869 AD.

There is no telling how much of these tales are true, as some of Ragnar's exploits are believed to be fantastical fabrications and urban legends. While this may be the case, there is historical evidence of the legendary deeds and adventures of Ragnar's sons.

8. The Great Heathen Army

The coasts of Britain were accustomed to raids from Norse seafarers. It was not uncommon for Vikings to plunder and pillage British soils every summer for as far back as 787 AD, even before the Lindisfarne attack. However, the invasion in 865 AD was no ordinary hit-and-run raid, nor did the soldiers who arrived intend to accept a Danegeld (a payment the English were taxed in exchange for protection). This invasion had its eyes on the land rather than just filling their coffers.

There are two intertwined tales describing the arrival of the Great Heathen Army. The first, which is more recognized, states that the Norsemen tribes had gathered under one banner, "The Raven Banner," after reaching the conclusion that uniting their army would reap more than the occasional portable wealth. They also believed that banding together would make it easier to conquer the disbanded kingdoms of England. They were not wrong.

The Raven Banner's flag depicted a raven flying upwards and was called Hrafnsmerki. The raven was thought to represent Odin, the Chief Viking god of the Norsemen, as he was often pictured with two ravens, Huginn and Munnin. They also believed that when their time came to leave the earth, ravens guided them to Valhalla (the Viking afterlife).

The number of troops that participated in the invasion has been under a lot of scrutiny. While many historians strongly believe they were in the thousands (probably 3,000), others argue that there is no evidence of this number based on the designs of the raiders' ships and that they were probably around 900 in total.

The fictional tale is more poetic, as it paints a picture of the three sons of Ragnar Lothbrok arriving on the shores of Britain to avenge their father's death at the hands of King Aella. This story is less plausible than the previous one because modern-day historians believe Ragnar raided Paris and settled in Ireland while the Great Army ventured from the east coast, but it does cast a whimsical air on the campaign. In the sagas, it is said that they defeated King Aella, and as punishment for killing their father, they performed the brutal and graphic Blood Eagle method of execution on him. The two stories do agree on one thing, though, which is that the leaders of the army, Ivor the Boneless, Halfdan Ragnarsoon, Bjorn Ironside, and Ubbe were the children of the Norse leader Ragnar Lothbrok.

The army spent the winter in East Anglia, where they reached a peaceful compromise stating that they would spare the locals if they provided them with horses. They headed North to Northumbria as winter broke to face King Osberht and King Aella of Bamborough. Following a swift victory, they secured York and placed a puppet leader under their service. They then headed south in 869 AD to conquer Edward the Martyr, defeating his forces in no time. The king faced a rather unpleasant ending, as he was tied to a tree and peppered with arrows for standing firm and true to his Christian faith.

In high spirits from their most recent victories, the Vikings then directed their attention to Wessex, where they faced King Alfred the Great. The battle of Ashdown was not as easy or pleasant as the previous battles they had fought. In fact, the fighting continued for around two years, all through 871 and 872 AD, during which the two armies faced off several times, and Wessex remained unconquered. King Alfred paid Danegeld to his foes in order to buy himself time before the next invasion. In 874 AD, the great army invaded Mercia, driving King Burgred out and cutting off Wessex's last support.

The army then split into two: one half went northward to raid Scotland led by Halfdan, and the other half moved south under the leadership of Guthrum, continuing the raids on Wessex. The final defeat of the great army at the hands of Alfred the Great came at the battle of Edington in Wiltshire. Following the defeat, Guthrum was baptized. A treaty was struck between the two parties, "The Treaty of Alfred and Guthrum," identifying the boundaries of their territories and agreeing to engage in peaceful trade.

This was the start of the Viking settlement in England and the transition from pirates to land owners. Halfland returned south, and the remaining army divided Northumbria among themselves and started plowing and planting the land, nurturing their own farms, forever intermingling with the English culture and influencing it.

9. Creation of the Danelaw

The Danelaw refers to the piece of land that the Danes settled on following the treaty brokered between Guthrum and Alfred. Guthrum converted to Christianity and was granted the name Aesthelstan, while King Alfred served as his godfather.

The Danelaw consisted of five main boroughs in the area of east Mercia. They were Derby, Leicester, Lincoln, Nottingham, and Stamford, with the center of power being in York (Jorvik). Each borough was independent and ruled by a Jarl, with the higher class in Jorvik holding most of the power. The Danelaw covered a huge area of England that today comprises 15 shire counties: Leicester, York, Nottingham, Derby, Lincoln, Essex, Cambridge, Suffolk, Norfolk, Northampton, Huntingdon, Bedford, Hertford, Middlesex, and Buckingham.

Following the treaty's guidelines, this area was where the laws, traditions, and customs of the Vikings held sway. It also detailed steps to reduce the hostility between the two parties and allow for the exchange of trade.

The Danes were also paid Danegeld, protection money in the form of tax, that prevented them from attacking English territories between the 9th and 11th centuries. Migrants moved from Scandinavia to live and settle in Danelaw, marrying into families of the Vikings. Norsemen rulers started minting their own coins and integrating social statures, mimicking the culture in Scandinavia. Some historians suggest that the Danelaw secured more freedom and maintained the rights of people.

One of the most important settlements was Nottingham, where Ivar the Boneless and Halfland Ragnarsson settled. For a good 80 years, there was peace between the Vikings and the Anglo-Saxons as they co-existed side by side.

As time passed, it was inevitable that this peace would come to an end. Alfred the Great had used the time to fortify and rebuild his armies and strongholds. His eldest daughter, Aethelfaed, and her brother, King Edward the Elder, led the assault on the Vikings to restore the lands occupied by the raiders. In 911 AD, Aethelfaed took over the governing of Mercia and became the lady of Mercians, establishing a burh nearby and starting to campaign against the Danish. She attacked the borough of Derby in 917 AD, bringing it back into the English fold.

In 954 AD, the five boroughs fell to King Edmund, and the Danelaw era came to a close after the defeat of Eric Bloodaxe, the Viking King of Northumbria, returning the land to English jurisdiction.

10. King Alfred the Great's Epic Struggle against the Vikings

King Alfred of Wessex was one of the only English rulers who succeeded in holding his ground against the Great Heathen Army.

The king was born in Wantage, Berkshire, in the year 849 AD. He was the youngest of five sons to King Aethelwulf, Lord of the West Saxons. Faced with the Viking's imminent invasion, through mutual agreement, the brothers came to the strategic decision with their father to rule in succession to each other instead of handing the kingdom over to one child.

A young prince at the time, it was said that in order to gather the sums to defend the land, he rode to a pierced Sarsen stone, known as the "Blowing Stone," and used it to encourage the people to defend their lands against the raiders. He secured a victory in the battle of Ashdown after a ferociously fought uphill assault. Unfortunately, the triumph was short-lived. By Easter, a defeat by the Vikings and the death of his brother followed.

Following the death of his older brother Aethelred, Alfred inherited both the crown of Wessex and the war with the Pagans. Young as he was (aged 22), he was one of the last remaining resistances in the face of the Norsemen's invasion, and he was not backing down. The young king was forced to pay off the Danes with Danegeld to buy himself time until he could rally his forces once again and force the heathen army to retreat to Mercian London. The Danes continued pillaging Dorset, breaking their oaths to the English and their own Gods (Thor).

In January of 878 AD, Guthrum, the Viking leader, attacked the king while he was celebrating the 12th night in Chippenham and laid waste to everyone he could find. Alfred managed to survive the attack and started planning his revenge upon reaching the conclusion that the Danes could not be bought; they had to be conquered.

He assembled a fort 60 miles southwest of Chippenham on the central Somerset Isle of Athelney. He gathered all the remaining soldiers still loyal to his cause from Somerset, Wiltshire, and Hampshire and marched to meet Guthrum in the Village of Edington. To say the battle that ensued was bloody is an understatement. The white horse of Westbury commemorated the battle, saying, "At last, he gained the victory. He overthrew the Pagans with great slaughter and smiting the fugitives; he pursued them as far as the fortress."

Following the battle, Guthrum held out in his own stronghold for two weeks, finally submitting to King Alfred the Great and agreeing to the Treaty of Wedmore (also known as the Treaty of Alfred and Guthrum), which led to his baptism and the establishment of the Danelaw.

King Alfred's reign lasted from 871 AD to 899 AD.

Chapter 3: Stories on the Norman Conquest of 1066

The Norman Conquest of England in 1066 was one of human history's greatest and bloodiest conquests. It claimed the lives of over 100,000 people, many of whom were civilians. It brought about several changes to the traditional English way of life; some were for the good of the country, while others were not.

The Anglo-Saxons, who ruled England for more than 600 years, were brought down from their elite status. The English language encountered a sudden influx of French words and phrases. The high-powered Anglo-Saxons in the government were replaced with Normans, and the laws were rewritten in Latin from Old English. The Normans also mingled with the native English people, and intermarriages became common practice. Most importantly, slavery was abolished in English society.

It all began when the English king, Edward the Confessor, met with the Duke of Normandy, William I, sometime during his reign.

The Norman Conquest of England in 1066 was one of the greatest and bloodiest conquests in human history.[3]

11. The Succession Crisis and the Battle of Stamford Bridge

Edward the Confessor was the son of the English king, Æthelred II (978 to 1013 and 1014 to 1016), and his Norman-born wife, Emma. She was the great-aunt of William I, in the sense that she was his grandfather's, Richard II, sister. It made William I a distant cousin of King Edward, very far back in the order of succession. Edward and Emma didn't have any children. Whether they couldn't have a child or didn't want one is a matter of debate. This lack of a direct descendant sparked the succession crisis following King Edward's death in 1066.

The next in line for the throne was Harold Godwinson, the Earl of Wessex and the most powerful aristocrat in the country. The Anglo-Saxon council of the king, the Witenagemot, was responsible for raising Godwinson to the throne and crowning him king. However, it didn't take long for two other rulers to dispute King Harold's ascension. One was the Duke of Normandy, William I, and the other was the Norwegian king, Harald III.

William may have had a weak claim in terms of blood relation to the late king, but he stressed that King Edward had named him his heir with Godwinson as a witness. King Harold simply dismissed the claims and continued ruling the country.

King Harald Hardrada's challenge of King Harold's crown had nothing to do with the similarity in their names. He was not related to the English kings in any way. The blood of the Vikings ran through his veins. His claim arose from an arrangement between the late Norwegian king, Magnus the Good (1035 to 1047), and one of the previous English kings, Harthacnut (1040 to 1042). They had agreed to let the other's heir rule over both Norway and England if either didn't have a child.

The reality was that Harthacnut had made this agreement when he was King of Denmark. Since he wasn't married and didn't have any children out of wedlock, he had named Magnus his heir. However, Magnus extended his claim to the throne of England during Edward the Confessor's time. He declared war on Edward a few years after he was elected as England's king, but he died under mysterious circumstances. King Harald decided to pick up where Magnus left off after Harold Godwinson was elected as the king of England.

King Harold knew that Duke William was the more dangerous of the two, a keen tactician with a larger and better-equipped army. So, he marched south with a huge army and camped to wait for William to begin his invasion. To his surprise, Harald struck first. Sometime in September, he attacked England from the north with a force of over 15,000. His army included the men of Tostig Godwinson, Harold's brother, who was dismissed from his service early in his reign.

King Harold had to rush northward, during which time Harald had crushed the army of Edwin and Morcar, Harold's brothers-in-law. It was called the Battle of Fulford and was over as soon as it had begun. Nevertheless, the Norwegian king suffered considerable losses during the battle. He later conquered York, where his army rested. It was at this time that King Harold reached their camp with his heavily bolstered force from London (over 15,000 strong).

In the early hours of the morning, Harold launched a surprise attack on the weary and depleted Norwegian army. Their advance was slowed down on the narrow Stamford Bridge, where they had to march in a small file. There, a handful of Vikings held their own against the entire army. Despite the numerical advantage of their enemy, they put up a good fight. This choking setback gave time for the rest of Harald's army to form and gather strength. However, the soldiers had to leave their armor behind due to lack of time.

It is said that the battle raged for hours on end despite the odds being clearly in favor of King Harold. Eventually, as the numbers of the Norsemen dwindled further, their defense faltered. The deaths of Harald and Tostig were the last straw, and despite being reinforced by Eystein Orre's army, who also led them to a final counterattack, the Norwegians were defeated.

More than 80% of their army was put to death. Those who surrendered or were captured, which included Olaf Haraldsson (son of Harald) and Paul Thorfinnsson (Earl of Orkney), took a pledge never to invade England again and were allowed to return to their homeland.

However, the victorious King Harold and his men barely had any time to celebrate. Three days after the Battle of Stamford Bridge, William I began his invasion of England from the south. Emboldened by his victory, Harold was confident of taking on the Duke of Normandy's army. It was William's turn to go down now, or so Harold believed.

12. William I, the Duke of Normandy

William I was born sometime in 1028 to the then Duke of Normandy, Robert I, and Herleva, his chamberlain's daughter. The two had William out of wedlock, and they never married. Robert had another child from a different lover, a daughter named Adelaide. He didn't marry that mistress either, or anyone else for that matter. It left William his only heir for the Duchy, and he proclaimed so before his death in 1035.

William's ascension to Duke wasn't smooth. His young age (around eight years of age) made him a target of many nobles hoping to gain power by controlling him. Since he had the support of the King of France, Henry I, and Archbishop Robert (his great-uncle), he was protected from the political machinations of the nobles during the first two years of his Duchy. However, when the archbishop met his death in 1037, the conniving nobles swooped on the young Duke William like vultures to a dead body.

William's guardianship changed hands quite a few times in the coming years. Every previous guardian was supposedly murdered by the one that followed, from Alan of Brittany to Osbern the Steward. Other important men in the realm – instead of trying to control William, were blatantly opposed to his Duchy. However, it wasn't until 1046 that a real rebellion gathered steam.

Guy of Burgundy, supported by many other Viscounts and nobles, was the leader of this rebellion. William was hidden and protected by his remaining family, in particular his maternal uncle, Walter, and his cousins, William FitzOsbern, Roger de Beaumont, and Roger of Montgomery. Despite their efforts, Guy of Burgundy almost managed to capture the duke.

After the failed attempt, William was given refuge in King Henry's halls, and a year later, he went back to his Duchy with the king's forces (including Henry I himself) to subdue the rebels. Needless to say, he emerged victorious. It didn't mark the end of the rebellion, though. Guy, the leader of the rebellion, was exiled in 1050, but other nobles and lords tried to take his place. It was around the same time that William's partnership with King Henry began to deteriorate.

It so happened that Geoffrey Martel, the Count of Anjou, laid claim over Maine in a direct move against William I and King Henry. Both of them wished to control the county. They managed to remove Geoffrey from Maine, but it wasn't a joint effort. William had come into his own, and he didn't need the support of the French king anymore. His influence in Normandy was growing. In an attempt to regain control of the region, King Henry switched sides and merged his power with Geoffrey Martel.

In 1054, the king and Geoffrey, along with several other nobles, launched an attack on William's duchy. They encroached on the region from two different sides. William was prepared for a possible attack, though. Taking half his army, he pushed King Henry and his men beyond his duchy's borders. His trusted supporters, like Roger of Mortimer and Walter Giffard, defended the other side of the invasion.

King Henry and Geoffrey may have lost one battle, but they had no intention of giving in. They launched another attack on William's duchy three years later, but they were thwarted again. It was time now for William to be on the offensive. He conquered the County of Dreux and laid siege to Thimert-Gâtelles. It was during this siege that King Henry and Geoffrey met their deaths. Then, the balance of power inevitably shifted in William's favor.

It has been claimed that Edward the Confessor probably reached out to Duke William when his duchy achieved stability. The then king of England may or may not have promised William his throne. There were no records of such a conversation, nor was there any confirmation from Harald III to have witnessed the promise. Nevertheless, the Duke of Normandy insists that there is truth to his version of the story.

With such a diverse and lengthy experience of war and politics under his belt, William I was ready to begin his conquest of England and claim his rightful (at least, according to him) throne.

13. The Battle of Hastings

As King Harold patiently waited with his army for William on the southern shores of England in August 1066, the latter's troops were ready to depart from Normandy. However, the fierce winds on the South Sea (now called the English Channel) prevented the Normans from setting sail. Those winds probably changed William's fate because if he had crossed the sea at that time, he would have landed in the waiting arms of King Harold and his large army (twice as large as William's).

The Battle of Stamford had depleted Harold's forces considerably. The surviving soldiers were exhausted and weak, and they didn't have much time to recuperate. Still, their numbers were slightly greater than William's, so it was more or less an even match. The Duke of Normandy's ships docked on the shores of Pevensey, a small village in Sussex. News of their raids in the village reached Harold's ears, and he hastened southward.

Meanwhile, William slowly marched east, raiding towns as he went, until he reached Hastings. There, he built a castle out of wood, which acted as his temporary base. Harold hoped to take the Normans by surprise, but William had scouts set up at discrete points around his base, and they let him know about the arrival of the English army well in advance.

William countered with his very own surprise by launching an attack on the English force, which was set up six miles north of his Hastings base. It was early morning on the 14th of October 1066 that the Norman forces commenced their charge on King Harold's defensive formation.

Their first few strikes were largely unsuccessful against the unshakable shield wall of the English. Many of William's soldiers were impaled on the pikes, which apparently prompted a few others to flee. A considerable number of Harold's soldiers went after the fleeing enemy troops, but as soon as they were out of reach of their main force, the Norman cavalry chased them down and killed them.

William used the same strategy successfully a few more times to chip away at Harold's army until their king was left relatively vulnerable. That was when the Normans struck in full force, and during the skirmish, King Harold was slain. It is unclear who hit the killing blow. From an arrow to the eye to William's broadsword in the gut, reports of Harold's death vary from soldier to soldier.

Some said that Harold didn't even die in the battle and lived on in complete isolation. Regardless of the English king's fate, one thing was as clear as day: William had won the Battle of Hastings and had solidified his claim to the throne of England. Alas, his dream of ruling England was not to be, not yet.

14. The Harrying of the North on King William, the Conqueror

Soon after news of the outcome of the Battle of Hastings reached the Witenagemot, they elected another Anglo-Saxon king, Edgar Ætheling. A furious William marched toward London, crushing any English forces that resisted his advance. No army, no matter how big it was, prevailed against the wrath of the Norman Duke, and eventually, Edgar and his supporters yielded.

William I, the Duke of Normandy, was crowned King of England on the 25th of December 1066. He was the first Norman king of England, William the Conqueror, as he came to be known later. In an attempt to quell any more rebellions, he granted lands to the nobles that revolted against him, including Edgar Ætheling. Thinking his kingship had been solidified in the realm, he went back to reside in Normandy in 1067, taking a few English nobles with him to ensure continued support. However, the rebellions continued.

William's half-brother, Odo (they shared the same mother, Herleva), was left in charge of the kingdom in his absence. During his time, Dover Castle in Kent was attacked by Eustace II of Boulogne, but it was well fortified, so they had to retreat. Eadric the Wild engaged the Norman troops in Hereford. Gytha, the late King Harold's mother, began staging revolts against the usurper from the town of Exeter. Odo was more of a warrior than a politician or a tactician, so he probably didn't know how to handle the rebellions that popped up in many parts of the country. Thus, at some point in December 1067, William had to return to England.

He laid siege to the Gytha's band of rebels and forced their surrender. The dawn of 1068 saw Edwin and Morcar's rebellion in partnership with the Welsh rulers. Even the Earl of North Umbria led a small uprising against the new king. However, William swiftly executed his suppression tactics, and one after the other, the revolters were forced to flee the country.

Nevertheless, rebellions, small and big, continued for a few more years. From the raids in Devon by the late King Harold's sons to the revolution of Sweyn II of Denmark. Through it all, Edwin and Morcar kept troubling William with incessant rebellions until Edwin was killed and Morcar was incarcerated for life.

Later, King Malcolm III of Scotland refused to recognize William's authority over the continent, so the latter had to march northward in 1072. During this time, rebellions cropped up in England again, most of which were taken care of after William returned victorious from Scotland in 1075. The Christmas of that year was a merry one for the Normans when William the Conqueror had finally asserted his control over England and its surrounding regions.

15. Chronicling the Radical Transformation of England

A direct impact of the Norman invasion was the complete eradication of the old English aristocracy. A new hierarchy was established as King William stripped off the lands of the English nobles and gave them to the Normans. English Earls were replaced by Norman Earls, and English sheriffs were replaced by Norman sheriffs.

When William ran out of castles to confer with his Norman followers, he constructed new ones in the form of *motte and bailey* castles. Norman-style Romanesque architecture was introduced in the country, with grand, magnificent structures that overshadowed the old English buildings.

The Catholic Church in England underwent a profound transformation as well. By 1096, barely any Englishmen held high-ranking posts at the church, and the place of God was entirely in control of the Normans.

King William adopted the old English governmental systems because they were effective, but he replaced the English employees with Normans. It was the language that changed drastically, though. All official governmental documents were translated from Old English to Latin. The intermittent usage of French words while speaking English became a common practice. Most of the Norman nobility, including the king himself, used the Norman French language while communicating, which came to be known as the Anglo-Norman dialect. It is said that although William understood English, he could speak in broken sentences at best.

Over 8,000 Normans and continentals emigrated to England from their homeland during William's reign. Most of them married amongst themselves, but quite a few intermarriages were found in the records, especially between Norman men and English women. Intermarriage became common in Norman, England, several decades after William's death.

An indirect consequence of William's conquest of England was the abolition of slavery. It so happened that the Norman-controlled church wasn't comfortable with the costs of maintaining enslaved people. However, slavery wasn't abolished overnight, but as the years went by, fewer and fewer slaves were registered until the 12th century, when not a single enslaved person was to be found in England.

This series of radical transformations didn't sit well with the Anglo-Saxons. Many of them left the country and settled down in Ireland and Scotland. A few English immigrants were also found in Scandinavia.

Despite the ruthless and forceful nature of the Norman Conquest of 1066, it brought about several beneficial changes to England, many of which were there to stay.

Chapter 4: Stories on the Magna Carta

The Magna Carta, also known as the "Great Charter," is one of the most significant documents in English and Western political thought history. It has its roots in the turbulent times of 13th-century England and played a pivotal role in the development of constitutional principles and the limitation of royal power. The Magna Carta was issued on June 15, 1215, during the reign of King John of England. King John's rule was marked by disputes with the nobility, heavy taxation, and a perceived abuse of royal power. In response to growing discontent among the barons and nobility, they forced King John to meet them at Runnymede, a meadow near the River Thames, where he agreed to seal the Magna Carta.

The Magna Carta consisted of a series of written promises and agreements between the king and his barons. Its primary purpose was to address grievances and establish certain fundamental principles.

King John's rule was marked by his insatiable greed.[4]

16. The Tyrant King

In world history, there are only a few monarchs as reviled as King John of England. Born in 1166, John was the youngest son of King Henry II and Eleanor of Aquitaine. He was thrust into the tumultuous world of medieval politics from a young age, and his upbringing left a mark on his character. John's nickname, "Lackland," was not a reflection of his wealth but rather a testament to his lack of success in acquiring land compared to his older brothers. From an early age, he harbored a deep-seated resentment toward his family and sought to assert his own dominance. This desire for power and his inherent sense of entitlement would set the stage for a reign marred by tyranny and oppression.

One of the defining characteristics of John's rule was his insatiable greed. He imposed exorbitant taxes on his subjects to fund his military campaigns and extravagant lifestyle, often driving them to destitution. This excessive taxation was not merely an unfortunate necessity but a deliberate policy to enrich the crown at the expense of the people. The common folk were burdened with an unfair tax system that squeezed them dry, while the nobility and clergy enjoyed significant exemptions. John's rapacity extended beyond taxation. He exploited his position to confiscate estates, seize inheritances, and exploit legal loopholes to extort money. This pattern of behavior eroded the trust and loyalty of his subjects, especially the powerful barons who had traditionally supported the monarchy.

The king's propensity for cruelty was also notorious. He was known for his quick temper and willingness to resort to violence to achieve his goals. His treatment of political opponents was often brutal, and he didn't hesitate to use torture to extract information or confessions. Even his own family members, including his wife Isabella of Angoulême, were not immune to his wrath. One of the most infamous incidents that fueled discontent was John's handling of his dispute with Pope Innocent III over the appointment of the Archbishop of Canterbury. In a daring move, the pope placed England under interdict, effectively cutting the country off from the sacraments of the Church. John responded with defiance, confiscating church properties and silencing dissenting voices. This conflict with the papacy further isolated him and weakened his moral standing.

As word of John's tyranny spread throughout the land, opposition began to coalesce around a group of disgruntled barons. The barons, led by figures like Robert Fitzwalter and Stephen Langton, the Archbishop of Canterbury, realized that they could no longer tolerate John's oppressive rule. They began to gather in secret, forming an alliance aimed at confronting the king and demanding justice. In the simmering cauldron of discontent, a rebellion was brewing, ultimately leading to the iconic moment in history when King John would be forced to reckon with the consequences of his actions at the meadow of Runnymede.

17. The Road to Runnymede

The journey to Runnymede was fraught with tension, intrigue, and a sense of impending reckoning. The barons who had united against King John knew that they were embarking on a perilous path. However, their determination to curb the king's unchecked power and establish the principles of justice and fairness in their kingdom drove them forward. Runnymede, a picturesque meadow along the banks of the River Thames, would become the stage for this pivotal moment in English history. As the barons and their advisors converged on this serene location, they were acutely aware of the gravity of their mission. They were demanding not just personal redress but a broader transformation of the political landscape.

The barons arrived at Runnymede with a clear agenda. They were armed with a list of grievances that they believed were the epitome of the wider injustices perpetuated by King John's rule. Foremost among these grievances were the heavy taxation and arbitrary confiscation of property that had left many barons financially crippled. The barons also sought to address the issue of scutage, a tax paid in lieu of military service. John had abused this levy, often demanding exorbitant sums even when there was no immediate threat of war. The barons were determined to curtail this practice and ensure that military service and taxation were fair and proportionate.

Another key concern was the abuse from the royal officials, known as sheriffs, who were responsible for collecting taxes and administering justice in local communities. These officials, appointed by the king, often acted with impunity, engaging in corruption, extortion, and other abuses of power. The barons demanded reforms to ensure accountability and fairness in the administration of justice. At Runnymede, the barons were not alone in their efforts. They were joined by religious leaders, including Archbishop Stephen Langton, who played a pivotal role in mediating the negotiations. Langton, a scholar well-versed in the principles of natural law, saw the opportunity to channel the barons' grievances into a broader framework of justice and human rights.

As the negotiations commenced, emotions ran high among the barons and King John. The barons were resolute in their quest for concessions, while John, aware of his position, was equally determined to maintain his authority. The discussions were characterized by debates, impassioned speeches, and moments of deadlock. In the midst of these negotiations, a council comprising both barons and clergy was established to oversee the process. This council played a role in ensuring that the agreements reached at Runnymede would be adhered to and enforced.

As time went on, it became apparent that a middle ground had to be found. The barons did not seek to overthrow the monarchy; they only aimed to curb the king's powers and safeguard their own rights and privileges. After weeks of negotiations, a preliminary document began taking shape – one that would later be renowned as the Magna Carta.

18. The Day of Destiny

The Day of destiny arrived at Runnymede, casting its light upon the beauty of the English countryside. It was in this tranquil setting that a momentous event would unfold. The barons, along with their advisors and witnesses, gathered around a table to mark this occasion. King John reluctantly stood on one side of his role in this unfolding drama. Though compelled to address the barons' concerns, he remained steadfast in safeguarding the authority of the crown.

Amidst weeks of negotiations, the Magna Carta materialized. Crafted clauses aimed at addressing the grievances of the barons and restraining the king's power were now read aloud. As these clauses echoed through the air, a mix of relief and apprehension filled their hearts. The document commenced by affirming the rights and liberties of the Church – a tribute to leaders who had joined forces with the barons for justice. It then delved into issues concerning taxation – the concern on everyone's mind.

Amongst all its provisions, Clause 12 emerged as one of significance within the Magna Carta. This clause established a principle; no scutage or aid (tax) could be imposed without seeking counsel from all corners of society. Henceforth, arbitrary taxes could no longer be levied by kings without securing consent from their trusted barons and advisors.

It served as a limitation on the king's authority and ensured that taxation would be fairer and more transparent. Other sections addressed the misconduct of sheriffs and established that justice would be administered impartially and without prejudice. Clause 39 proclaimed, "No individual of status shall be detained, imprisoned, dispossessed, banished or harmed in any way unless it is through the lawful judgment of their peers or by the established laws." This particular clause laid down the principle process of safeguarding people from arbitrary arrests and punishments.

As each section of the Magna Carta was read aloud, it received approving nods from the barons and their advisors. They recognized that this document had the potential to transform the relationship between the ruler and his subjects, paving the way for a fairer society. Finally, after all sections were read and agreed upon, it was time for King John to affix his seal on the Magna Carta. As he pressed his seal into the wax, there was a moment of silence, as if even Mother Nature herself held her breath. The ink had barely dried on this parchment; its impact would reverberate throughout history.

The signing of the Magna Carta marked the beginning of an important chapter in English history. It brought about a change in the relationship between the king and his subjects. It established principles such as justice, fairness, and individual rights. This document had an impact on law and governance, shaping their course for years to come.

19. The Birth of Rights

The Magna Carta was not merely a list of objections and demands; it was a profound statement of principles that laid the foundation for the rule of law, individual rights, and constitutional government. Its clauses, carefully crafted at Runnymede, were not just about curbing the excesses of a tyrannical king but about establishing enduring principles that would shape the course of history. Among the most significant clauses was Clause 39, which declared that no free man could be imprisoned except by the lawful judgment of his peers or the law of the land. This clause, often referred to as the "law of the land" or "due process" clause, established a fundamental principle of justice: that individuals had the right to a fair trial and protection from arbitrary punishment.

Clause 12, which mandated that no scutage or aid (tax) could be levied without the common counsel of the kingdom, was a groundbreaking provision that placed limits on the king's power to tax his subjects. It introduced the concept that taxation required the consent of those being taxed, setting the stage for more accountable and representative fiscal policies. Another crucial clause was Clause 40, which ensured that justice would be administered promptly and without delay. It stated, "To no one will we sell to no one will we refuse or delay, right or justice." This principle underlined the importance of a timely and accessible legal system, a key component of a just society.

The Magna Carta also tackled the issue of misconduct among officials, especially the sheriffs who held significant power at the local level. Clause 17 introduced guidelines for appointing sheriffs, ensuring that they were individuals who would carry out their duties impartially. This provision aimed to combat corruption and misuse of power within the justice system. Apart from these clauses, the Magna Carta safeguarded the rights and privileges of groups, including merchants. These clauses acknowledged the importance of freedom and recognized trade as a key factor in the kingdom's prosperity.

While primarily addressing concerns raised by barons, the Magna Carta's principles had an impact on society. It laid down a foundation for law, gradually extending rights and liberties to a broader range of people over time. The Magna Carta was not a fixed document but rather an evolving one, open to revisions and reinterpretations in line with needs. Its lasting legacy lies not only in its clauses but also in its overarching principles of justice, fairness, and individual rights that it championed. These principles would go on to shape law development, not only in England, but across numerous nations worldwide.

20. The Global Legacy

The Magna Carta, born out of the complex political climate of 13th-century England, has left an indelible mark on the world. Its impact transcended its time and place, shaping the development of constitutional principles and legal systems in nations far beyond the borders of England. One of the most remarkable aspects of the Magna Carta's legacy is its profound influence on the formation of the United States of America. The Founding Fathers of the United States, deeply influenced by Enlightenment ideals and a commitment to individual rights, looked to the Magna Carta as a foundational document in the development of their own constitution. The principles of limited government, due process, and the protection of individual liberties found in the Magna Carta resonated strongly with the American colonists as they sought to break free from British rule. The concept that no one, not even a king, was above the law was a fundamental tenet of both the Magna Carta and the U.S. Constitution.

One of the most direct echoes of the Magna Carta in American history is the inclusion of the Fifth Amendment, which guarantees due process of law and protection against self-incrimination. This amendment, along with other elements of the Bill of Rights, reflects the deep-seated belief in individual rights and the rule of law that the Magna Carta helped to popularize. Furthermore, the idea of taxation with representation, a core grievance of the American colonists leading to the American Revolution, was rooted in the Magna Carta's demand for consent in taxation. The cry of "No taxation without representation!" echoed the spirit of Runnymede and was a defining principle in the founding of the United States.

The Magna Carta's influence extends far beyond the English-speaking world. In the aftermath of World War II, the international community came together to draft the Universal Declaration of Human Rights (UDHR). This historic document, adopted by the United Nations General Assembly in 1948, laid out a comprehensive framework for the protection of human rights on a global scale. Eleanor Roosevelt, the driving force behind the UDHR, explicitly acknowledged the Magna Carta's influence on the declaration. The UDHR drew upon centuries of thought on individual rights, and the Magna Carta was a key precursor to this evolving concept. The UDHR enshrined principles such as the right to life, liberty, and security of person, as well as the right to a fair and public trial, echoing the Magna Carta's enduring legacy of justice and rights protection.

The Magna Carta's impact is not limited to the United States and the UDHR. Its principles have reverberated throughout the world, influencing the development of constitutional frameworks in numerous countries. For instance, Canada's constitution, including the Canadian Charter of Rights and Freedoms, incorporates principles inspired by the Magna Carta. The Charter guarantees fundamental rights and freedoms to all Canadians and serves as a cornerstone of the country's legal system. The Australian Constitution reflects the Magna Carta's emphasis on the rule of law and individual rights. It has played a crucial role in shaping Australia's legal and political landscape.

The post-apartheid South African constitution, adopted in 1996, draws from the Magna Carta and other sources of human rights principles. It emphasizes equality, justice, and the protection of individual rights. India's legal system incorporates many elements from British common law, which – in itself – is heavily influenced by the

Magna Carta. The Indian Constitution guarantees a range of fundamental rights to its citizens, including equality before the law and protection from discrimination.

Apart from its implications, the Magna Carta is also a representation of broader concepts such as the rule of law and justice. It serves as a reminder that everyone, regardless of their status or authority, must adhere to the law. This principle resonates across cultures and beliefs, providing guidance to those who strive for fairness and accountability in governance. In countries where the rule of law's under threat or human rights are violated, the Magna Carta remains an inspiring source and a rallying cry for justice advocates. Its legacy reminds us that the struggle for rights and freedoms transcends time and place – it is a pursuit that spans generations.

The Magna Carta originated in 13th-century England and has proven to be an enduring document of utmost significance. Its principles have influenced the formation of nations and have served as a benchmark for safeguarding rights. From its inception in Runnymede to its lasting impact on systems, the Magna Carta stands as evidence that individuals and communities possess immense power to challenge tyranny and uphold the values they hold so dear.

Its lasting impact continues to inspire individuals dedicated to creating a society. It serves as a reminder that the pursuit of freedom and commitment to principles is a journey that goes beyond borders and endures throughout generations.

Chapter 5: Stories on the 100 Years' War

If there is anything detrimental in world history that human beings have proven time and time again to be proficient at, it would be wars. The history of humanity is built on conquests and the aftermath of conflict, with civilizations rising and falling like dominoes. Disputes over power, resources, and land have always been a strong enough incentive to shed a fellow man's blood. The story of the 100 Years' War is no different. Despite its name, the Hundred Years' War didn't last for 100 years; it lasted for 116. From 1337 to 1453, the English and the French went head-to-head over the control of the French throne.

The war lasted for 116 years.[5]

21. Origins of the Conflict

The history of France and England has always been stained with blood. There was barely a period in their joint history where these two countries didn't seize an opportunity to cross swords. Some believe that the seeds of war were planted almost 300 years earlier than its recorded start.

In 1066, the Duke of Normandy (at the time a French province), William, attempted to invade England. At the battle of Hastings, the Duke's army triumphed over the Anglo-

Saxons, and he was crowned King William I of England. It's safe to say that this was an unusual situation where a monarch was considered simultaneously a sovereign of England and a liegeman of France. Subsequently, he would control fiefs in France as well. This meant that all future kings of England kept their control and the Dukedom of Normandy. By the year 1154, the English crown's control over the French lands was growing, with King Henry II holding titles like the Duke of Normandy, Count of Anjou, and Duke of Aquitaine, along with his kinsmanship.

This new arrangement remained intact until 1205, when King John lost control of the French lands to the French King Phillip II Augustus. The lands lost to the French were Normandy, Anjou, Aquitaine, Gascony, Poitou, and Maine. This defeat earned King John the nickname Lackland, giving him and his lineage a stronger motivation to reclaim the lost areas. Try as they would to take it back, the French firmly resisted.

Several attempts at peace were made in the coming years to avoid an armed conflict. In 1259, a treaty between Henry III and King Louis IX of France was struck, allowing King Henry control over the province of Guyenne in exchange for the surrender of Anjou, Normandy, and Poitou.

While this treaty seemed like a real path to a truce, it didn't sit well with future generations of both kingdoms, causing more power-grab attempts and more treaties with every passing king.

These little skirmishes continued for a long time, well into the beginning of the 14th Century, ushering in the start of the 100 Years' War.

22. Edward, The Black Prince

In February of 1328, King Charles IV of France died, leaving behind no male heirs to rule. During that time, there were no clear guidelines on how to handle a lack of heirs to the throne. There were, however, two main claims to the throne. The first claim came from the King of England, Edward of Windsor (King Edward III). Like his ancestors, he tried to claim the French crown, and in his declaration, he relied on the concept of inheritance of titles. As it happens, his mother was Isabella of France, daughter of King Philip IV and sister to Charles IV.

The second possible heir was Philip VI, Count of Valois, first cousin of Charles IV, and son of Philip III. Essentially, Edward's maternal uncle.

According to French law, a monarch is to rise to power only if they were related through the paternal side of the previous king, which caused a point of dispute between the two parties. However, in the English rule book, this was not a requisite, for it stated that the blood relation can be maternal or paternal, adding emphasis to the concept of the "blood of kings."

This started a feud between the two candidates, ending in a battle won by the French. It also led to the official declaration of Philip VI as King of France and the unanimous blessing of the French community.

Shortly after this conflict, King Edward was blessed by the arrival of his first son, Edward of Woodstock (later known as the Black Prince), from his wife, Philippa of Hainault. He was born in June of 1330 in Woodstock near Oxford. He received his first armor at the young age of seven, an honor that would shape his life immensely.

The king granted his son funds from the Duchy of Cornwall, making him the Duke of Cornwall along with his other title, Earl of Chester. By 1343, the 13-year-old Prince was granted the title of Prince of Wales.

The Battle of Crécy

In 1337, the conflict heightened between France and England over the claim to the French Throne. It seemed that war was inevitable. The King of England knighted his son and other young knights in July of 1346 to prepare for the war.

Prince Edward was said to have earned the title of the Black Prince from his black armor, while the most favorable theory suggests it came from his "scorched earth" method of war (chevauchée). His technique involved the burning of French Villages and towns and terrorizing the locals, which provided plentiful bounty and food for his troops. It was a well-known method of economic warfare to financially weaken your opponent, making it harder for them to gather and assemble an army from the rubble. It was also a very effective method to provoke King Philip to engage in battle.

In August 1346, the two armies faced off in the battle of Crecy. The Prince was only 16 years old when he led the army's right wing with Sir Godfrey Harcourt. The young Prince fought ferociously against unfavorable odds (12,000 to 25,000). He guided the army into a defensive position on a rise by the river Maine, efficiently employing his Welsh and English archers. The battle was settled in favor of the English, with only 300 English casualties as opposed to the 14,000 fallen French men. The great losses that the French suffered were a direct result of them raising the banner to give no quarter. This resulted in the annihilation of the crème de la crème of the French nobility, including King John of Bohemia, the Count of Blois, and the Count of Flanders.

Following the fateful battle, the Prince earned his spurs (the mark of knighthood that is awarded in a full knighting ceremony). Legend states that following the battle, the Prince assumed the emblem and motto of the fallen Bohemian king, the 3 white Ostrich feathers, and the saying, "Courage, I serve" (homout; ich dene).

In July of 1347, the English king and his black Prince marched with 26,000 soldiers, effectively laying siege to Calais for a whole year before capturing it.

The Battle of Poitiers

King John II was newly crowned the King of France in 1350. Continuing the tradition of his predecessor, he went to war with the English. In a strategic move on the Black

Prince's part, he moved in 1355 to raid Gascony and capture Bordeaux, a land that served as a main patron to the French Kings' coffers.

Edward adopted the same strategy of torching cities, farming lands, and villages as he moved forth. Once again, this proved very effective in pushing the unwise King John to engage in battle. A French army was assembled in an effort to cut off the link between the southeast English forces and their counterparts in Normandy. This interception surprised the Black Prince's corps. The battle of Poitiers was fought the next day, on 19th September 1356, in the mixed topography of woods, farmland, and marshes, 4 miles away from Poitiers. Once again faced with adverse odds (35,000 to 7,000 Englishmen), the Black Prince triumphed over the muddled leadership of the French and, through employing the English longbows to his advantage. Prince Edward captured 2,000 French knights, as well as King John II, who was escorted back to England, where he remained in captivity for four years.

It's important to mention that the Prince was well-known for his manners and proper behavior. He treated his captives with respect and courtesy, displaying chivalry in his actions. Additionally, he generously shared gold among his followers and soldiers while also making donations to the churches in England.

In 1362, the Prince was appointed as the Prince of Aquitaine by his father after their failed attempt to seize the throne in Reims. This particular stronghold proved to be impenetrable in 1359. After enduring a winter during their endeavor, an agreement was reached between the King and England through the signing of the Treaty of Bretigny in 1360, which ensured peace between both nations for a span of two years. Following this period of peace, the Black Prince shifted his focus towards Spain in 1367 by aiding King Pedro the Cruel of Castille against his brother Henry of Trastamara, who had challenged him for the throne. Edward emerged victorious over Henry at Nájera in Castille, and as a token of gratitude, he received a gem known as the Black Prince's Ruby from the King. To this day, it remains part of England's crown jewels.

In 1361, at Windsor Castle, the Prince entered into matrimony with his cousin Joan, who held the title Countess of Kent. The couple had two sons, Edward and Richard, who later became known as Richard II of England. The circumstances surrounding the Black Prince's death are uncertain; some believe it was due to injuries sustained during wars, while others suggest it was an illness. Ultimately, the Prince, who had dedicated a portion of his life in service to the monarchy, passed away before having the opportunity to assume the throne.

23. Joan of Arc

Joan of Arc stands as one of history's greatest female warriors and saints. She was born in Domrémy la Pucelle, France, in January 1412 during the period of the 100 Years War. At that time, England appeared to be gaining the upper hand, asserting control over portions of French territory. This shift in power was largely attributed to King Henry V's triumph at the Battle of Agincourt in 1415.

King Henry V enjoyed a series of victories against the French forces. In 1420, he compelled them to acknowledge his descendants as legitimate heirs to the French throne through the terms outlined in the Treaty of Troyes. Additionally, he forged an alliance by marrying Cathérine of Valois, daughter of the King. This union further solidified his ties with Philip the Good, Duke of Burgundy. However, Charles of Valois' supporters succeeded in assassinating Philip's father.

By 1422, when Henry V tragically passed away, the Anglo-Burgundian Union had firmly established its presence across much of Northern France. The baton was then handed down to his son, Henry VI.

The village where Joan of Arc lived was right at the border of the French lands that the English controlled. At the young age of 13, Joan started experiencing visions and hearing voices. She claimed that those manifestations came to her from St. Michael the Archangel, St. Margaret of Antioch, and St. Catherine of Alexandria. The voices she heard instructed her to give aid to the man who was the rightful heir to the French crown, the dauphin Charles of Valois, son of Charles VI.

The young Prince was growing restless as five years had passed since his father's death, and he was no closer to being crowned. It was tradition to crown the new king in Reims, a land that was currently in the middle of the English territories. As long as the Prince remained unconsecrated, his claim to kinsmanship was open for dispute.

The Siege of Orleans

One of the reasons many believe Joan of Arc was having divine visions was her audience with Prince Charles. In 1428, Joan traveled to meet Charles in a temporary court he had set up in Chinon on the Loire River. She wanted to explain her divine mission to earn him back the throne. After being turned away, she returned with the same claim a year later, convincing the captain to allow her an audience with Charles. Upon meeting the Prince, it is said that she divulged information about him that no one else knew. After further examination and questioning, the young maiden was able to win over the dauphin and his followers.

She was then recruited to provide assistance in Orléans, a French city under siege by the English. Joan dressed herself in white armor, cut her hair short like a man, and headed to Orléans. On her way, she ordered the clergy of St. Catherine's Church to dig up a sword under the stone floor near the altar. No one knows how she knew of the location of the weapon or the story behind it, but a sword was found, nonetheless.

Prior to her arrival in Orléans, Joan sent a letter to the English commander, asking him to gather his soldiers and exit Orléans and France. Though the English didn't take the letter seriously, they considered it an alert to an approaching force. Hundreds of the French troops situated in Blois made their way toward Orléans on 27th April 1429. When

Joan arrived with La Hire, one of the French commanders, with supplies, she was advised that any action should be postponed until reinforcements arrived.

The young maiden was resting when she suddenly roused from her sleep, stating that her "counsel" had advised her to attack immediately.

She put on her armor and hurriedly left in the direction of an English fort to the east. When she arrived, she found that an engagement was already taking place, and the French were suffering many casualties. The French troops were inspired and renewed their attack on their enemies upon seeing Joan's arrival. This led to a victory and the French securing the English fort. Following several other battles led by Joan, she freed the city of Orléans and eliminated the English at Patay, earning herself the title of the maid of Orléans. In the battle of Les Tourelles, she was wounded by an arrow but continued to stand her ground until the French secured their victory.

Joan was present during the coronation of the dauphin in July of the same year when he was officially named King Charles VII. Following these victories, the maiden made it clear that she wished to restore all of France, making advances to secure Paris that were, unfortunately, futile.

The End of Joan of Arc

In May of 1430, Joan of Arc was captured by John of Luxembourg in Compiègne, where she was unhorsed and could not remount. News of her capture spread through France, and the King, working towards a truce with the Duke of Burgundy, did not attempt to rescue her. By January of 1431, she was surrendered to the Bishop of Beauvais, Pierre Cauchon, in exchange for 10,000 francs. She was put on trial and accused of over 70 crimes (later reduced to about 12), with heresy and dressing as a man at the top of the list. After being forced to sign a confession denying that she ever received divine visions, she later defied her captors' orders and donned men's clothing again. She was then sentenced to death by burning at the stake on May 30th, 1431.

20 years following her death, King Charles VII ordered a new trial be held where her name was finally cleared.

24. Battle of Agincourt

King Henry V was a well-known antagonist/protagonist during the 100 Years' War, depending on how different people viewed him at the time. The King, continuing the legacy of his predecessors, fought against the French to claim the French crown.

Two months prior to the battle of Agincourt, he had led 11,000 soldiers across the English Channel and laid siege to Harfleur in Normandy. The siege lasted for about five weeks. Many of the King's men were either deserters or became afflicted with disease and battle fatalities. Eventually, they surrendered. The King marched northeast to Calais, where he would meet the English fleet and sail back home.

King Henry, however, didn't anticipate the 20,000 French men intercepting his over-exhausted soldiers in Agincourt on their way home. The battle was a bloodbath, with most of the details of what went down disputed by both parties.

The French force was led by Constable Charles D'Albert and Marshal Jean II Le Meingre.

On 25th October 1415, the battle was held on a muddy field flanked by woods, which minimized the chances of large-scale maneuvers. Henry positioned his archers on either side of his remaining men in arms. At 11 a.m., the French started a slow advancement, weighed down by their heavy armor. The English archers armed with longbows with a range of 250 yards rained hell on the enemy. The French cavalry and knights tried to assert their positions and catch the English off guard but failed miserably. Their predicament arose from the tight, muddy space that wasn't accommodating to their large numbers and the protective stakes that the English archers were shielded behind.

King Henry then ordered his archers to raise their axes and swords and attack the French, essentially creating a bloody massacre. 6,000 French men fell on the battlefield that day, while the English lost about 400, marking this victory as one of the greatest and most impressive encounters in Henry's military history.

Five years later, following several other victories, the French recognized King Henry V as heir to their throne. Unfortunately, he didn't live long to enjoy his triumph as he died two years later from camp fever near Paris.

25. The End of the War

The end of the bloodbath between the English and French came in the battle of Castillon on July 17th, 1453. If a comparison is to be made between the state of the lands before and after the war, it will be noted that almost no change occurred, for most of the areas that the English took possession of were, in the end, reclaimed by the French.

King Henry VI was the first and only English King to receive the honor of coronation in France. Following the crowning of Henry VI (who was 10 years old at the time) in 1431 at the church of Notre Dame, the territories that the English acquired across the channel started to slip through their fingers. By 1436, Paris was retrieved by the French, and by 1450, so was Normandy. In 1451, the French attacked Aquitaine and gained control of Bordeaux, which they had lost 300 years previously to the English.

Loyalists to the English crown traveled from Bordeaux to England, seeking aid from the King.

The English retaliated with 3,000 men under the command of the Earl of Shrewsbury, John Talbot, recovering most of western Gascony in October 1452. In July 1453, the French army faced John Talbot's forces in Castillon, where they defeated him and he was killed.

By October of the same year, it was clear that no more English reinforcements were on the way. And so, the surrender of Bordeaux commenced, and the English left the French lands apart from Calais, which was officially reclaimed in 1558 by the French.

There was one final attempt to attack France in 1475, which quickly dissipated after King Louis XI bribed the English army led by Edward IV to go back home.

The Anglo-French war did not end with a peace treaty or a truce. For some time following the last battle, the French were apprehensive and ready for another English attempt to invade their lands.

Without a doubt, it impacted both nations immensely. Even though both nations suffered numerous losses and had similar societal struggles as a result of the war, these similarities did not bring the two nations any closer together but rather widened the rift that was already there.

As a result of the raids, France was greatly ravaged by the war. They were meant to undermine the French ruler by murdering citizens, torching the crops and houses, and pillaging its riches. The economy was gravely damaged, with taxes on the rise to compensate for the lost funds in the war. However, it wasn't long before the country started rebuilding itself from the rubble. The future French monarchy was quick to assert itself after the recovery of its rightful crown. Meanwhile, the English were enjoying the riches they plundered from France over the course of the war, building churches and new houses.

It is safe to say that patriotism and the national identity in both countries rose after the war, with several generations knowing nothing but the conflict between them. England distanced itself from the rest of Europe, developing parliamentary democracy, despite the English Kings still claiming to be Kings of France all the way until George III.

Chapter 6: Stories on Henry VIII and the Reformation

Most readers find refuge from their daily hectic lives by delving into fantastical modern tales of love, power, and betrayal. However, if examined closely, history provides a bottomless well of unbelievable, incredible stories of romance, greed, and redemption with the most unexpected twists imaginable. These historical characters are not works of a writer's imagination in countless pages of books. They lived, breathed, and thrived on the same earth that humanity inhabits today.

It is wise to consider that not all recorded accounts were documented accurately. Personal gain, ego, and vanity usually lend a hand to the ink painting the pictures of those characters. With this in mind, the story of Henry VIII continues to be an inspiration to the creative minds of our time. From television and movie interpretations to novel and abstract stories, the tale of Henry's love life entanglements, family, politics, and conquests is, as they say, one for the books. Those who are not into perusing books probably recognize this famous name from the TV show "The Tudors" or the big screen masterpiece "The Other Boleyn Girl." These works of art have transported their viewers into the 16th-century royal palaces of England.

However, one of the most controversial monarchs of England was not actually meant to be king at all. The young prince was the second-born son of Henry VII and was promised a life free of responsibilities and full of pleasures until his brother's untimely death.

The story of Henry VIII continues to be an inspiration to the creative minds of our time.[6]

Henry Tudor (Henry VII) was one of the last surviving descendants of the House of Lancaster, following the vicious power struggle over the throne during the War of the Roses. Henry VII ascended the throne after defeating Richard III, the last remaining son of the House of York and the Lancasters' sworn enemy.

As a newly ordained King, Henry VII wished to end the ongoing dispute between the English families and decided to wed Elizabeth of York, a well-thought strategic move to reunite the nation economically and politically. Together, they had four children: Arthur, Henry, Margaret, and Mary.

So, who exactly is Henry VIII?

26. Who Is Henry?

Henry VIII made his grand appearance in the world at Greenwich Palace on June 28th of the year 1491. For most of the country and royal family, the young prince was considered the spare royal in case any misfortune was to befall his elder brother. Prince Arthur was growing up to be a bright and sporting young man.

While most historians cannot say for sure whether the brothers were cordial towards one another, it is mentioned that throughout his life, Henry kept his late brother's garter robes with him. Soon after the second heir to the throne was christened, he was sent to live away from his older brother with his sister Margaret at Eltham palace, under the care of his mother.

In 1502, at age 15, Henry's older brother died of an illness that to this day remains a mystery. Overnight, Henry's life was turned upside down. His father, Henry VII, assigned him several male stewards to prepare the young man for his new duties. Due to a difficult pregnancy, Elizabeth, Henry's mother, rarely spent time with him. By February, the queen had given birth prematurely to a baby girl in the tower of London. Sadly, both mother and daughter passed away days later, renewing the shadow of grief over the royal family.

At the young age of 13, Henry moved to the royal household. His father proved to be an overbearing parent, protective of his only and last male heir. The prince was not allowed to wander alone or hunt or joust without someone accompanying him at all times. These overprotective tactics did nothing for Henry's independence and frustrated him no end. He suffered unpleasant comments from other royals and officials, such as the Spanish ambassador, who remarked that the prince was hidden away like a girl.

This annoying phase didn't last long, though. As he grew older, the young prince flourished. He had a knack for writing poetry and creating music —and was well-versed in subjects. He developed an interest in art. Enjoyed participating in noble sports like wrestling, tennis, falconry, jousting, hunting and sword fighting. It didn't take long for him to earn the titles of a " prince" and a "renaissance man" due to his charm and wit.

In 1509, King Henry VII passed away. At the time, Henry VIII was an impressive 17-year-old with a height of six feet and an athletic build. His rise to the throne marked England's first transfer of power in over a century. His mixed heritage symbolized an era of unity following his father's reign. It is said that upon learning about the public's dissatisfaction with his father's rule, Henry promised conditions to win his people over.

Following tradition, the prince spent the night of his coronation at the Tower of London before being crowned at Westminster Abbey. This act represented not only his ascent to power but also his control over the entire nation.

27. Henry's Romantic Escapades

Henry could probably be named the playboy of the 16th century, with six wives, three legitimate children, and many illegitimate ones, one of whom, Henry Fitzroy, first Duke of Richmond and Somerset, was acknowledged.

Catherine of Aragon

Six weeks following his ascension to the throne, Henry married his late brother's widow. Originally, Catherine, a Spanish Princess, was betrothed to his brother at the age of two, and they wed in 1501 when they were teenagers. A few months later, Arthur met his sudden demise, leaving his widow stranded in England. When Henry became heir to the throne, Catherine was betrothed to him in 1503. They got married in 1509 with a five-year age difference (Catherine was 23, and Henry was 17).

It was uncommon at the time for a brother to take his sibling's widow for a wife. In order to do that, a special pardon had to be granted to the couple from the pope. They remained married for 15 long years, with Catherine giving birth to six children, three sons and three daughters, with only one of the children, Mary 1, surviving in 1526.

By the year 1525, Catherine withdrew more and more from the festive and loud court life that her husband indulged in. She became increasingly pious and reserved. Frustrated with his wife's inability to deliver a male heir and believing that his marriage may be cursed, the king opted to get his marriage annulled so he could take a new wife. This action struck a nerve with the Roman Church, which denied him the right to do so, leading to the church reform in England.

In his demand, the King advocated for separation by using the scripture that indicated that a man cannot wed his brother's wife. Meanwhile, Catherine fought the claim by announcing that she was still a virgin when Arthur died. She was also backed by her nephew, the Holy Roman Emperor Charles, who basically controlled the pope.

After the break from the Roman Catholic Church and their divorce in 1533, Catherine, now called the Princess Dowager of Wales, was ordered out of the royal court. She was forbidden from seeing their daughter Mary and spent the last three years of her life in seclusion with only a few servants waiting on her. She passed away in January of 1536 at Kimbolton Castle and was buried in Peterborough Abbey.

Anne Boleyn

Nearing the end of his marriage to Catherine, Henry became infatuated with one of his wife's ladies-in-waiting, Anne Boleyn.

Anne was one of Sir Thomas Boleyn's daughters. In her youth, she had spent her time in the French court with her sister Mary, one of the mistresses of King Henry VIII. In 1519, Anne was ordered back to England, with rumors of her promiscuous behavior running wild. She was appointed as one of Queen Catherine's ladies-in-waiting. It wasn't long before the King started to notice her and took her as one of his mistresses. This new development elevated Anne's status. By 1522, she returned to England, becoming a popular figure in court. By 1526, it was a sure fact that the King had become deeply in love with the charismatic young woman.

Henry's close friend, Cardinal Thomas Wolsey, was not a fan of his mistress and called her "the night crow."

In the late 1520s, the King sent numerous letters to Anne, promising her loyalty and love and that she would forevermore be his only mistress.

After the King's seven-year trials to break off dealings with the Roman Church, he managed to wed Anne in 1533. The King divorced Catherine, declaring their marriage null and void due to her relations with his brother, consequently proclaiming his first child, Mary I, illegitimate. All hopes for a male heir now resided with Anne.

In 1533, a pregnant Anne gave birth to her first child, the future Queen Elizabeth I, at Greenwich. Her two later pregnancies, one of which was a boy, ended in miscarriage.

Their marriage lasted for three years, with Ann unable to grant the King a male heir. This failure marked the beginning of Anne's downfall. Supporters of the Old Catholic regime, which the King denounced, exchanged rumors about her fidelity, going as far as accusing her of adultery and forging plans to assassinate the King. The adultery charges were outrageous enough to include relations with her own brother and four other commoners. These rumors were believed to have been brought upon her by Thomas Cromwell and backed by her uncle, the Duke of Norfolk.

In order to acquire a male heir, King Henry VIII accused Anne of treason and practicing witchcraft, sentencing her to death after a sham trial on the 19th of May 1536.

Anne was allowed a small mercy from Henry by performing her execution using a sharp sword instead of an unreliable dull ax.

Jane Seymour

It wasn't long before the King found his third wife. Only 10 days following Anne Boleyn's execution, the King married one of her ladies-in-waiting, Jane Seymour. The wedding took place in Whitehall Palace. The King finally got his heir and the son that he desired. Jane gave birth to Henry's first male heir, Edward VI, on the 12th of October 1537 at Hampton Court Palace.

Three days following the birth, the young prince was christened in the Chapel Royal. However, tragedy struck the family yet again when Jane suffered postnatal complications and died on October 24th.

The birth of a male heir strengthened Henry's resolve in his choices, believing that he was favored by God now.

Jane was buried at Windsor Castle, becoming the only wife of Henry, who lay in the same tomb with him.

Anne of Cleves

The King remained unmarried for two years after the death of his third wife. As time passed, the ministers felt that the kingdom could possibly do with an alliance with a foreign country. The King decided to send his trusted painter Hans Holbein to the German court to bring him back paintings of the daughters of the Duke of Cleves, Anne, and Amelia. Upon seeing her picture, the King was attracted to Anne, and arrangements were made to seal the union. This marriage can easily be classified as a political tactic to strengthen the ties with Anne's brother, who ruled a protestant duchy in Germany.

Upon meeting Anne, the king was not impressed and started referring to her as "Flanders Mare." He informed his ambassadors and courtiers that he had no interest in performing his marital duties on the grounds of Anne's unfavorable looks. The marriage was soon annulled, and Anne was granted income and several homes in the English country, including Hever Castle. She was a frequent visitor to the Royal court as an honored guest.

Cromwell was not so lucky, though, for the King executed him based on bogus charges of treason for arranging the match.

Kathyrn Howard

Following an accident in one of the tournaments where his horse rolled over him, the King was left with an injured leg. This accident led to him being unable to exercise and thus gaining so much weight he was unable to walk.

At the time, the King was not in a good mental state and longed for a second male heir to secure the succession of the throne. A young, petite, and beautiful Katheryn Howard caught his eye. She was the daughter of the younger brother of the Duke of Norfolk of the powerful Howard family. Katheryn was Anne Boleyn's cousin, and like her cousin, she had a reputation for adultery prior to her marriage to the King.

They sealed their marriage in July 1540, when the King was 49 years old. King Henry was smitten with his new wife, showering her with gifts and calling her "his rose without a thorn." This honeymoon phase didn't last long, though. After two years, the young bride, like his second wife, was accused of infidelity by resuming her relations with an old lover, Thomas Culpepper. The King was heartbroken, and as a result, like her cousin in 1542, she was beheaded at Tower Green.

Catherine Parr

The last love interest and wife of Henry VIII was Catherine Parr. Catherine was just starting a relationship with Thomas Seymour, Jane Seymour's brother, when the King took an interest in her. Catherine was widowed twice by that time and was 31 years old. She was well-educated and clever. She spoke French and Italian fluently and could read Latin. Catherine married the King on July 12th, 1543. She was a devoted wife and a good stepmother to his three children, Mary, Elizabeth, and Edward. Her religious interests in Protestantism almost led to her downfall. These beliefs created many animosities within the royal court. Following a religious debate with the king, he issued a warrant for her arrest on the grounds of heresy. The Queen then hastened to remove all banned religious books and pleaded with the King that her debate was only to distract him from the pain of his injured leg.

As proof of his trust in her, he declared her regent in his absence while on a quest to invade France in 1544, a role that was only held by his first wife, Catherine of Aragon.

28. The Creation of the Church of England

The separation and creation of the Church of England was more of a romantic act than a religious one, with the King wishing to marry Anne Boleyn and divorcing his first wife, Catherine of Aragon. The King was hell-bent on getting his wishes that this predicament was named "the Great Matter." According to the Roman Catholic Church, without Catherine's consent, they were reluctant to annul the marriage. With protestant reformers backing his desires, Henry moved to break away from the Roman Church through a series of acts that were passed between 1532 and 1534.

Following the King's marriage to Anne Boleyn after his new chief advisor Thomas Cromwell (who was appointed after Thomas Wolsey was stripped of all his royal offices for failing to resolve the matter) declared his first marriage annulled, the Roman Pope excommunicated the King in 1533. This was the start of the break with the Roman Church.

In 1533, the English parliament declared the act in restraint of Appeals, which dictated that the Roman Pope no longer had jurisdiction or religious authority in England and that England was an empire. By 1534, the Act of Supremacy was passed, making the King and all his heirs "the Supreme head of the Church of England," which granted him unchallenged power to reform religious institutions. Henry Appointed Thomas Cromwell as vicegerent in spiritual affairs.

Henry was quite pleased with himself at this point; he mixed the faith that he knew as a boy with the salvation he was seeking as a man but without the blessings of a priest. He went as far as demanding that all acknowledge him in place of the pope as God's representative on Earth. Those who opposed him, like Thomas More, were executed for treason at the Tower of London in 1535.

29. The Dissolution of the Monasteries

Following the break with the Roman Church came the dissolution of the monasteries. Henry started seizing the lands and wealth of the Catholic churches and monasteries in England and selling them off. This motion was led by Thomas Cromwell, who, between 1536 and 1540, demolished, shut, and seized over 800 monasteries and religious houses like Riveaulx, Byland, and Fountains. They went on to accuse the clergy of "Vicious, carnal, and abominable sin."

The riches and money that he acquired from the monasteries were employed in more than one direction. He stored some in the royal treasury, gave some to his new ministers, and used the rest to develop and enlarge the English navy from 5 to 53 ships and build new dockyards. The Mary Rose, one of the ships, lies to this day in the Portsmouth Naval Museum). He made sure to invest in the arts and sciences and the central and local government.

30. Political Conquests

Henry didn't quite fit the archetype of a military commander. However, that didn't stop him from attempting to cement his name as a war hero. Against the advice of his much older and wiser councilors, Henry embarked upon a military adventure with his father-in-law, Ferdinand II of Aragon. In an effort to settle rivalries between the French and the Spanish that were centered on Italian claims, their target was France. The conquest ended shortly in 1520 with a peace treaty with Francis I, King of France. Henry was generous with funding displays and tournaments at the field of the Cloth of Gold, an act to show the unity between the two nations. It is safe to say that his wars with France were rather costly and unnecessary.

Henry did secure a victory in 1513, which was won by the Earl of Surrey, Thomas Howard, against an attempted invasion from the Scots at Flodden.

31. Henry's Death

Henry died at the age of 55 on January 28th, 1547. He was buried next to his third wife, Jane Seymour, in St. George's Chapel at Windsor Castle. He was survived by his last wife, Catherine Parr, who was then free to marry her old lover, Thomas Seymour.

His male heir, Edward VI, ascended the throne at only nine years old but died six years later. He was followed by Mary I, who spent the total of her five reigning years trying to restore the Catholic regime in England. She was then succeeded by Elizabeth I, who restored her father's Protestant vision. Elizabeth was considered the longest monarch to hold the throne of the Tudor Dynasty.

Chapter 7: Stories on the Era of Enlightenment

The English Enlightenment was a time of intense intellectual exploration and cultural evolution. To set the scene, this chapter begins by linking the roots of the Enlightenment to the preceding Scientific Revolution and changes in the cultural milieu. And in order to illuminate this dynamic period of intellectual and cultural evolution, the next story scouts the minds and theories of key Enlightenment thinkers like John Locke and Adam Smith, unraveling their impact on society and subsequent thought.

The third story traces the intensive evolution of modern political theories, explaining how Enlightenment ideas laid their foundations. The penultimate tale explores the vibrant literary culture of the time, focusing on the emergence of satire and notable works of the period. To conclude your journey through the Enlightenment, the last narrative examines the lasting influence of this era on English society, education, and religious perspectives, including the rise of secularism, fully bringing the transformative spirit of the Enlightenment era to life.

Adam Smith – a key figure during the Enlightenment Era.[7]

32. The Roots of the Enlightenment: Scientific Revolution

Preceding the Enlightenment, the Scientific Revolution brought fundamental transformations in theories and philosophies revolving around nature and the universe. Based on the progression principle, which dictates that continuous efforts in scientific research help people understand the words around them, the movement revolutionized scientific methodology between the early 16th and 18th centuries. It also laid the foundations for modern scientific theories and research.

One from whom many British scientists took inspiration was Nicolas Copernicus, the Polish astronomer who first proposed the idea of the Earth revolving around the Sun and not the other way around as previously believed. While shocking to cosmologists at the time, the discovery that the Earth isn't the center of the universe represented a concept that was way beyond the grasp of this scientific field at the time. As a result, people started to question many other long-held traditions and beliefs.

Another groundbreaking theory of the 16th century was the blood circulation thesis proposed by the anatomist Andreas Vesalius. Marking the beginning of the scientific revolution across multiple fields, scientists were now challenging and altering previous conceptions of the universe and society. This was fueled by technical revolutions, which allowed people of all classes to access knowledge and learn about anything that sparked their interest.

After its invention in the 15th century, printing became widespread, disseminating information to the masses. Posters and pamphlets that would inspire countless debates (encouraging people to think more rationally and radically) were printed on a daily basis.

During the Scientific Revolution, one of the figures who had a great impact was Francis Bacon. He is considered the pioneer of the empiricism theory, and he made substantial contributions to learning and knowledge. Bacon introduced a method of research that emphasized continuous observation and logical reasoning to draw conclusions based on what was observed. This approach also allowed for experimentation to either prove or challenge theories. As people became curious about the accuracy of accepted knowledge, traditional beliefs about the universe started being questioned.

Bacon also advocated for the dissemination of knowledge, emphasizing that the government had a role in expanding people's understanding. His colleague, Thomas Hobbes, further supported progress as a means to overcome challenges in comprehending nature.

In parallel, William Gilbert formulated a hypothesis based on magnetism principles, explaining how the Earth rotates on its axis due to forces.

Another influential figure during this period was John Flamsteed, an astronomer from Derby. Flamsteed established "The King's Astronomical Observatory," which became known as the Royal Greenwich Observatory. Through his expertise and research conducted there, Flamsteed made great contributions in his field. However, his groundbreaking achievement, known as "Historia Coelestis Britannica," was published posthumously.

The contributions of court physician William Harvey were truly groundbreaking and would shape the future of medicine. Through dissections, he comprehensively explained the mechanism of blood circulation. In 1628, he published his findings, elucidating the role of the heart in propelling blood through the system.

During the period of the Civil War (1642-1649), England's Scientific Revolution continued unabated. In fact, after the war's end, there was enthusiasm for embracing science and technology's positive impact on political, social, and economic progress.

In the 1600's, a distinguished body called the Royal Society was established with a mission to advance research across scientific disciplines. It boasted members such as Robert Boyle, Sir William Petty, Sir Christopher Wren, and undoubtedly Sir Isaac Newton – whose monumental works, like "Mathematical Principles of Natural Philosophy" and "Principia" solidified his status as one of the revolution's foremost figures. By 1703, Newton had ascended to become President of the Royal Society.

These publications not only presented a structure for mechanics and formulated laws regarding gravitation and motion, but they also revolutionized people's comprehension of science. The remaining part of the century was characterized by the breakthroughs achieved in the preceding years. Alongside establishing the groundwork for industrialization, these discoveries had an influence on politics and culture, igniting a movement that would shape the nation's destiny for generations to follow. This imminent era, known as the Enlightenment, was about to commence.

33. Minds of Enlightenment Thinkers - John Locke and Adam Smith

There were many English Enlightenment thinkers. Two particularly notable individuals who played a significant role in changing society's perception of long-standing ideas were John Locke and Adam Smith. John Locke is famously associated with the concept of the contract, which aimed to establish an agreement between the government and its citizens outlining their respective responsibilities. Under this agreement, citizens would surrender some privileges for freedom while the government would ensure their safety and protect their rights. Locke arrived at this idea after studying the state of nature, which provided insights into how society operated under laws.

Although others before him had also explored returning society to an established authority-led government era, Locke was unique in successfully pursuing this notion during his time. Unlike his contemporaries who relied on metaphors or their own subjective experiences (as our brains often tend to do), Locke was among the first to transcend these limitations and envision a state.

Therefore, he reached the conclusion that each individual (although this applied to men then) is inherently endowed with a sense of morality rooted in natural rights. However, these morals can become tainted through life experiences. The solution to prevent people from deviating from this order is to establish governing bodies that safeguard their rights and enable them to remain faithful to their principles.

Locke's idea that the government had the duty to uphold the natural rights people are born with was quickly adopted by other European thinkers, including Rousseau, who, putting his own spin on it, proposed that the social context should be based on the general will (a government ruled by a collective, not an individual).

Scotsman Adam Smith is the father of the modern economy. After devoting a considerable amount of time to vigorously studying how markets function, this social scientist came up with several suggestions on how to boost the market, including the concept of free market capitalism. In his most comprehensive work, "The Wealth of Nations," Smith prefaced that if a market could operate without the government's constant interference, this would lead to economic growth of never-before-seen proportions. One of the ways Smith proposed to achieve this prosperous state was by abolishing protectionist taxes and monopolist practices, as these hindered international trade at a higher rate. Smith claimed that without these practices, the market would blossom, bringing greater general prosperity to the entire nation.

Smith transferred the same Enlightenment principles and beliefs to economics as other intellectuals did to politics, science, morals, etc. According to Smith, economics are ruled by the same natural laws that people could easily unveil and explain through rational thinking.

Smith based his confidence in the market's development on his belief that if permitted (not limited by taxes and land monopoly), every citizen would want to put their capital into supporting domestic trade, so there would be no need for import. Seeking only their security and prosperity, individuals would also promote the public interest, much to the benefit of the entire nation. Many view these ideas outlined in Smith's The Wealth of Nations as a sequel to his previous work, "The Theory of Moral Sentiments," which laid down the foundation of Smith's naturalistic outlook on society's future.

34. Development of Modern Political Theories

From the 1500s, Europe was in a constant state of political upheaval. Religious leaders and monarchs caused numerous conflicts as they fought over resources and territories and tried to impose different versions of Christianity. Britain saw some of the deadliest battles, not to mention their devastating effects, during the early 17th century. One of the consequences of this was the harsh criticism directed toward the religious and political leaders for allowing the continuous conflict and the loss of so many lives. The other one was the birth of sovereignty. European countries could now seize control over what was happening within their borders without another country interfering with their actions. This law of domestic affairs laid the foundations for modern political theories regarding international relations.

John Locke's proclamation that no ruler should have absolute power over their subjects was another prominent change in the English political scene. Instead of referencing commands from God, the leaders were slowly forced to accept that the authority must come from the people. They had no choice. Incited by Locke's and other Enlightenment thinkers' ideas, the masses were prepared to replace the rules with one that would listen to people. It was the birth of democracy as it is known today. It was the first time that leaders were made accountable by their subjects.

Following these revolutionary changes, another shift happened, not just in Britain but all across Europe. Intellectuals started pushing the idea of the separation of power. They argued that by dividing the responsibilities between legislative, judicial, and executive authorities, a much greater balance could be achieved. Besides dismissing the notion of countries led by one leader, Enlightenment thinkers argued against religious interference in state affairs. This idea was bolstered by generations of conflict and the religious influences on political decisions seen on the continent.

John Locke presented the notion that all people possess natural rights to property, liberty, and life from birth. Moreover, people's rights can't be constrained or dismissed by law or any other power. It marked the beginning of a long and still ongoing fight for individual rights. While the campaign led to improved religious tolerance and minorities across Britain gained more liberty to worship, the country still has a long way to go on this front.

In contrast to the era before the Enlightenment in Britain, where inequality was widespread and religious and political leaders enjoyed rights to land ownership, certain professions, and tax exemptions, a new wave of thinkers emerged. They argued that every individual is born equal, so why should some have it all while others struggle to survive? Initially, this notion of "people" only applied to men. Women, enslaved individuals, and ethnic minorities did not enjoy the rights. However, leveraging the effects of the Enlightenment movement, these marginalized groups gradually began advocating for their equality. Remarkable activists like Mary Wollstonecraft and Mary Astell were at the forefront in England, fighting for women's rights alongside men.

Another significant transformation brought about by the Enlightenment was witnessed in politics through free market capitalism. Prior to Adam Smith's introduction of this concept, mercantilism prevailed – a system where countries relied on production while limiting imports from abroad. However, Smith's theories on free market capitalism emphasized supply and demand dynamics, stringent regulations, and comparative advantage. This led England and numerous other nations to seize the opportunity for increased wealth through trade. Additionally, it prompted them to forge relationships with one another.

Although the system had its flaws, it served as the basis for future trade policies.

35. The Vibrant Literary Culture of the Enlightenment

The British Enlightenment's achievements weren't only limited to the political scene and scientific fields. They also made their way into English literary culture. The 18th-century writers achieved accomplishments in many domains, including periodicals, novels, drama writing, and poetry.

Many authors even started crossing the divide between fact and fiction in their writing. Sir Walter Scott was one of the pioneers in historical novel writing, combining his knowledge of history with plenty of imaginative license.

While unimaginable before, even travel writers started to take the liberty to engage their descriptions with creative fictitious techniques. James Bruce was particularly successful in this genre. However, this was also due to his previously established good reputation, as the introduction of fiction made many readers question the author's authority.

Tobias Smollett, a novelist and a doctor, combined his love for writing with his long-nourished interest in medical practices and foreign cultures. In his works, he explores the use of herbal medicine in different cultures. Likewise, John Gabriel Stedman's accounts of his experiences in the Dutch colony of Surinam paint a fascinating picture of the local, national, and global literary networks established in the 18th century.

Besides the vibrant book culture contributed to by published authors from several genres, the English Enlightenment period is also known for its abundantly consumed literature. This allowed the readers to make the connection between elite and popular culture, which people created since the movement's beginning. As in neighboring Scotland, where ballads played a crucial role in crossing the divide between the different sides of the cultural hierarchy, literary achievements in Britain made people more hopeful of ending inequality.

Another literary field that rose to popularity in the 18th century was satire. The ecclesiastical genre was particularly widespread, often sparking debates among the supporters of the different branches of Christianity trying to establish authority at the time.

Drama and rhetoric also played critical roles in the era. Several plays were created around philosophical concepts introduced during the Enlightenment. The authors often followed the most popular Enlightenment theories so they could provide a faithful rendition of human nature and revolutionary communication methods. Others explored the questions of human nature through science, particularly psychology.

The second half of the Enlightenment's literary culture is loaded with equally illuminating and intriguing works, often focusing on the mysteries of space. However, the author wasn't the only one benefiting from the proof, inspiring enlightened ideas, and the interest these sparked in the public. Publishers also capitalized on other writers' successes, often making a fortune on one or more better-selling publications. This continued well into the next century. Emulating earlier works, publishers often re-made older editions and established collections of authors' works to continue capitalizing on revolutionary ideas of the Enlightenment.

The influence of the vast amount of literary achievements in the Enlightenment continued to inspire authors even in the Romantic era. Moreover, numerous writers across France cited some English authors of the movement. The French were particularly engrossed by 18th-century English poems that captivated their audience with very subtle techniques.

British Enlightenment literary influences are also seen in American literature. The first American novel, William Hill Brown's "The Power of Sympathy" (1789), is full of Enlightenment ideas. The Enlightened literary culture also influenced some of Britain's most renowned early 19th-century novels. Austen, Scott, and Dickens were famous for creating plots around a mutual duty, one of the key motivational concepts that pushed the Enlightenment movement forward.

36. The Lasting Influence of the Enlightenment on English Society

The new and exciting ideas of the Enlightenment spread like wildfire across Britain. At first, the royals and the church tried to censor and even ban public demonstrations of enlightened thinking, along with books and other publications. They were alarmed because they saw people questioning everything wrong with the government and considering changes. Their fears eventually materialized when the concept of the social contract was proposed, inferring that authoritarian leaders could no longer rule without their decisions being questioned by their subjects. After the French and American revolutions, the religious leaders and monarchs lost their supreme authority. While they were still respected by English society, their influence wasn't even a fraction of what it once was.

The theories of ethics and psychology proposed by enlightened thinkers also had a lasting influence. With the popularization of natural sciences, philosophers started to take vastly different approaches to their thinking. Applying rules of natural phenomena to societal issues became a commonality. John Locke's argument that people are subject to the laws of nature just like every other creature influenced England's political scene for years to come. While this prominent impact was also aided by the efforts of Rousseau and other Enlightenment thinkers outside Britain and their influence on

Europe's and the United States' political changes, Locke inspired many of them in the first place.

On the purely science front, the Enlightenment led to the theories of deduction and induction and, ultimately, the creation of a very different cosmology than was known before. Based on this, mathematicians proposed that everything in this world operates by a few universal rights. Since then, many of these laws have been discovered, proven, and used to create the biggest masterpieces of mankind.

Enlightenment also encourages people to seek rational reasons behind everything, including religion. This is how deism, atheism, materialism, skepticism, and other radical concepts related to religious belief came to be.

The extreme notions put an end to the Enlightenment. As the new cultural force named Romanticism emerged, people started to turn away from radical and rationalist ideas. It allowed people to explore emotional concepts rather than relying solely on reason. Still, the high optimism brought on by the radical changes of the Enlightenment remained. The British People now knew that progress was possible if there was enough force to prompt it, and this is one of the Enlightenment's most enduring legacies.

Chapter 8: Stories on the Rise of the Empire

This chapter delves into the ambitious imperial interests of Great Britain. You will learn about three of the most significant events of world history, how they contributed to the rise of the British Empire, and how they affected other parts of the world. This chapter explores the conflicts, causes, and aftermaths of the Scramble for Africa, the East India Company, and the Opium Wars.

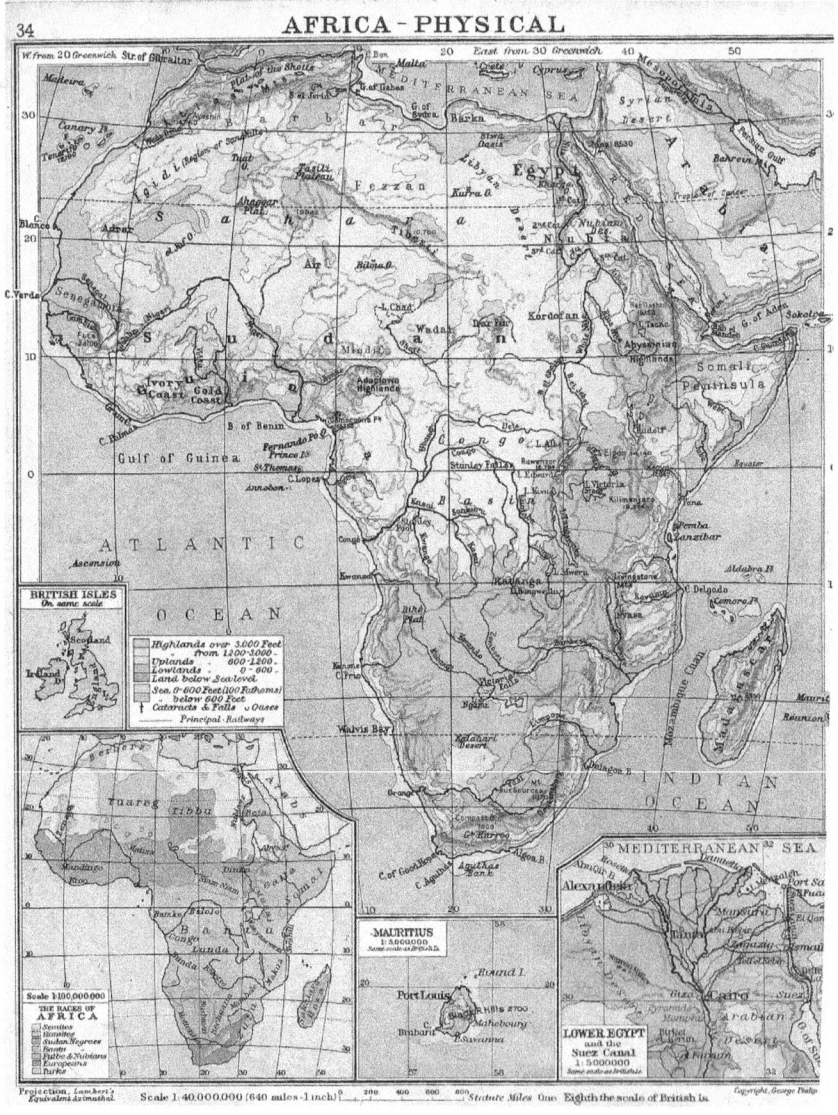

Africa was a rich cultural center.[8]

37. The Scramble for Africa

Starting in the late 19th century and ending in the early 20th century, the Scramble for Africa was a period that shaped the world's geopolitics for years to come. At this time, European colonizers moved at a rapid rate and grew their empires extensively. Contrary to popular belief, Africa, before it was subject to European encroachment, was a rich cultural center.

Colonizers' excuse for invading Africa was that they wanted to "civilize" the continent. While Europe was more technologically advanced at the time, Africa was deprived of the opportunity to utilize its resources to thrive and develop. If it hadn't been robbed of its natural and human resources, the continent would eventually have incorporated European technological and industrial advancements and even built on them.

Before the Europeans arrived in Africa, the continent was home to numerous empires, cultures, and societies, each with its own efficient economic and political systems. In the West lay the wealthy Mali and powerful Songhai empires. In the East, there was the beautiful Swahili Coast. In Central Sudan, there was the prosperous Hausa Kingdom, which was known for being a flourishing trade center, and in the North of Africa, Carthage and the Ancient Egyptian civilization were already making history.

While it wasn't until the Scramble that Europe overtook Africa, Europeans were already sneaking their way through the continent centuries back. For instance, the trans-Atlantic slave trade started when Europeans began their exploration expeditions in the 15th century. There were also interactions between both continents through the trans-Saharan trade routes. These transactions contributed to Europe's expanding influence.

The Causes of the Scramble for Africa

The Industrial Revolution was among the key factors resulting in the Scramble. As demand and supply increased during the Industrial Revolution and rapid economic growth, Europe needed access to more raw materials to keep up. Africa was targeted because it was rich in diamonds, rubber, gold, cocoa, cotton, and other sought-after materials.

At some point during the industrialization, the supply exceeded the population's demand, which is why Europe needed to find new markets to sell their goods. Africa was the ideal marketplace because of its large population. The Europeans would also be introducing new goods to Africa, which people would be curious about and excited to buy.

At the time, the prestige and prowess of a nation were determined by the size of its empire. Dominating Africa benefited Europe's perceived status and geopolitical strategies. Europeans established their military bases in Africa after the colonization. This domination also allowed them to secure profitable trade routes.

Europe's advanced weaponry and strong military power made it easy for them to gain control over Africa, where they still relied on primitive weaponry. They also made innovations in transportation and were skilled at navigation, which aided land exploration. Europeans were able to survive the rough African living conditions with their medical advances.

The Berlin Conference: How Colonial Powers Divided Africa

Africa was officially divided among the interested colonial powers in the Berlin Conference, which took place in 1884 and 1885. The conference was led by Otto von Bismarck, who was a German Chancellor and was attended by European and American representatives. This conference was held to dissipate the rising tension, which might have slowly escalated into armed conflict between nations who wanted territorial claims over Africa. In this meeting, guidelines and agreements were laid out to solidify each nation's territorial rights. The Congo River basin, which was rich in rubber and ivory, making it highly coveted, was declared a free-trade zone to which all colonial powers had access.

This conference led to the exploitation of Africa's land and resulted in the death of millions of its people. Africa was regarded as no more than a commodity that Europeans could divide, share, and rob. No one cared about the continent's inhabitants, traditions, religions, or cultures. Colonizers never involved African representatives in these discussions.

Countries that treated their colonies as extensions of their nations, such as France, spread their cultures, beliefs, laws, and languages there. Others, such as Britain, used indirect means of ruling. Instead of implementing their laws and government structure, they retained the existing power dynamic. British officials were ranked higher than indigenous leaders, who then served as intermediaries between the British government and the people. They made sure that everyone followed the government's rules. The United Kingdom and Great Britain were among the most powerful colonial powers in the Scramble. Its colonies extended all over the region and included Kenya, South Africa, Uganda, Ghana, Nigeria, Sudan, and several others.

The Exploitation of the People and the Land

The economic system that the colonials implemented in Africa was designed to ensure that the continent's resources benefited European commerce and trade. They extracted a wide range of precious metals and stones, numerous agricultural products, and even forced human labor. The African population suffered from food shortages because they were obligated to grow crops that generated profit rather than food crops. Many colonials implemented cruel forced labor systems. King Leopold II of Belgium was known for being the most brutal, as his tactics resulted in the death of millions of workers.

Africans eventually adopted their colonizers' languages, which included French, English, Dutch, and Portuguese. Christianity also spread throughout the continent as missionaries actively converted them, encouraging them to let go of their traditional religions. Some colonials created educational systems for the African population. However, these were not intended to teach them important skills and information but to mold them into an obedient workforce. This limited the skills and education of the population, which is a problem that lasted even after decolonization.

Resilience and Rebellion

Africans frequently resisted and rebelled against the colonizers despite the brutal punishment and treatment they would receive. At first, they resisted by engaging in armed conflict. The Battle of Adwa, which occurred in Ethiopia in 1896, the several wars led by the Xhosa and Zulu people, and the Maji Maji Rebellion that took place in Tanzania between 1905 and 1907 are among the most notable uprisings.

As powerful African leaders emerged, the resistance movements started becoming more powerful and organized. African societies realized that armed conflict wasn't their strongest suit, which is why they started utilizing political strategies instead. During the early 20th century, the African population began advocating for civil and constitutional rights. A few decades later, they also started the fight for independence.

The Decolonization of Africa

World War II and its aftermath and consequences were the main factors influencing the decolonization of Africa. European powers were significantly weakened after the war in terms of military power, political strength, and the economy. This hindered their ability to effectively maintain their policy. The underlying notion of the Scramble that deemed the Europeans racially superior to Africans was also discredited during the war.

There was also a redistribution of global power following the war, with the Soviet Union and the US emerging as the most powerful. The US supported the decolonization of Africa because it was similar to the nation's past fight against colonialism, while the Soviet Union supported decolonization as an opportunity to spread socialist beliefs and stand against Western influence.

Many colonies fought for their independence through atrocious wars, such as Mozambique and Angola, which were Portuguese colonies, and Algeria, which was ruled by French powers; others were decolonized peacefully. While other African countries, such as Egypt, broke away from British control earlier, Ghana was the first sub-Saharan country to break free in 1957, allowing other British colonies to follow with ease.

The French, however, implemented an "association" policy, which encouraged integration and cultural exchange. This allowed their colonies to gain political independence while still maintaining aspects of the French culture and language and keeping economic ties with the nation. The UK was also keen on maintaining strong cultural, economic, and political relations with its formal colonies. They usually continued to invest in these nations and offer assistance with development. The British Commonwealth was primarily responsible for maintaining these ties.

38. The East India Company

The East India Company was also popularly known as the English East India Company. It was established on December 31, 1600, mainly to exploit and monopolize all trade with India, East Asia, and Southeast Asia. This monopolistic entity helped expand the British Imperial interest in Asia. Britain also established the company to get a share of the East Indian spice trade, which was very profitable and was monopolized by Spain and Portugal until 1588.

The company encountered a lot of resistance from the Portuguese and the Dutch, who occupied Indonesia then but were eventually allowed to trade. Its commerce activities started with South Indian goods like silk, saltpeter, cotton, and spices but soon branched out to benefit from trades in Southeast Asia, East Asia, and the Persian Gulf.

The East India Company made use of slave labor from the 1620s to the 1770s. They transported enslaved Africans to India, Southeast Asia, and St. Helena Island to increase production and profits. Enslaved individuals were mostly from East African countries, particularly Madagascar and Mozambique. During the late 18th century, however, the interest in cotton goods declined, and the British developed a liking for Chinese tea. They financed these imports with illegal opium trades, which resulted in the outburst of the Opium Wars in 1839.

The East India Company then faced a lot of backlash for monopolizing the market, giving rise to a rival company. This competition didn't last long, as both entities merged and created the United Company of Merchants of England in 1708. The company had a court that consisted of 24 directors and was organized into several committees. As shareholders could vote on important regulations and changes, they could influence trade policies. However, many problems arose, leading to government intervention. The government established acts that gave them control of political policy. They created a regulatory board that responded to parliament, which resulted in the gradual loss of the company's control over commerce and trade. The company was no longer monopolistic and only a managing tool for India's British government. The company was dissolved in 1873.

39. The Opium Wars

The mid-19th century witnessed a turning point in history known as the Opium Wars. China engaged in the Opium War with Great Britain from 1839 to 1842 and confronted both Great Britain and France in a second conflict from 1856 to 1860. Unfortunately, China experienced defeat in both wars leading to severe consequences. As a result, they were compelled to cede Hong Kong to the powers and establish treaty ports for trade, thereby granting special privileges to foreigners. Additionally, it is worth noting that the British authorities actively facilitated and encouraged the trade of opium among citizens under the guise of free trade.

The First Opium War

Numerous Asian countries, such as India, Vietnam, Malaysia, Vietnam, and Burma, experienced the consequences of the expanding dominance of powers. Despite the influence exerted by the United States, France, Great Britain, and other colonial powers on China's affairs, China itself was never formally colonized. While Confucianism permeated all spheres of governance, society, and culture, unlike resistance movements, it faced less opposition from colonial powers due to its secular nature.

While Great Britain believed that Confucianism wouldn't stand in the way of modernity as some religions did, China wasn't entirely effective in responding to the colonial efforts of Westernization. China was already a bureaucratic, mercantilist country characterized by its military strength and advances in industrialism. Everything about China's social, cultural, economic, and political dynamics was drastically different from the systems of European powers at the time, making it really difficult for the people to deal constructively with encroachment. This caused internal upheaval and political conflicts, repetitive external invasions, and unfair treaties.

During the years that preceded the first opium war, China-based its trade operations with the West in the city of Guangzhou. This was the only place in China in which licensed merchants could trade with foreigners. Great Britain adhered to this trade system for years, as it offered Indian Cotton and British Silver to China in exchange for tea, porcelain, silk, and other goods. While the British enjoyed Chinese goods, the Chinese weren't very interested in British goods, which caused Britain to replace cotton with opium, also from India. The balance was now shifted in Britain's favor, and the Chinese became the ones who had to pay for goods using silver.

Opium was being used for both medical and recreational purposes in China and other parts of Eurasia. To capitalize on this interest in the product, Britain invested more money in opium plantations and processing. They eventually monopolized the industry of opium cultivation and trade. As their investments increased, more Chinese citizens started smoking opium for recreational purposes, which became a widespread addiction. In 1800, the Chinese government recognized that it was a serious issue and banned the production and importation of the product. By 1813, the smoking of opium was outlawed, and whoever was caught smoking it was subject to harsh punishment.

The British still found ways to transport opium to China through private British and American traders who sold it to Chinese smugglers. The Chinese opium trade picked up in 1830, but the British East India Company lost its monopoly over the drug four years later. This caused the price of British opium to decrease, making it more attainable and widespread among Chinese citizens. Members of the government and army, and even those who were studying to take up political and military positions, smoked opium, too. In 1836, the Chinese government went as far as executing Chinese smugglers and dealers.

Over time, the opium issue grew out of hand. Officials were torn between taking the pragmatic approach, which was legalizing the use of opium and applying tax laws on the product, and taking a harsher approach, which involved punishing imported and sold opium. The latter approach was eventually implemented and led by Lin Zexu, a Chinese government official.

Lin tackled the opium issue through many phases. He started by writing an open letter to Queen Victoria in which he questioned British morals. He then arrested over 1,600 Chinese opium dealers and destroyed thousands of drug pipes. He also asked foreign companies to hand over the opium inventories in exchange for Chinese tea. When they refused, Lin ceased all foreign trade and quarantined the area where the foreign merchants were. After a month and a half in confinement, the foreign merchants finally gave up over 20,000 chests of the drug. Lin's troops also seized the opium that was found on British ships around Chinese islands. He mixed the drug with lime and salt to damage its effectiveness before dumping it into the sea. With pressure from Lin, the British ended up moving to Hong Kong after they were expelled from Macao, a Portuguese colony,

All of these events caused British dignity to take a hit, giving rise to the first Opium War. The British government vowed to compensate merchants for their opium losses, which were worth millions of sterling pounds. This gave Great Britain the excuse to expand their colonies into China. The war officially started when conflict arose between British merchants and Chinese warships in 1839. A year later, a British fleet arrived at Guangzhou and started battling, bombarding and invading cities, and negotiating their way through China. China was forced to give up Hong Kong to Great Britain in a settlement. The nation also had to pay reparations and establish full diplomatic relations with the British Empire. As a consequence, the Chinese government also had to send Lin Zexu into exile. The Chinese forces had weaker and less advanced naval ships and weaponry, making them unable to fight against the British forces.

The war ended in 1842 with the Treaty of Nanjing, which was in favor of the British. This treaty gave Great Britain access to five Chinese ports and a profitable port in Hong Kong, which were also now subject to British laws. China was also forced to pay compensation and apply any rights that foreign countries gained to Britain. China, however, didn't receive any benefits from this treaty.

The Second Opium War

The second Opium War started in 1856 when Beijing was encroached on by French and British invaders. New treaties and compensations that harmed China, along with the legalization of the opium trade, were also in effect. In 1856, the Chinese authorities arrested Chinese people who worked on a British ship and executed a French missionary around the same time. Britain and France used these incidents as opportunities to get China involved in more trade. In 1858, China agreed to fulfill several Western demands. However, they refused to sign the treaty, which worsened their situation.

British and French armies invaded Beijing and tore down the Imperial Summer Palace in 1860. The Emperor then fled to Manchuria while his brother negotiated with the French and British authorities in the Convention of Beijing. He signed the treaty, agreed to compensation, and gave up the Kowloon Peninsula to the British.

The Scramble for Africa, the East India Company, and the Opium Wars are among the most significant events in world history that resulted in far-reaching consequences. Great Britain's ambitious imperial interests and its desire to grow its power across continents were what fueled these events. Great Britain's influence played a great role in shaping today's global geopolitics.

Chapter 9: Stories on the World Wars

The two World Wars had a huge impact on history and led to the collapse of many empires. It is impossible to talk about these wars without mentioning Britain's role in them. This chapter covers some of the most interesting stories that took place in the World Wars.

Britain had a vital role to play during WWI and WWII.[9]

40. The Christmas Truce of 1914

Nobody understands the struggles of war like the brave soldiers fighting and the innocent civilians caught in its wake. In the midst of World War I, British soldiers held onto hope to spend Christmas with their loved ones. However, the intensity of battle forced them to fight for their survival during the holiday season.

On Christmas Eve, British and French troops found themselves huddled together, reminiscing about their families and friends left behind. Then something remarkable unfolded – a moment that could only be described as a Christmas miracle.

Before midnight struck, an unfamiliar sound reached their ears. Usually accustomed to explosions, gunfire, and anguished cries during wartime, this sound was different – it carried a soothing melody.

As they strained to listen, they discovered it was the German soldiers singing "Stille Nacht," their rendition of "Silent Night." Like their counterparts, these German soldiers were also yearning for home and missing their loved ones dearly; thus, they resorted to carols in an attempt to evoke the spirit of Christmas.

Without hesitation or reservation, British and French troops joined in harmony by singing "Silent Night" in their languages.

They all felt a longing for home and tried to make the best of their terrible situation. It was a moment when these men transcended their roles as soldiers and embraced their shared humanity, coming together to celebrate this sacred night.

Something extraordinary occurred on that night. Amidst the singing of the Allied Forces, another sound broke through. It wasn't a song; it was someone shouting. The singing ceased momentarily as they tried to discern the source of that voice. To their surprise, it came from the enemy line. The words weren't in German. An English shout emerged from one of the soldiers, inviting the troops to "come over here." Cautious, the British soldiers proposed meeting in the middle instead. The intentions of their counterparts were met with skepticism; few could have anticipated what would transpire next – most would have dismissed such a tale as unbelievable.

Both sides ventured into no-man's land with trepidation – uncertainty filled the air as they didn't know what awaited them. As they finally converged, British soldiers found Germans waiting for them. Although they had faced each other in battle several times, this encounter felt entirely different. They gathered not as adversaries – but as men who chose words over bullets to communicate.

With mutual trust growing between them with each moment, both Allied and German soldiers laid down their weapons and warmly shook hands.

They exchanged good wishes for Christmas and then gathered together to sing traditional Christmas songs. They enjoyed the company of one another, sharing laughter and conversation while indulging in cigars, wine, and chocolate –and even exchanging gifts. There was a sense of camaraderie as they played football and proudly displayed family pictures. Some soldiers even shared their addresses, hoping for visits once the war came to an end. In an act of compassion, they also supported each other in burying their fallen comrades.

The soldiers found themselves in a state of disbelief. Hours before, they had been locked in combat. During that brief period, they had become friends who shared stories and laughter. For that one night, all feelings of hatred, anger, and bloodshed were set aside. Instead, there was a connection between human beings who sought solace in each other's presence on this sacred occasion. Amidst the chaos and danger that surrounded them daily on the battlefield, this holy night offered them respite from the deafening explosions and the constant fear for their lives.

However, not everyone among the ranks approved of this truce. Certain sergeants and commanders believed that humanizing their enemies would only lead to complications. By forming connections with these men through shared stories about their families, it would become harder to shoot at faceless foes during conflicts. There was one soldier who accused his comrades of dishonoring themselves by accepting this truce; this man was Adolf Hitler.

No matter who opposed the ceasefire it was crucial for the soldiers to remember their humanity before anything.

41. The Evacuation of Dunkirk

During the events of the Second World War in 1939, Germany made its move by invading Poland. The next year, they expanded their invasion to Belgium. In response to these actions, Britain dispatched the British Expeditionary Force (BEF) to aid France and its allies in the fight against Germany. These significant events reshaped history and ultimately led to the evacuation of Dunkirk.

On May 10th, 1940, Germany caught the Allied Forces off guard with a surprise attack along the border of Holland. They employed ground assaults, parachute drops, and air raids from all directions. This strategic move was unexpected, not just for the Allies; it also surprised the Germans themselves. Adolf Hitler had reservations about this decision due to its risks but eventually approved it.

The attack left Holland and Belgium in a state of shock, forcing them to surrender. British soldiers stationed in France valiantly fought against attacks until they found themselves gradually retreating towards Dunkirk, a port city in France.

The scene that unfolded in Dunkirk on May 26th, 1940, was distressing beyond words. The cacophony of weaponry reverberated throughout every corner of the city.

The British, French, and Belgian troops found themselves surrounded from all sides. The Allied forces felt trapped with no escape. The beaches of Dunkirk offered no shelter, and the German air forces relentlessly attacked them without mercy.

Britain was determined not to abandon their soldiers and allies. In response, Sir Winston Churchill, the Prime Minister of England at the time, initiated an operation named Dynamo with the objective of rescuing their troops and bringing them home. Every available sea vessel was deployed to Dunkirk, ranging from battle ships to fishing boats. It was a massive undertaking, and both soldiers and civilians alike acted swiftly and selflessly to save their army.

Churchill knew what was at stake here. If this rescue mission failed, Britain and the rest of Europe would fall. So, he desperately needed to rescue his men to save his country.

On May 27th, the first destroyer vessels took the journey to rescue the stranded soldiers. However, German air forces attacked any ship and made it impossible to reach the British troops. Luckily, the British air forces quickly intervened, but the battle was ruthless, and their planes were destroyed. The pilots fell on the beaches of Dunkirk, stranded with the soldiers.

Although it seemed like an impossible situation with the Germans attacking by air and on the ground, the British didn't give up. For nine days, they fought relentlessly under harsh conditions, but their persistence paid off, and Operation Dynamo was a success. They managed to evacuate the British and French soldiers. The mission is often called the "Miracle of Dunkirk" because they were expected to rescue 45,000 soldiers or less. However, they managed to save over 300,000 of the stranded troops from England and France. Sadly, 17,000 soldiers didn't make it.

The Dunkirk Evacuation changed the course of the Second World War. By achieving the impossible, Dunkirk gave the British soldiers and the Allies hope and inspired them to keep fighting. The British people were proud of their troops and supported them during these critical times. The soldiers were now more confident than ever. They had proved Hitler and the Nazis wrong since they believed the British soldiers wouldn't return, but they did. The Allied Forces conquered the Axis Powers (Germany, Italy, and Japan) on D-Day and won World War II.

42. The Battle of the Somme

The Battle of the Somme occurred during World War I and stands out as one of the most devastating conflicts in history. By 1916, British and French forces had engaged in combat for over two years. Both sides possessed immense tactical capabilities, making victory elusive for either party.

In an attempt to weaken their adversaries, the Allied Forces devised a strategy to simultaneously assault the Germans from the north and south, intending to inflict damage to their defenses. British troops held great expectations about this offensive believing it could potentially pave their way to triumph. Little did they suspect that two British soldiers had betrayed them by divulging the plan to their enemies. Consequently, German forces were well aware of the assault, leading them to fortify their defenses and await the Allies' arrival.

Meanwhile, the Germans had formulated their own plan aimed at diverting attention from the impending Allied attack and disrupting their forces. They initiated an offensive against troops stationed near Verdun – a city in France – before any opportunity arose for executing the Allies' intended strategy.

The situation faced by the British was dire. They lacked soldiers for their plan as the French were engaged in the battle at Verdun. Simultaneously, they had to initiate their plan to alleviate pressure on the troops who were defending themselves against German attacks. This played into the hands of the Germans.

Despite the circumstances, British commander Douglas Haig maintained a positive outlook and believed the Allied forces could inflict damage on enemy lines. The plan itself was flawless; it just fell short due to an act of treachery.

On July 1st, 1916, a massive army comprising British soldiers from parts of the Commonwealth (including Canada, New Zealand, Australia, India, and South Africa) was assembled by the Allied Forces. They split into two groups; one launched an attack in the south and managed to harm their adversaries, while the second group attacked in the north but faced less success. Within one hour, 20,000 British soldiers were lost in battle, with another 37,000 suffering injuries. This was only the beginning. The conflict dragged on for five months, resulting in a loss of 600,000 soldiers.

The brave soldiers of the Allied army fought valiantly, seeking to exploit any weaknesses in the enemy's defense. However, the Germans consistently stayed a step ahead, accurately anticipating the British army's every move. On July 19th, they launched another assault against the Germans, enduring three days of fighting and suffering another devastating loss. Tragically, 5,000 Australian soldiers lost their lives on this day, marking it as one of the worst moments in Australia's history.

Following the Australians' efforts, the South Africans were eager for their opportunity to prove themselves on the battlefield. The Allied Forces launched an attack against the Germans with hopes of securing their flank. Months of battles ensued, and they ultimately achieved their mission; however, this victory was bittersweet. The South Africans alone mourned the loss of 2,500 soldiers while more Allies also perished.

The British army faced setbacks throughout their campaign. Communication issues plagued them, making it challenging to coordinate attacks. Consequently, there were increased casualties, which forced commanders to halt their offensive and devise an alternative strategy. Unfortunately, during this pause in action, enemy forces capitalized on the opportunity to launch counterattacks, resulting in a prolonged battle that surpassed expectations.

In September, though, fortune smiled upon the Allies as they successfully captured both Guillemont village and Ginchy town from German control. The British forces triumphed in their attack against German defenses, but these victories were relatively insignificant. They did not significantly impact the enemy's defense. With the soldiers exhausted and disheartened from witnessing the loss of comrades, General Haig had to make the difficult choice to bring an end to the Battle of Somme.

In this battle, neither side emerged victorious, with the Germans suffering a loss of approximately 500,000 soldiers. Despite casualties on both sides, the German defensive line remained unbroken.

43. Britain's Role in the Treaty of Versailles

On 28 June 1919, the Allied forces and Germany signed a peace treaty ending the First World War. This took place at the Palace of Versailles in France. US President Woodrow Wilson, French Prime Minister George Clemenceau, and British Prime Minister David Lloyd George all attended to represent their countries and sign the treaty. The war had caused devastation on both sides, with towns and villages in France and Belgium disappearing completely. British lands, on the other hand, only suffered minimal devastation but many casualties.

The signing of the treaty didn't go smoothly. Emotions were running high, and many people were blaming Germany for the war. French Prime Minister George Clemenceau wanted Germany to pay reparations to the Allied forces for all the damage they had caused. British Prime Minister David Lloyd George had a different opinion. He knew that his people were angry and wanted vengeance for all the casualties Germany had caused. He had promised the British people that he would do whatever it took to make Germany pay. However, that was what he said in public; privately, he didn't want to destroy Germany.

George was worried about the Russian Revolution and its impact on Britain and the rest of Europe. He believed Germany could be their strongest line of defense against communism. If Germany fell, the left could prevail. He agreed that Europe shouldn't go easy on Germany, but destroying it wasn't the best idea.

George was also looking for Britain's best interests. He understood that reconciliation was necessary since Germany was a great trading partner, so its economy must not suffer. He also wanted Germany to remain strong to create a power balance between it and France. If Germany fell, France could be the dominant European power. George also wanted to neutralize the German navy so the British Royal Navy would be the most powerful in Europe.

American President Woodrow Wilson wanted to punish Germany, but not as an act of vengeance. He hoped the Europeans would reconcile and prevent further bloodshed.

The Versailles treaty didn't destroy Germany as Clemenceau hoped. However, it suffered greatly. It lost 13% of its territory, returned Alsace and Lorraine to France, was prohibited from having submarines and an air force, and paid 6.6 billion euros in reparations. They also accepted blame for the war.

The treaty was a victory for the Allies as it secured world peace and protected French borders from any future attacks. However, the German people were outraged and found the terms of the treaty to be unfair. The clause that angered them the most was Germany's acceptance of war guilt.

The German government felt pressured by its people, so they decided to renegotiate the treaty. This led to more issues between Germany and the Allied forces, which eventually seeped into the Second World War.

44. Did Churchill Save Britain?

Sir Winston Churchill holds the distinction of being Britain's only prime minister to have served for a total of ten years in nonconsecutive terms from 1940 to 1945 and again from 1951 to 1955. He gained recognition as one of the greatest political figures globally and continues to be held in high esteem by many.

Churchill assumed office during one of the periods in British history, specifically during the Second World War. His first day as Prime Minister coincided with Germany's invasion of France, Holland, and Belgium. Moreover, he confronted the events at Dunkirk, where his leadership demonstrated his aptitude for the role. By making the decision to mobilize all water vessels, both military and civilian, to rescue Allied troops, Churchill played a pivotal role in saving hundreds of thousands of soldiers and ultimately securing victory against Germany.

The majority of citizens showed unwavering support for Churchill. They had complete faith in his ability to lead them towards triumph over Hitler. Renowned for his intellect and astute decision-making skills during times of adversity, he devised political strategies that repeatedly safeguarded Britain's interests. This was most evident during Dunkirk, a moment that put Britain's resilience to its greatest test yet.

With his commanding presence, he forged the Big Three Alliance alongside Russia and the United States. Had Britain been led by a different prime minister during the Second World War, Europe's destiny could have taken a very different path.

To answer the question, yes, Sir Winston Churchill saved Britain and even the whole Western civilization. Thanks to his wise leadership, the country managed to stay in the Second World War and achieve victory. He was different from David Lloyd George, who admired Hitler, which might have clouded his judgments at the time. However, Churchill didn't share the same sentiment and was only focused on saving his country.

45. The Blitz and the London Underground

During World War I and II, the British sought refuge in the London Underground to escape the horrors of the raids. The First World War shocked the people as it was the first time they had experienced this kind of brutality in modern history. They found their only refuge was in the tube stations.

In the Second World War, people knew what to expect, but many were reluctant to use the Underground again. However, with the extensive attacks on London, they had no other choice.

On May 31, 1915, London experienced its first airstrike, leading people to hide in the tubes. Living underground was extremely hard, but they had to sacrifice their comfort to survive and keep their families safe.

The English also experienced their first blackout. Indoor lights were concealed, and streetlights were extinguished to prevent the Germans from finding their targets. Even underground lights were turned off, leaving the Londoners anxious and terrified.

As with any war, it was heartbreaking how people gathered in one place, sitting in the dark with their suitcases and crying children holding their teddy bears, hoping all of this would end soon. The English believed that Great Britain would be victorious. They kept their "Keep calm and carry on" spirit. They hung statements like "Bombed but not defeated" and "London can take it" on the underground walls. Their patriotism never wavered, which resulted in the term "the Blitz spirit."

During the war, Germany attacked London 17 times, and 667 people lost their lives. If it wasn't for the London underground, there would have been much more casualties.

These stories show how Great Britain went through many trials and tribulations over the years. Through the wars and struggles, the British also had hope and perseverance for a better day.

Chapter 10: Stories on the Dawn of Modern England

Welcome to the dawn of modern England. It was a long journey to get here, but as you can see from the previous chapters, Britain has a very rich history. And all these aforementioned events have impacted the British world we know today. You may be familiar with some of the stories featured in this chapter. You either have lived through them or heard about them from an older family member.

The Beatles – one of the many British bands that transformed the music scene.[10]

46. The Rise of British Music

Can you even imagine what the world would be like if we didn't have music from bands like The Beatles? Would the music industry be as vibrant without the influence of the Queen? It's impossible to discuss history without acknowledging its profound impact on music.

Back in the 1960s, a new term emerged; "The British Invasion." But this invasion didn't involve Britain conquering nations; rather it was a phenomenon that completely revolutionized the global music scene. It referred to acts, such as The Beatles, Queen, and The Rolling Stones, gaining popularity in the United States and reshaping the entire landscape of music.

In the 1950s, British musicians were captivated by the image projected by rock and roll bands. However, despite their attempts to replicate it, they fell short. Eventually, things changed with the rise of jazz music. Many young people were drawn to its "do it yourself" ethos and found inspiration to start writing their songs.

Bands from all corners of the UK decided to blend British influences to forge their distinctive musical movement. One of the prominent movements in Britain was Merseybeat, which originated in Liverpool. It served as a source of inspiration for artists, including a small band from Liverpool who chose to name themselves "The Beatles."

At the time, British musicians were gaining immense popularity. Many sought to captivate audiences. The first British song to climb the Hot 100 Summit was "Telstar" by The Tornados. Teenagers and young Americans who identified as Mods and Rockers showed great interest in British music.

The British invasion reached its peak with the emergence of The Beatles, considered one of the greatest bands ever. The obsession with The Beatles initially took hold in Britain before spreading. An article published by The Washington Post highlighted how young people in England were going wild over them.

On November 4th, The Beatles performed in front of the Queen Mother, capturing much attention. Their performance had an impact on audiences and the media couldn't get enough of them, gradually forming a cultural phenomenon that became known as "Beatlemania."

Beatlemania quickly spread throughout America; discussions about them dominated news outlets while their songs received airtime on TV and radio stations. Americans fell head over heels for The Beatles, a love that has continued to this day.

There is a captivating tale about a girl who wrote a letter to a radio station after watching The Beatles on TV. She wondered why America didn't have proper music.

On December 17th, the radio station played The Beatles song "I Want to Hold Your Hand." Americans fell head over heels for this song and hurried to record stores to buy it. They even called the radio station requesting it to be played again. Beatlemania had infected the nation. There seemed to be no cure for it. In 1964, "I Want to Hold Your Hand" topped the charts as the number-one song in the country.

Following this, The Beatles made their way to America, leading a news anchor to declare that the British invasion was now known as Beatlemania. Their first appearance on television took place on the Ed Sullivan Show and set TV records that night with nearly half of the US population tuning in.

This was just the beginning of the British Invasion. Numerous other bands, such as The Animals and The Rolling Stones achieved success in America.

Decades have passed since these bands emerged, and their influence remains strong and vibrant today.

Numerous musical groups and individual artists originating from the United Kingdom, such as Adele, Oasis, Blur, and One Direction, have achieved great levels of popularity and triumph in the United States and the world as a whole.

47. The Suffragette Movement

Throughout history, women have faced severe discrimination, being treated as second-class citizens and considered inferior to men. Numerous movements emerged to advocate for equality, one of which was the Suffragette movement.

Emmeline Pankhurst and her daughters. Christabel, Sylvia, and Adela Pankhurst initiated the Suffragette movement in Manchester with the aim of demanding women's right to vote. Their efforts made history when the government granted voting rights to women over 30 years of age, female university graduates, and female property owners. While this was a milestone for women's rights, it was clear that there was still a way to go. In 1903, they established the Women's Social and Political Union (WSPU) as a means of raising awareness about the Suffragette Movement. The WSPU firmly believed in "actions speaking louder than words."

The Suffragette movement predominantly advocated for rights for women through various means. They tirelessly worked towards their cause for more than a decade. Unfortunately, they fell short of achieving their goals. It was at this point that Emmeline realized that the peaceful approach adopted by her predecessors wasn't yielding the desired results, prompting her to shift strategies.

The women grew weary of relying on their words as nobody seemed to pay attention to them. Instead, they decided to embrace their motto and allow their actions to speak for themselves.

Emmeline and the women in her group used violence to express their demands. They destroyed shop fronts and pillar boxes, and some even bought gun licenses to give the impression that they were ready for a revolution.

They moved WSPU headquarters to London, giving them the chance to protest near the government so they were seen and heard. They protested at Downing Street, heckled members of Parliament, and some went to the extent of chaining themselves to government buildings. Some protesters tried to destroy classic works of art like The Toilette of Venus by François Boucher.

In 1908, the WSPU held a meeting with all its members. Women came from every part of Britain. It was the first time all the members came together. They agreed to march in different parts of the country to protest against voting inequality. 300,000 women took to the streets demanding to be treated as human beings.

Although they had good intentions, their actions weren't acceptable to society, and they were arrested and thrown in prison. They were tortured and treated horribly. The women went on a hunger strike in protest. However, this made the situation worse. The woman who got weak or ill because of the hunger strike was allowed to leave prison with a permit. Once they regained their health and felt better, the police would arrest them again and return them to prison.

However, if they protested or joined the Suffragette movement, they would return to prison, even if they hadn't recovered! This new law was called "The Cat and Mouse Act."

During World War I, the government banned any type of protest. The Suffragettes spent their time supporting the troops. The women were also released from prison during this time, putting an end to the hunger strikes.

Even though the Suffragette women did everything in their power, they couldn't achieve the vote. However, this paved the way for many other women to speak up and take active roles in society.

The Impact of the Industrial Revolution on Modern Britain

The Industrial Revolution had a huge impact on Modern Britain. It didn't only change the country's economy but also the daily lives of the people. The British people were farmers and lived in rural areas. The Industrial Revolution introduced factories and machines and changed the lives of British people forever. Manual labor like stage coaches businesses and hand-weaving became a thing of the past as people were relying on machines.

The Industrial Revolution also changed the way people commuted. Methods of transportation were revolutionized, with trains and railroads taking off, making life faster and easier. People didn't have to travel for days just to visit their families in another city. They just got on a train and reached their destination in a couple of hours. People felt connected and close to each other as everyone they knew was just a ride away.

People were able to afford many products and goods as the economy was booming, and there were many job opportunities. New factories were built every day, providing jobs for people from all walks of life. However, nothing is free. Britain moved away from the clean and quiet rural life into the loud, crowded, and polluted industrial cities. Crime increased, and life became more dangerous than it used to be.

Life was faster than ever before. With the invention of new machines, people could make whatever they wanted in minutes rather than hours. For instance, in Prehistoric England, they used to sew using animal bones; then they discovered threads and needles. In the Industrial Age, they used sewing machines so they could make clothes in days rather than weeks.

Britain was changing rapidly. It was no longer a simple agricultural country. Thanks to the Industrial Revolution, they were able to build viaducts, bridges, and buildings.

Britain became a developed country, a far cry from what it was like during the Prehistoric era and Viking age.

Farmers also reaped the benefits of the revolution. It was an era of innovation, with the invention and manufacturing of tools that farmers relied on to cultivate their lands and simplify their lives.

Moreover, the industries of steel, iron and coal thrived during this age. These resources served as fuel for machines and were essential for factories to operate effectively.

As factories sprouted in cities, urban life experienced a boost. The city's population swelled while villages and small towns saw a decline. People flocked to reside near these factories due to the job opportunities they offered – both men and women, even children, found themselves in demand.

The advent of transportation methods further enticed people to settle in cities where accessibility was paramount. Although trains were a novice invention, they became an important means of travel for people from various social classes.

The Industrial Revolution showcased Britain's flourishing state to the world and subsequently spurred its spread across other European nations. This revolution played a role in boosting Britain's population from 6 million people to 21 million during the century. Cities like Halifax, Sheffield, Liverpool, and Manchester became some of the most densely populated areas in the country.

In this shift, the British population experienced a disinterest in rural living and instead opted to relocate to urban areas.

Although living in the city provided them with great opportunities, it had its disadvantages. The factories increased pollution levels in the air. They also were poorly sanitized, making people ill and contributing to the spread of various diseases.

Another disadvantage to the Industrial Revolution was child labor. There weren't any laws protecting children, and they had to work under tough conditions. Poor parents preferred their children to work in the factories rather than go to school as they needed extra income.

Like anything in the world, the industrial era had its advantages and disadvantages. There is no denying that it was a big part of Britain's history, and its impact is still felt to this day.

48. The Swinging Sixties

The era known as the Swinging Sixties occurred between 1964 and 1970, leaving a lasting impact on history by transforming British culture and society. Without a doubt, Britain would have looked remarkably different if it hadn't been for the influence of this period.

During those years, Harold Wilson served as Britain's Prime Minister and supported the shifting dynamics and scientific advancements taking place in the country. Wilson cleverly appealed to the public's desire for progress, promising to propel the nation if they voted for him. Recognizing that people were primarily focused on innovation and growth, this promise secured his victory.

The 1960s witnessed changes in society, culture, and values. A spirit of rebellion swept through the people who found themselves leading different lives from their parent's generation and grappling with finding common ground. These teenagers grew up amidst prosperity while their parents endured the hardships of the Great Depression. Given their circumstances, they had the freedom to simply be themselves – enjoying their youth, having fun, or pushing against societal norms.

This new generation was well-educated and understood that they shouldn't blindly adhere to outdated traditions or conventions. They began questioning established norms and beliefs while also having time, resources, and liberty to explore ideas in order to discover their own identities and aspirations.

During the 1960's, there were styles that appealed to people. Some embraced the Mod style, opting for fashionable attire while riding scooters. On the other hand, there were those who identified as rockers, donning leather jackets and riding motorcycles. Mods and rockers often displayed anger, rebelliousness, and antisocial behavior.

Teenagers and young individuals in that era were greatly influenced by radio, magazines, and TV shows. As they embarked on a journey of self-discovery, the media capitalized on their confusion by featuring The Beatles or slim models on magazine covers, creating a perception that they should emulate their appearance and style. This is somewhat similar to the way social media currently promotes airbrushed photos and sets beauty standards.

Despite experiencing freedom and financial stability during the 1960's in Britain, certain groups (such as women) still faced struggles with inequality. Feminism was an emerging movement at that time, with many taking to the streets to demand rights like legalized abortion. Moreover, thousands of individuals protested against Britain's involvement in the Vietnam War outside of the US Embassy. These protests turned aggressive at times, resulting in riots and hundreds of arrests.

49. Queen Elizabeth II

One can't talk about Britain's modern history without mentioning the woman who shaped it, Queen Elizabeth II. Queen Elizabeth II's reign lasted for a little over 70 years, making her the longest-reigning British monarch. Interestingly, Elizabeth wasn't supposed to be a queen. She was the third in line to the throne after her uncle and father. She wasn't raised to be a queen but to lead a normal life, or as normal as it could be for the king's niece.

Her uncle Edward was the King of England, but he fell in love with a divorced American woman called Wallis Simpson and wanted to marry her. Marrying a divorcee wasn't allowed, so he chose to follow his heart and abdicated the throne. His brother Albert, Elizabeth's father, became the new King of England. She was 10 at the time, and her life turned upside down as she had to be prepared for her new role.

She married her first love, Royal Navy officer Philip Mountbatten, when she was 21 and had four children with him. She gave birth to Charles and Anne before she became queen – and Andrew and Edward afterward.

When Elizabeth was 26 years old, she was on a trip to Kenya with her husband. There, she received news that turned her world upside down. Her father had passed away, and she was the Queen of England. She was very young at the time, and this wasn't an easy responsibility. However, she vowed to the people of Britain to spend her life serving them and the country.

Whether a person is a royalist or not, no one can deny that Queen Elizabeth II was one of the most significant figures in modern English history. She only cared about her country and the royal family. She always presented a united front even when scandals of members of the royal family were headlines in the papers, like Prince Charles and Princess Diana's divorce or the feud between her grandsons, Prince William and Prince Harry.

In her 70 years of leadership, the Queen achieved so much for the country and monarchy. She modernized the royal family by giving its female members the same rights as the males. She also supported thousands of charities in Britain and other countries around the world. She was the first monarch in 100 years to visit Ireland. The historic visit strengthened the relationship between the two countries and was a message of love and peace.

She was loved and highly respected by her people. This was evident after her death, with the whole nation mourning her, and why wouldn't they? Queen Elizabeth II served her country well with class, dignity, and strength. Even when the royal family faced their toughest tests, she always met the public with a smile and followed the family's motto of never complaining, never explaining.

Britain's modern history is as rich as its ancient history. The country has influenced the whole world in every aspect. Whether it was the Industrial Revolution, classical literature, or music, all eyes have always been on Britain.

Conclusion

Throughout history, we can learn many lessons by studying the experiences of those who came before us. Britain, as an empire, has a captivating history filled with intriguing stories, controversies, and significant events that shaped the course of time.

This book delves into each era of history, starting with Prehistoric England. It takes readers on an enthralling journey to one of the country's landmarks, Stonehenge. The book explores theories surrounding its construction and purpose while providing insights into the lives of people during those times.

Continuing the adventure, the book then transports readers to the era of Vikings. Beyond folklore and mythology, it uncovers events that had an impact on Britain's fate, offering captivating stories about how these invaders shaped its destiny.

Among the most important moments in British history lies the Norman Conquest. Following King Edwards passing, Britain underwent a tremendous transformation. The battles for power and the rise and fall of rulers make it reminiscent of a tale from Game of Thrones.

History is replete with royals, unlikable more than likable ones. However, these are often the ones that cause a stir and incite people to reshape history. The book provides an account of King John's nature and how the people rebelled against him and removed him from power. This narrative illustrates the strength of action and how it can bring about change.

Moving on, we delve into the Hundred Years War, an era brimming with tales of conflict featuring prominent figures such as Joan of Arc.

The book also transports you to two captivating figures from history; King Henry and Anne Boleyn. You may be familiar with their love story as it has been portrayed in numerous films and television shows. King Henry was deeply enamored with Anne to the point that he altered his country's laws for her. However, he also made the decision to have her executed, a choice that haunted him for the remainder of his life.

England has always been celebrated for its minds and literary luminaries. The stories surrounding the Age of Enlightenment demonstrate how Britain transitioned from the Dark Ages to embracing advancements while fostering a culture steeped in literature. Witnessing their transformation from an existence during times to becoming one of the world's most cultured nations is undeniably fascinating.

The story of the rise of the British Empire is truly fascinating. Often surrounded by controversy, especially when considering its evolution over the centuries. In this part of the book, the initial section narrates the experiences of soldiers during both World Wars and their immense struggles to safeguard their nation. These stories offer lessons emphasizing the importance of maintaining hope in dire circumstances. The final chapter explores moments such as The Beatles' impact on the music scene.

Throughout Britain's history, from ancient times to today, every event has played a crucial role in shaping its society, culture, and politics. Just imagine how different England would be today if King Henry hadn't separated the state from the church. Similarly, consider what might have happened in Europe if no one had come to rescue soldiers at Dunkirk!

We hope that by deep-diving into English history throughout this book, you have gained an understanding and appreciation for its characters and compelling events.

Check out another book in the series

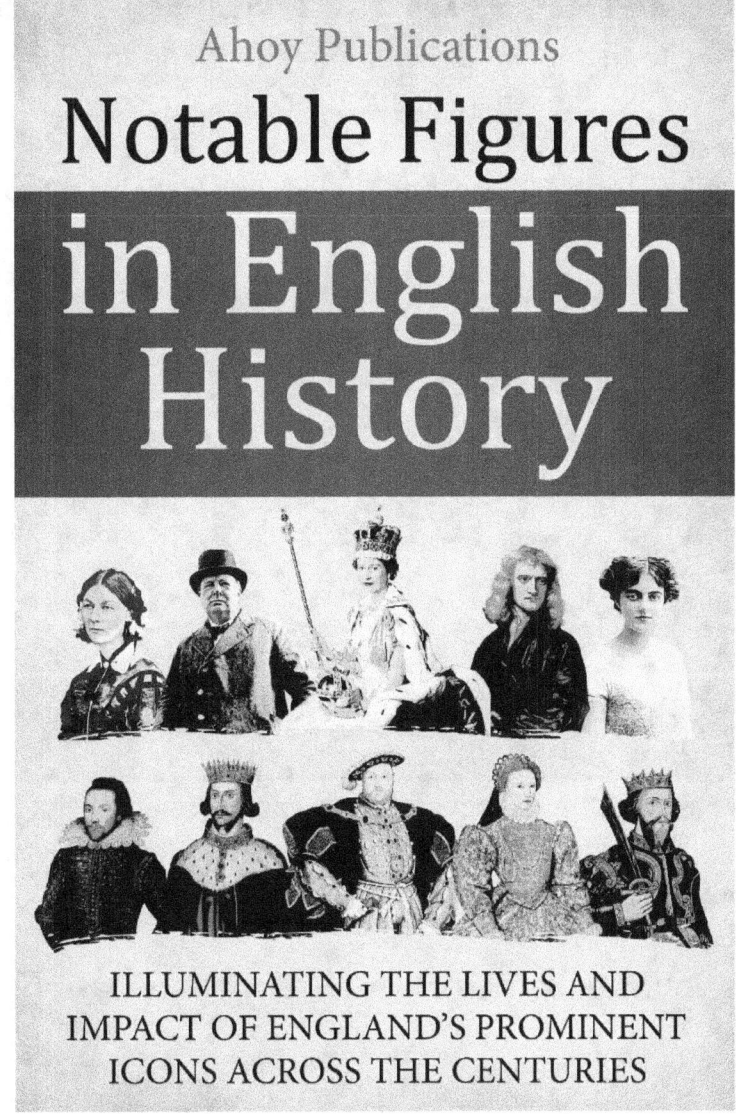

Welcome Aboard, Check Out This Limited-Time Free Bonus!

Ahoy, reader! Welcome to the Ahoy Publications family, and thanks for snagging a copy of this book! Since you've chosen to join us on this journey, we'd like to offer you something special.

Check out the link below for a FREE e-book filled with delightful facts about American History.

But that's not all - you'll also have access to our exclusive email list with even more free e-books and insider knowledge. Well, what are ye waiting for? Click the link below to join and set sail toward exciting adventures in American History.

Access your bonus here: https://ahoypublications.com/

Or, Scan the QR code!

Sources and Additional References

Part 1

Hines, John. *The Anglo-Saxons from the Migration Period to the Eighth Century: An Ethnographic Perspective.* Boydell and Brewer, 1997.

Stenton, Sir Frank M. *Anglo-Saxon England.* Oxford University Press, 1971.

Barlow, Frank. *The Feudal Kingdom of England 1042-1216.* Routledge, 2002.

Gillingham, John. *The Norman Conquest.* Routledge, 2002.

Bates, David. *William the Conqueror.* Yale University Press, 2009.

Keegan, John. *The Face of Battle.* Viking Press, 1976.

Barron, Caroline M. *The Reign of Edward III: Crown and Political Society in England, 1327-1377.* Yale University Press, 1990.

Bartlett, Robert. *England under the Norman and Angevin Kings, 1075-1225.* Oxford University Press, 2000.

Hindley, Geoffrey. *A Brief History of the Hundred Years War.* Robinson, 2006.

Vaughan, Richard. *The Hundred Years War: The English in France, 1337-1453.* University of California Press, 1999.

Ross, Charles. *The Wars of the Roses.* Thames and Hudson, 1976.

Bainton, Roland H. *The Reformation of the Sixteenth Century.* Beacon Press, 1952.

Wernham, R. B. *The Making of Elizabethan Foreign Policy, 1558-1603.* Stanford University Press, 1980.

Williams, Neville. *Elizabeth I: Queen of England.* Atheneum, 1967.

Adamson, John. *The Civil Wars: A Military History of England, Scotland, and Ireland, 1638-1660* (Oxford University Press, 1998).

Burrow, John A. *History of Histories of the English Civil War* (Cambridge University Press, 2008).

Durston, Gregory. *The Later Stuarts, 1660-1714* (Longman, 1996).

Harris, Tim. Revolution: *The Great Crisis of the British Monarchy, 1685-1720* (Penguin Books, 2006).

Porter, Roy. *The Creation of the Modern World: The Untold Story of the British Enlightenment* (W.W. Norton and Company, 2000).

Goose, Nigel. *The Industrial Revolution* (Routledge, 2005).

Hobsbawm, Eric. *Industry and Empire: An Economic History of Britain Since 1750* (Weidenfeld and Nicolson, 1968).

Palmer, Colin A. *The Slaves of Britain: Blacks in Britain, 1780-1850* (Oxford University Press, 2014).

Walvin, James. *The Slave Trade: The Story of the Atlantic Slave Trade, 1440-1870* (Simon and Schuster, 1997).

Morris, Rose. *The Oxford Illustrated History of the British Monarchy*. Oxford University Press, 1988.

Thompson, R. M. *The War in the Crimea*. Kessinger Publishing, 2007.

Butler, Joseph. *The Great Famine and the Irish Diaspora in America*. University of Massachusetts Press, 1994.

Finnan, Joseph. *The Irish Famine: A Documentary History*. Irish Academic Press, 2009.

Kastner, Jens. *The Great Exhibition of 1851: A Nation on Show*. Bloomsbury Academic, 2014.

Fay, C.R. *The Boer War*. Oxford University Press, 2010.

Horne, John. *The Great War: 1914-1918*. Penguin, 2003.

Prior, Robin. *To Arms: The Great War 1914-1918*. Oxford University Press, 2003.

Jones, Mary. *The British Labour Movement and the General Strike of 1926*. Routledge, 2008.

Rosenberg, Jennifer. "Overview of World War II." ThoughtCo, Aug. 28, 2019, thoughtco.com/world-war-ii-1779792.

Powell, Martin. *The Welfare State in Britain since 1945*. Palgrave Macmillan, 2007.

Bull, Stephen J. *Britain, Egypt, and the Middle East: Imperial Policy in the Aftermath of the Suez Crisis, 1957-1961*. Routledge, 2004.

"Margaret Thatcher (1979–90)." BBC, BBC, www.bbc.co.uk/history/historic_figures/thatcher_margaret.shtml

"Margaret Thatcher and the 1980s." The British Library, www.bl.uk/20th-century-literature/articles/margaret-thatcher-and-the-1980s

"Falklands War." Encyclopedia Britannica, www.britannica.com/event/Falklands-War

"Good Friday Agreement: 20 Years On." The British Library, www.bl.uk/20th-century-literature/articles/good-friday-agreement-20-years-on

"The Good Friday Agreement: What Is It?" The Guardian, www.theguardian.com/world/2018/mar/19/the-good-friday-agreement-what-is-it

"Brexit Timeline: How Britain Voted to Leave the EU." BBC, BBC, www.bbc.co.uk/news/uk-politics-32810887

"Brexit: A Very British Revolution." The British Library, www.bl.uk/20th-century-literature/articles/brexit-a-very-british-revolution

Part 2

(N.d.). Org. uk. https://www.historic-cornwall.org.uk/the-power-of-stonehenge-a-pagan-perspective/#:~:text=For%20many%20pagans%2C%20Stonehenge%20is,to%20seek%20guidance%20and%20clarity.

(N.d.). Parliament.uk. https://www.parliament.uk/about/living-heritage/evolutionofparliament/originsofparliament/birthofparliament/overview/magna carta/

(N.d.). Royal.uk. https://www.royal.uk/alfred-great-r-871-899

(N.d.). Royal.uk. https://www.royal.uk/henry-viii

(N.d.). Yourstory.com. https://yourstory.com/2023/05/operation-dynamo-dunkirk-evacuation-world-war-2-may-26

An introduction to prehistoric England. (n.d.). English Heritage. https://www.english-heritage.org.uk/learn/story-of-england/prehistory/

Asia Pacific Foundation of Canada. (2017). The Opium Wars in China. Asia Pacific Curriculum. https://asiapacificcurriculum.ca/learning-module/opium-wars-china#:~:text=The%20Opium%20Wars%20in%20the,China%20lost%20both%20wars.

AstroPages. (n.d.). Wwu.edu. https://www.wwu.edu/astro101/stonehenge.shtml

Barrett, C. (2018, April 6). Hundred years' war: Joan of arc and the siege of Orléans. HistoryNet. https://www.historynet.com/hundred-years-war-joan-arc-siege-orleans/

Battle of Agincourt. (2010, July 21). HISTORY. https://www.history.com/this-day-in-history/battle-of-agincourt

Beyer, G. (2023, April 14). Ragnar Lodbrok and his viking family. TheCollector. https://www.thecollector.com/ragnar-lodbrok-and-family/

Beyer, G. (2023, July 30). Battle of the Somme: A sunlit picture of hell. TheCollector. https://www.thecollector.com/battle-of-somme/

Boddy-Evans, A. (2019). Events leading to the Scramble for Africa. ThoughtCo. https://www.thoughtco.com/what-caused-the-scramble-for-africa-43730

Britain Express. (n.d.). Bronze Age England and Wales, the beaker people. Britain Express. https://www.britainexpress.com/History/Bronze_Age.htm

BRITAIN-The official magazine. (2015, June 23). Henry VIII: King of England. Britain Magazine | The Official Magazine of Visit Britain | Best of British History, Royal Family, Travel and Culture. https://britain-magazine.telegraph.co.uk/features/the-two-sides-of-henry-viii/

British Library. (n.d.). Www.bl.uk. https://www.bl.uk/people/william-the-conqueror

British Library. (n.d.-b). Www.bl.uk. https://www.bl.uk/magna-carta/articles/magna-carta-an-introduction

British Library. (n.d.-c). Www.bl.uk. https://www.bl.uk/magna-carta/videos/what-is-magna-carta

Cartwright, M. (2019). The impact of the Norman conquest of England. World History Encyclopedia. https://www.worldhistory.org/article/1323/the-impact-of-the-norman-conquest-of-england/

Cartwright, M. (2020a). Battle of Agincourt. World History Encyclopedia. https://www.worldhistory.org/Battle_of_Agincourt/

Cartwright, M. (2020b). Edward the Black Prince. World History Encyclopedia. https://www.worldhistory.org/Edward_the_Black_Prince/

Cartwright, M. (2020c). Hundred Years' War. World History Encyclopedia. https://www.worldhistory.org/Hundred_Years'_War/

Cartwright, M. (2023). The impact of the British Industrial Revolution. World History Encyclopedia. https://www.worldhistory.org/article/2226/the-impact-of-the-british-industrial-revolution/

Cavendish, R. (n.d.). End of the Hundred Years War. Historytoday.com. https://www.historytoday.com/archive/end-hundred-years-war

Cohen, J. (2010, December 14). Solving the riddle of Stonehenge's construction. HISTORY. https://www.history.com/news/solving-the-riddle-of-stonehenges-construction

Edward The Black Prince. (2019, November 8). Historic UK. https://www.historic-uk.com/HistoryUK/HistoryofEngland/Edward-The-Black-Prince/

Enlightenment Thinkers. (n.d.). StudySmarter UK. https://www.studysmarter.co.uk/explanations/history/european-history/enlightenment-thinkers/

Enstam, G. (2017, November 7). "The Scottish Enlightenment and Literary Culture" edited by Ralph McLean, Ronnie Young, and Kenneth Simpson. The Bottle Imp. https://www.thebottleimp.org.uk/2017/11/scottish-enlightenment-literary-culture-edited-ralph-mclean-ronnie-young-kenneth-simpson/

Forbes, S. (2014, September 30). The man who saved Western civilization -- and how he did it. Forbes. https://www.forbes.com/sites/steveforbes/2014/09/30/what-we-owe-churchill/?sh=21f19bd6e71f

Galvez, C. (2022, September 8). Remembering Queen Elizabeth II and her achievements. Toast Life; Toast Media Inc. https://mytoastlife.com/remembering-queen-elizabeth-ii-and-her-achievements/

Henry VIII - Reformation, Divorce, Monarchy. (n.d.). In Encyclopedia Britannica.

Henry VIII wives: facts for kids. (2023, May 3). National Geographic Kids. https://www.natgeokids.com/uk/discover/history/monarchy/wives-of-henry-viii/

Henry VIII. (2016, October 9). Historic UK. https://www.historic-uk.com/HistoryUK/HistoryofEngland/Henry-VIII/

Henry VIII. (n.d.). Historic Royal Palaces. https://www.hrp.org.uk/hampton-court-palace/history-and-stories/henry-viii/

History Hit. (n.d.). Why did the Vikings invade Britain? History Hit. https://www.historyhit.com/why-did-the-vikings-invade-britain/

How Churchill led Britain to victory in the Second World War. (n.d.). Imperial War Museums. https://www.iwm.org.uk/history/how-churchill-led-britain-to-victory-in-the-second-world-war

How long did Queen Elizabeth last as Queen? - Google Search. (n.d.). Google.com. https://www.google.com/search?sca_esv=565412338&sxsrf=AM9HkKkEvo_Vx6s20uBZ5exVcEJKv0_x5Q:1694740978816&q=How+long+did+Queen+Elizabeth+last+as+Queen%3F&sa=X&ved=2ahUKEwj67ZyQuquBAxW0XaQEHQBHAYAQzmd6BAgiEAY

How many children did Henry VIII have? (n.d.). Rmg.co.uk. https://www.rmg.co.uk/stories/topics/how-many-children-did-henry-viii-have

Hundred Years' War - From the Treaty of Brétigny to the accession of Henry V (1360–1413). (n.d.). In Encyclopedia Britannica.

Hundred Years' War - Significance of the Hundred Years' War. (n.d.). In Encyclopedia Britannica.

Introductory Astronomy: Stonehenge. (n.d.). Wsu.edu. http://astro.wsu.edu/worthey/astro/html/im-lab/stonehenge/stonehenge.html

Janssen, V. (2018, October 29). WWI's Christmas truce: When fighting paused for the holiday. HISTORY. https://www.history.com/news/christmas-truce-1914-world-war-i-soldier-accounts

Jarus, O. (2020, March 11). Lindisfarne: The "Holy Island" where Vikings spilled the "blood of saints." Livescience.com; Live Science. https://www.livescience.com/lindisfarne.html

Jarus, O. (2022, September 27). Did druids build Stonehenge? Live Science. https://www.livescience.com/did-druids-build-stonehenge

Jarus, O. (2023, March 21). Where is Stonehenge, who built the prehistoric monument, and how? Livescience.com; Live Science. https://www.livescience.com/stonehenge-england-ancient-history

Joan of Arc. (2009, November 9). HISTORY. https://www.history.com/topics/middle-ages/saint-joan-of-arc

Kaplan, A. (2022, September 9). Elizabeth wasn't originally raised to be queen. How she became Britain's longest-reigning monarch. TODAY. https://www.today.com/news/news/elizabeth-wasnt-originally-raised-queen-became-britains-longest-reigni-rcna46982

Lochun, K. (2020, May 6). Alfred the Great and Edington: how the King of Wessex became great. HistoryExtra. https://www.historyextra.com/period/anglo-saxon/king-alfred-why-great-battle-edington-somerset-marshes-burn-cakes/

Mackenzie, L. (n.d.). What was the significance of the Viking attack on Lindisfarne? History Hit. https://www.historyhit.com/what-was-the-significance-of-the-viking-attack-on-lindisfarne/

Magna Carta summary (1215), Petition of Right - human rights. (n.d.). United for Human Rights. https://www.humanrights.com/what-are-human-rights/brief-history/magna-carta.html

Magna Carta. (2015, October 6). National Archives. https://www.archives.gov/exhibits/featured-documents/magna-carta

Marco, S. (2021, October 30). Beaker people and Stonehenge. Odysseytraveller.com; Odyssey Traveller. https://www.odysseytraveller.com/articles/bronze-age-beaker-people-of-stonehenge/

Marsh, A. (2022, June 21). In 793AD, Vikings attacked Lindisfarne. Here's why it was so shocking. National Geographic. https://www.nationalgeographic.co.uk/history-and-civilisation/2022/06/in-793ad-vikings-attacked-lindisfarne-heres-why-it-was-so-shocking

Martinez, J. (2022). Battle of Agincourt. In Encyclopedia Britannica.

McCrum, R. (2015, September 26). Agincourt was a battle like no other … but how do the French remember it? The Guardian. https://www.theguardian.com/world/2015/sep/26/agincourt-600th-anniversary-how-french-remember-it

McLean, A. P. J. (n.d.). The hundred years' war. Lumenlearning.com. https://courses.lumenlearning.com/atd-herkimer-westerncivilization/chapter/the-hundred-years-war/

Military History Monthly. (2022, January 12). Edward III, the black prince, and the battle of crécy. The Past. https://the-past.com/feature/edward-iii-the-black-prince-and-the-battle-of-crecy/

Museum of London. (2021, July 27). Who were the Suffragettes? Museum of London. https://www.museumoflondon.org.uk/museum-london/explore/who-were-suffragettes

Nadeau, S. (2016, December 24). How did the 1914 WWI Christmas Truce happen? Solosophie. https://www.solosophie.com/wwi-propaganda-and-christmas-truce-1914/

Nikel, D. (2022, October 22). Danelaw explained: When the Vikings ruled in England. Life in Norway. https://www.lifeinnorway.net/danelaw-explained/

No title. (n.d.-a). Study.com. https://study.com/academy/lesson/the-100-years-war-england-vs-france.html

No title. (n.d.-b). Study.com. https://study.com/academy/lesson/joan-of-arc-and-the-end-of-the-100-years-war.html

Norman conquest. (n.d.). Nationalgeographic.org. https://education.nationalgeographic.org/resource/norman-conquest/

Owens, J. (2017, January 21). Stonehenge. National Geographic. https://www.nationalgeographic.com/history/article/stonehenge-1

Paese, M. (n.d.). British invasion. Thehistoryofrockandroll.net. https://thehistoryofrockandroll.net/british-invasion/

Plesz, O. (2017, March 17). Joan of Arc and the hundred-year war. Manchester Historian. https://manchesterhistorian.com/2017/joan-of-arc-and-the-hundred-years-war/

Porter, G. (2021, February 10). The holy island of Lindisfarne - the Viking attack. Org.uk. https://www.lindisfarne.org.uk/793/

Prehistoric Britain. (2015, March 28). Historic UK. https://www.historic-uk.com/HistoryUK/HistoryofEngland/Prehistoric-Britain/

Prehistory: Daily life. (n.d.). English Heritage. https://www.english-heritage.org.uk/learn/story-of-england/prehistory/daily-life/

Ragnar Lothbrok: the legend of the immortal Viking and his sons. (2019, December 6). HistoryExtra. https://www.historyextra.com/period/viking/ragnar-lothbrok-the-immortal-viking/

Rebellions against William. (n.d.). Gcsehistory.com. https://www.gcsehistory.com/faq/rebellions.html

Royal Collection Trust. (2009, November 9). Henry VIII. HISTORY. https://www.history.com/topics/european-history/henry-viii

Shaw, I. P. (2023). Edward The Black Prince. In Encyclopedia Britannica.

Short, E. (2023, January 29). Dunkirk and the real story of the World War II military disaster. MovieWeb. https://movieweb.com/dunkirk-true-story-ww2/

Shuttleworth, M. (n.d.). Neolithic astronomy. Explorable.com. https://explorable.com/neolithic-astronomy

Sir Winston Churchill. (n.d.). Gov.uk. https://www.gov.uk/government/history/past-prime-ministers/winston-churchill

Sky HISTORY. (n.d.). The Three Greatest Viking Battles. Sky HISTORY TV Channel. https://www.history.co.uk/shows/the-real-vikings/articles/the-three-greatest-viking-battles

St. Joan of Arc - French Heroine, Martyr, Trial. (n.d.). In Encyclopedia Britannica.

Stonehenge. (2010, June 1). HISTORY. https://www.history.com/topics/european-history/stonehenge

Swinging sixties: Definition, Culture & Meaning. (n.d.). StudySmarter UK. https://www.studysmarter.co.uk/explanations/history/modern-britain/the-swinging-sixties/

The Battle of Hastings. (2016, April 18). Historic UK. https://www.historic-uk.com/HistoryMagazine/DestinationsUK/The-Battle-of-Hastings/

The battle of Stamford Bridge. (2021, August 30). Historic UK. https://www.historic-uk.com/HistoryMagazine/DestinationsUK/The-Battle-of-Stamford-Bridge/

The Editors of Encyclopaedia Britannica. (2023, September 10). East India Company | Definition, History, & Facts. Encyclopedia Britannica. https://www.britannica.com/money/topic/East-India-Company

The Editors of Encyclopedia Britannica. (2022). The Enlightenment Causes and Effects. In Encyclopedia Britannica.

The Editors of Encyclopedia Britannica. (2023). Druid. In Encyclopedia Britannica.

The Editors of Encyclopedia Britannica. (2023). Ragnar Lothbrok. In Encyclopedia Britannica.

The Enlightenment: Adam Smith: 1723 – 1790. (n.d.). Saylor Academy. https://learn.saylor.org/mod/book/view.php?id=54704&chapterid=40124

The five boroughs of Danelaw. (2019, July 25). Historic UK. https://www.historic-uk.com/HistoryUK/HistoryofEngland/The-Five-Boroughs-Of-Danelaw/

The Great Heathen Army of Vikings that invaded England. (2021, April 12). HeritageDaily - Archaeology News. https://www.heritagedaily.com/2021/04/the-great-heathen-army-of-vikings-that-invaded-england/138660

The great heathen army. (2019, March 20). Historic UK. https://www.historic-uk.com/HistoryUK/HistoryofEngland/Great-Heathen-Army/

The history of the Magna Carta. (2019, May 31). Historic UK. https://www.historic-uk.com/HistoryUK/HistoryofEngland/The-Origins-of-the-Magna-Carta/

The history of the Vikings in England. (n.d.). English Heritage. https://www.english-heritage.org.uk/visit/inspire-me/the-history-of-vikings-in-england/

The history press. (n.d.). Thehistorypress.co.uk. https://www.thehistorypress.co.uk/women-s-history/suffragettes/

The Importance of the Eclipse in Ancient Society. (n.d.). Encyclopedia.com. https://www.encyclopedia.com/science/encyclopedias-almanacs-transcripts-and-maps/importance-eclipse-ancient-society

The National Archives. (n.d.). The national archives - homepage. https://www.nationalarchives.gov.uk/education/resources/magna-carta/british-library-magna-carta-1215-runnymede/

The Norman conquest. (2017, September 30). Historic UK. https://www.historic-uk.com/HistoryUK/HistoryofEngland/The-Norman-Conquest/

The origins of the Hundred Years War. (2021, August 31). Historic UK. https://www.historic-uk.com/HistoryUK/HistoryofEngland/Origins-Hundred-Years-War/

The real Ragnar Lothbrok. (2018, November 13). Historic UK. https://www.historic-uk.com/HistoryUK/HistoryofEngland/Ragnar-Lothbrok/

The Scientific Revolution. (2020, April 20). Historic UK. https://www.historic-uk.com/HistoryUK/HistoryofBritain/The-Scientific-Revolution/

The Scramble for Africa | St John's College, University of Cambridge. (n.d.). https://www.joh.cam.ac.uk/library/library_exhibitions/schoolresources/exploration/scramble_for_africa

The Viking Raid on Lindisfarne. (n.d.). English Heritage. https://www.english-heritage.org.uk/visit/places/lindisfarne-priory/History/viking-raid/

The Vikings in Britain: a brief history. (2011, January 13). The Historical Association. https://www.history.org.uk/primary/resource/3867/the-vikings-in-britain-a-brief-history

Théry, J. (2017, April 13). How Joan of Arc turned the tide in the hundred-year war. National Geographic. https://www.nationalgeographic.com/history/history-magazine/article/joan-of-arc-warrior-heretic-saint-martyr

Treaty of Versailles centennial: British aims in Paris. (n.d.). Peacepalacelibrary.Nl. https://peacepalacelibrary.nl/blog/2019/treaty-versailles-centennial-british-aims-paris

Treaty of Versailles. (n.d.). Sky HISTORY TV Channel. https://www.history.co.uk/history-of-ww2/treaty-of-versailles

TVH. (2023, July 30). What was the North Sea Empire?

Understanding Stonehenge. (n.d.). English Heritage. https://www.english-heritage.org.uk/visit/places/stonehenge/history-and-stories/understanding-stonehenge/

Waxman, O. B. (2017, July 20). What to know about the miraculous true story behind Dunkirk. Time. https://time.com/4865358/dunkirk-history-christopher-nolan-film/

Welford, J. (2022, August 22). The end of the Hundred Years War. Medium. https://medium.com/@johnwelford15/the-end-of-the-hundred-years-war-1a315c73c91b

What Is the Enlightenment and How Did It Transform Politics? (n.d.). World101 from the Council on Foreign Relations. https://world101.cfr.org/contemporary-history/prelude-global-era/what-enlightenment-and-how-did-it-transform-politics

What was the "Scramble for Africa"? (n.d.). History Skills. https://www.historyskills.com/classroom/modern-history/scramble-for-africa/

When the Vikings ruled in Britain: A brief history of Danelaw. (n.d.). Sky HISTORY TV Channel. https://www.history.co.uk/articles/when-the-vikings-ruled-in-britain-a-brief-history-of-danelaw

Why did Henry VIII break with Rome? (n.d.). Rmg.co.uk. https://www.rmg.co.uk/stories/topics/why-did-henry-viii-break-rome

Why did the Vikings raid? (2021, March 26). BBC. https://www.bbc.co.uk/bitesize/topics/z939mp3/articles/z7jd8xs

Why the Enlightenment still matters today. (n.d.). Gresham College. https://www.gresham.ac.uk/watch-now/why-enlightenment-still-matters-today

Why was Stonehenge built? (2013, April 10). HISTORY. https://www.history.com/news/why-was-stonehenge-built

Wilde, R. (2009, December 5). Effects of the Hundred Years War. ThoughtCo. https://www.thoughtco.com/aftermath-of-the-hundred-years-war-1221904

William I - Norman Conquest, England, Normandy. (n.d.). In Encyclopedia Britannica.

Wong, D. (2023, April 25). What if Africa was Never Colonized? - Dwayne Wong (Omowale) - Medium. Medium. https://dwomowale.medium.com/what-if-africa-was-never-colonized-cd480ecb5390#:~:text=Had%20Africa%20not%20been%20colonized,ability%20to%20effectively%20develop%20itself.

Shelter in wartime. (n.d.). London Transport Museum. https://www.ltmuseum.co.uk/collections/stories/war/shelter-wartime

The blitz spirit. (2018, October 6). Historic UK. https://www.historic-uk.com/HistoryUK/HistoryofBritain/Blitz-Spirit

Images Sources

1 https://pixabay.com/photos/sunrise-stonehenge-mystical-england-3901312/

2 https://pixabay.com/photos/ai-generated-man-helmet-7718746/

3 https://pixabay.com/photos/horse-soldier-warrior-war-battle-4596827/

4 https://pixabay.com/photos/england-king-artus-royal-3431451/

5 https://pixabay.com/photos/art-sculpture-medieval-knight-6598445/

6 https://pixabay.com/photos/hans-holbeing-king-henry-viii-91067/

7 https://pixabay.com/photos/adam-smith-edinburgh-statue-4637193/

8 https://pixabay.com/photos/map-map-of-africa-world-map-globe-7299481

9 https://pixabay.com/photos/soldiers-grave-dig-war-buried-67510/

10 https://pixabay.com/photos/beatles-statue-lennon-mccartney-4612416/